Radical Reality

Radical Reality

*Documentary Storytelling and the Global
Fight for Social Justice*

CATY BORUM AND DAVID CONRAD-PÉREZ

OXFORD
UNIVERSITY PRESS

Oxford University Press is a department of the University of Oxford.
It furthers the University's objective of excellence in research, scholarship,
and education by publishing worldwide. Oxford is a registered trade mark of
Oxford University Press in the UK and in certain other countries.

Published in the United States of America by Oxford University Press
198 Madison Avenue, New York, NY 10016, United States of America.

© Oxford University Press 2025

All rights reserved. No part of this publication may be reproduced, stored in a retrieval system,
transmitted, used for text and data mining, or used for training artificial intelligence, in any form or
by any means, without the prior permission in writing of Oxford University Press, or as expressly
permitted by law, by license or under terms agreed with the appropriate reprographics rights
organization. Inquiries concerning reproduction outside the scope of the above should be sent
to the Rights Department, Oxford University Press, at the address above.

You must not circulate this work in any other form
and you must impose this same condition on any acquirer

Library of Congress Cataloging-in-Publication Data
Names: Borum Chattoo, Caty, author. | Conrad-Pérez, David, author.
Title: Radical reality : documentary storytelling and the global fight for
social justice / Caty Borum and David Conrad-Pérez.
Description: New York, NY : Oxford University Press, [2025] |
Includes bibliographical references and index.
Identifiers: LCCN 2024056060 (print) | LCCN 2024056061 (ebook) |
ISBN 9780197604250 (hardback) | ISBN 9780197604267 (paperback) |
ISBN 9780197604281 (epub)
Subjects: LCSH: Documentary mass media—Social aspects. | Social justice.
Classification: LCC P96.D62 B68 2024 (print) |
LCC P96.D62 (ebook) | DDC 070.1—dc23/eng/20250115
LC record available at https://lccn.loc.gov/2024056060
LC ebook record available at https://lccn.loc.gov/2024056061

DOI: 10.1093/9780197604298.001.0001

With a wide grin, I recently learned that "Comrade" has the same Latin root as the word "Camera." They both derive from "in the same room"—those that are in it together—and indeed, we are all on the same beautiful, fragile planet.

—Jess Search, Cofounder, Doc Society

This book is dedicated in loving memory of the inimitable Jess Search, whose brilliance, tenacity, and radical approach to nonfiction storytelling and human rights—and joyful collaboration with many, many comrades—helped create a thriving global documentary community.

Contents

Acknowledgments	ix
List of Images	xiii

1. Fighting the Good Fight Around the World	1
2. Confronting Government Power	27
3. Witnessing Conflict and Resilience	48
4. Upholding Freedom of Expression	73
5. Demanding Human Rights	102
6. Demonstrating Activism	132
7. Creating Spaces for Reconciliation and Healing	156
8. Building a Future for Global Independent Documentary Storytelling to Survive and Thrive	181

Appendix A: Interviews	207
Appendix B: Filmography	209
Notes	211
Index	233
About the Authors	243

Acknowledgments

This book is truly the work of a large community of creatives and activists, still living and past, whose efforts, time, and risks are the wellspring from which this research was made possible. To say that we are indebted to the trust and perspectives offered by them—through hours of formal and informal conversations, interviews, and collaborative discussions—would only begin to scratch the surface of our appreciation and respect. This includes all of the documentary filmmakers, impact strategists, executives, and civil society leaders we interviewed, often more than once. We hope our readers will check out Appendix A to see the full list of individuals whose direct voices are reflected in these pages.

Likewise, as is the case with the films and activism initiatives featured here, this research would also not have been possible without the support of a cadre of organizations and their leaders. We would like to recognize the particular support of Megha Sood and Nikki Heyman from Doc Society, who helped make connections with documentary people all around the world, as well as other trusted documentary colleagues who took time out of their schedules to read draft versions and shared valuable feedback, personal connections, and resources, including Nanfu Wang, Marcia Smith, Jacqueline Olive, Chloe Genga, and Beadie Finzi. Their broader leadership in the documentary field serves as the inspiration and driving force for this entire book, and their personal contributions to sharing their perspectives and experiences through multiple interviews over the course of the last few years has enriched its contents in a multitude of ways. Without their courage to overcome immense challenges in pursuit of telling vital stories, and their willingness to also share honest reflections on the state of the field and their own work, this book would not be possible. Additionally, a good deal of our insights were originally sparked and investigated through our work at the Center for Media & Social Impact, through documentary studies supported by the Perspective Fund (Denae Peters, Jacob Taylor), Ford Foundation (Chi-hui Yang, Jon-Sesrie Goff), and MacArthur Foundation (Jennifer Humke, Kathy Im, and Lauren Pabst), and we express our deep gratitude for their belief in our efforts.

X ACKNOWLEDGMENTS

At our home institution, American University, we appreciate a handful of close colleagues whose leadership and efforts enrich the book, particularly the Center for Media & Social Impact's operations director, Varsha Ramani, and our research collaborator Aras Coskuntuncel. Additionally, Hannah Lipstein, a student in AU's MA in Strategic Communication program, provided invaluable editorial assistance. We thank them all.

Last but not least, we are profoundly grateful for Norman Hirschy and Zara Cannon-Mohammed, our editors at Oxford University Press, who furnished a positive and encouraging editorial process as we crafted this volume.

Our individual notes follow.

David Conrad-Pérez:

I thank the incredibly kind and brilliant community of people behind the Center for Media & Social Impact, especially Caty Borum (who opened the doors that made it possible for me to contribute to this book, and whose incredible mentorship, collaboration, humor, and support I value immensely), Varsha Ramani, and Aras Coskuntuncel. I am absurdly fortunate to be able to count any time spent with these amazing individuals as working hours. I also want to share appreciation for a dear friend and colleague, Nancy Katu-Ogundimu, who passed during the writing of this book; her critical work in nonfiction storytelling and journalism for peace and justice serves as its own force of evidence and guidance for the potential of media in making the world a better place, and her friendship and warm generosity improved the world of everyone around her.

Finally, and beyond all else, the powers of film and language aren't enough to capture my gratitude for the encouragement and love of Ana Maria Pérez, the most inspiring and supportive wife and partner I could have ever dreamed of, who lifted my posture and spirit on many occasions in the writing of this book.

Caty Borum:

Working with David Conrad-Pérez on anything—a documentary jury, research project, piece of writing—is an absolute delight, and this book is the pinnacle of our many collaborations over the years. Every idea is better when David is involved, not only due to his incredible aptitude as a thinker and a writer, but because of the spirit and humanity he brings to everything he does. I am similarly grateful to our beloved CMSI colleague and friend

Varsha Ramani, whose many talents make our work possible. On a personal level, my love Jeffrey Jones is a bottomless well of encouragement, brilliance, brainstorming, ideas, affirmations, and creativity, and I thank him for all the support he provides me on a daily basis. And finally, my gorgeous, amazing children—Elias and Simone—fill my heart with love and pride. Everything I do is for them and the world they will inherit.

* * *

Parts of Chapter 1 ("Fighting the Good Fight Around the World") were previously published in: Caty Borum, David Conrad-Pérez, and Bryan Bello (2022), "Creative Independent Investigative Documentary Storytellers in the Streaming Age: Toward A Community of Practice Framework," *Journalism Practice*, https://doi.org/10.1080/17512786.2022.2126993.

Part of Chapter 3 ("Witnessing Conflict and Resilience") was previously published in: David Conrad (2018), "Misguided Benevolence: How 'Moments of Need' Came to Motivate American Journalism" (PhD diss., University of Pennsylvania).

Part of Chapter 7 ("Creating Spaces for Reconciliation and Healing") was previously published in a case study series produced by the authors: David Conrad-Perez et al. (2024), "Beyond the Impact Report: What's Really Needed to Produce and Sustain Social Impact in Documentary Film?" Case Study series. Center for Media & Social Impact (CMSI), American University.

Part of Chapter 8 ("Building a Future for Global Independent Documentary Storytelling to Survive and Thrive") was previously published in: Caty Borum Chattoo (2020, December 17), "Looking Beyond 2020, Why Do Documentaries Matter to Democracy?," *Documentary* magazine, https://www.documentary.org/online-feature/looking-beyond-2020-why-do-documentaries-matter-democracy.

Oxford University Press and the authors gratefully recognize these publishers.

Images

1.1, 1.2, 1.3:   Description: Arvind Kejriwal in *An Insignificant Man*.
Images courtesy of Khushboo Ranka.   2–3

1.4:   Description: *An Insignificant Man* poster. Image courtesy of
Khushboo Ranka.   4

2.1:   Description: *All In*: AllInForVoting campaign bus.
Image courtesy of Amazon Content Services LLC.   34

2.2.   Description: *The Silence of Others:* María Martín sits by the road
that covers the mass grave containing her mother's remains. Photo
Credit: Almudena Carracedo. © Semilla Verde Productions.   39

2.3.   Description: *The Silence of Others:* Jose Maria "Chato" Galante
in the jail where, as a 24-year-old, he was imprisoned for fighting
against the dictatorship. Photo Credit: Almudena Carracedo.
© Semilla Verde Productions.   40

2.4.   Description: *The Silence of Others*: The statues featured in
The Silence of Others, on a mountaintop in the Valley of Jerte,
by sculptor Francisco Cedenilla. Photo Credit: Almudena Carracedo.
© Semilla Verde Productions.   40

2.5.   Description: *The Silence of Others*: Seville Screening—November
2018 Pre-Premiere of *The Silence of Others* in Seville.
Photo Credit: Beatriz Macias.   42

3.1.   Description: *No Simple Way Home*: Family portrait. From left to
right: Standing: Mabior Garang de Mabior, Chol Garang de Mabior.
Seated: Gak Garang de Mabior, Akuol Garang de Mabior, John
Garang de Mabior, Rebecca Nyandeng de Mabior, Nyankuir Garang
de Mabior. Image provided by: Akuol Garang de Mabior.   64

3.2.   Description: *No Simple Way Home*: Rebecca Nyandeng de
Mabior arriving in South Sudan. Image provided by:
Akuol Garang de Mabior.   64

3.3.   Description: *No Simple Way Home*: Akuol and Nyankuir. From left to
right: Nyankuir Garang de Mabior, Akuol Garang de Mabior.
Image provided by: Akuol Garang de Mabior.   65

3.4.   Description: *No Simple Way Home*: Main film poster.
Photo Credit: Thomas Morley. Image provided by:
Akuol Garang de Mabior.   65

xiv IMAGES

4.1. Description: *Writing with Fire*: Codirector and cinematographer Sushmit Ghosh filming Meera Devi on location in Uttar Pradesh. Image Copyright: Black Ticket Films. 87

4.2. Description: *The First Step*: Van Jones advocating for criminal justice reform in Washington, D.C. Credit: Meridian Hill Pictures. 93

4.3. Description: *The First Step*: A coalition from West Virginia and Los Angeles come together to discuss criminal justice reform. Credit: Meridian Hill Pictures. 93

5.1. Description: *Welcome to Chechnya* BTS VFX SHOOT. Image credit: Courtesy of the *Welcome to Chechnya* Film Team. 116

5.2. Description: *Welcome to Chechnya* poster. Image credit: Courtesy of the *Welcome to Chechnya* Film Team. 117

5.3. Description: *Uýra*: Film national premiere at Nossa Senhora de Fátima, Uýra's neighborhood—Manaus, AM. Image credit: Matheus Belém. 125

5.4. Description: *Uýra*: Film national premiere at Nossa Senhora de Fátima, Uýra's neighborhood—Manaus, AM. Image credit: Matheus Belém. 126

5.5. Description: *Uýra* film poster. Image courtesy of *Uýra* film team. 127

6.1. Description: *Delikado*: Tata Balladares rests on a fallen tree while searching for illegal loggers in forests of southern Palawan, Rizal, Palawan—April 2018. Photo Credit: Karl Malakunas. 135

6.2. Description: *Delikado*: Tata Balladares and other PNNI para-enforcers walk through a patch of destroyed forest. *Delikado*: Photo Credit: Delikado LLC. 135

6.3, 6.4. Description: *Delikado*: The film's participants receiving a standing ovation at the Philippine premiere of the film to a full house of 1,500 people in Manila in 2022. Copyright Delikado LLC. 137

6.5. Description: *Thank You for the Rain*: Kisilu Musya leaves Christina Wayua Kisilu. Photos credit: Julie Lillesæter. Copyright Banyak Films & Differ Media 2017. 148

6.6. Description: *Thank You for the Rain*: Kisilu Musya at the "red line" protest in Paris. Photos credit: Julie Lillesæter. Copyright Banyak Films & Differ Media 2017. 149

7.1 Description: Members of the *In My Blood It Runs* film and impact team during an impact strategy planning workshop. Photo Credit: *In My Blood It Runs* film team. 167

7.2, 7.3. Description: A screening event and resource table for the film *Pray Away* in Washington, D.C. Photo courtesy of *Pray Away* film team. 172, 173

7.4.	Description: Left to right: Earl S. Mowatt (one PULSE Foundation), Rev. Stanley Ramos (Alabanza MCC), Patty Sheehan (conversion therapy survivor, Orlando City Council), Heather Wilkie (Zebra Youth), and *Pray Away* impact producer Shae Washington. Photo courtesy of *Pray Away* film team.	174
8.1.	Description: Shanida Scotland, Doc Society Codirector, Head of Film, speaking at Doc Society's inaugural Democracy Story Lab in London in November 2023. Photo courtesy of Doc Society and Shanida Scotland.	182

1

Fighting the Good Fight Around the World

In 2016, the acclaimed Indian political documentary *An Insignificant Man* premiered at the prestigious Toronto International Film Festival. It was a critical hit, astonishing viewers with its intimate access to political figures and its open showcase of public dissent—reflections rarely seen in mainstream Indian news. In observational form, the documentary follows the real-time developments of what became a crucial moment for the country's democracy in 2013—the political rise and impending dominance of the right-wing religious Hindu-nationalist party, Bharatiya Janata Party (BJP), a restless uprising sparked to life within pockets of India's multiethnic, multireligious populace. A new collective voice clapped back—the Aam Admi Party (AAP), or "Common Man's Party"—and its founding leader, politician Arvind Kejriwal, didn't demur in criticizing the corruption he saw in the country's two major political parties.

As directors Khushboo Ranka and Vinay Shukla said in press interviews at the time, Kejriwal and his AAP provided a jolt of energy for prodemocracy Indian citizens who responded to his calls to fight malfeasance and shed light on perceived murky political machinations. Within a political system that is, as the filmmakers characterize it, "extraordinarily opaque," the documentary reveals it all, despite the impossible odds stacked against this kind of critical, in-depth storytelling in India.[1] By the time Ranka and Shukla were ready to launch the film in their own country, the BJP had become the dominant party under India's Prime Minister Narendra Modi, the right-wing stalwart elected in 2014.

But in an unanticipated twist, the Indian government stepped in to block the film. In 2017, the country's national censor, the Central Board of Film Certification (CBFC), refused to provide the official certificate required to distribute the film in India—that is, unless the filmmakers removed all references to BJP and Congress, and unless they also received written permission from Prime Minister Modi and the titular figure Kejriwal, the activist politician pushing for change.[2] Ranka and Shukla knew the proposed

---

Radical Reality. Caty Borum and David Conrad-Pérez, Oxford University Press. © Oxford University Press 2025.
DOI: 10.1093/9780197604298.003.0001

Image 1.1 Description: Arvind Kejriwal in *An Insignificant Man*. Image courtesy of Khushboo Ranka.

Image 1.2 Description: Arvind Kejriwal in *An Insignificant Man*. Image courtesy of Khushboo Ranka.

changes to the film would be catastrophic. In neutered form, it would be useless as an authentic eyewitness to a meaningful political moment.

The tide only turned after the directing team launched a social media campaign in protest, vocally amplified by the International Documentary Association and others, when India's Film Certification Appellate Tribunal

FIGHTING THE GOOD FIGHT AROUND THE WORLD 3

Image 1.3 Description: Arvind Kejriwal in *An Insignificant Man*. Image courtesy of Khushboo Ranka.

(FACT) finally cleared the film for release.[3] But there was still another hurdle to pass: the country's highest court. By the end of the year, the Indian Supreme Court ruled in favor of the film and freedom of expression, a crucial moment for directors Ranka and Shukla and for documentaries that would follow.[4] The decision was a pathbreaking precedent for nonfiction storytellers working within the country's media censorship system. With its notoriety well-established due to the controversy, *An Insignificant Man* opened immediately in India, blasting open a rare window to witness political resistance and opposition in the country.

For its makers, the film was a turning point. As codirector Vinay Shukla said years later in an interview for this book, he was motivated by idealism for his country when he began, and he was even more compelled by the nonfiction form when the commotion was all over. His original compulsion—tell true stories that speak truth to power in some way—was even stronger:

> That film gave me the opportunity to explore idealism, to understand what happens when a new political party full of idealism enters the current system of politics. What are the challenges that it faces? How does it deal with it? What kind of impact does the party have on the political culture and vice versa? And I was also constantly thinking about the larger question of how we should be framing our politics. But I went into that film

Image 1.4 Description: *An Insignificant Man* poster. Image courtesy of Khushboo Ranka.

with an inherent lens of being excited about idealism. When the film came out, because Khushboo and I faced so many challenges, our idealism had taken a solid beating on the release of that process. . . . But I was also pushed to a space wherein I was suddenly questioning, I was in a new phase in life wherein I began to contemplate what my role as an author is in the society around me. Because India currently is, without a doubt, going through a massive phase of transformation. . . . When I decided to make films, I really wanted to make them because I thought films can change the world and make it a better place. It's very, very idealistic. And it's in my core DNA.[5]

The story of *An Insignificant Man* exemplifies the motivations, opportunities, and constraints facing a tenacious network of global documentary makers and film organizations fighting for social justice—transparency, right to dissent, anticorruption, freedom of expression, human rights—against tides of increasingly oppressive climates that often seek to silence inconvenient voices of protest or uncomfortable narratives of reality. The film's battle against censorship and its hard-won legal victory would be notable in nearly any juncture, but it may seem particularly salient today, especially if we peer more closely at the bigger picture. In 2019, India, the world's largest democracy, dramatically plummeted nearly 10 places on the annual global Democracy Index report—a compilation published by *The Economist* that ranks democratic functioning based on indicators including an open press, freedom of expression, and activities of civil society—landing in the bottom half of the second-tier, "flawed democracy" category, where the United States also resides.[6] As the report noted, "the primary cause of the democratic regression [in India] was an erosion of civil liberties in the country," and its government's tendency to silence media references to taboo topics.[7] While this is a particular story within a specific political context, it echoes in other corners of the world, in liberal democracies and authoritarian climates alike. And yet, it only begins to reveal the dynamic opposition and increasing pressures that documentarians face.

Radical Reality: Documentary Storytelling and the Global Fight for Social Justice reveals how and why independent documentary makers around the world are producing nonfiction film and TV programs that reveal hidden or neglected stories and fight for social justice, how they collaborate with supportive civil society organizations and activists to amplify their efforts, and why contemporary documentary storytelling matters for social change and progress in a global context. The book's stories spotlight documentary's place in the participatory media era and its challenges for an evolving future: surveillance technology, misinformation, suppression of free speech, consolidated commercial media systems, and other constraints. In countries around the globe, documentary films like *An Insignificant Man* are standing for freedom of expression, serving as witnesses to conflict and resilience, maintaining cultural memory of human rights abuses, and opening intimate windows into acts of protest, activism, reconciliation, and resistance that often go unseen in dominant news and other media portrayals. They are pushing against boundaries of oppression, centering underrepresented communities and leaders, providing spaces for community healing and recognition, and challenging authoritarian narratives that dispel controlled and often inaccurate portraits of people and their problems and triumphs.

And they are doing so in significant times. In disparate places, including within democracies historically lauded for their support of various freedoms, governments are ramping up forms of repression against those who would challenge power—independent media and journalists, civil society organizations that collectively advocate for the public interest, and ordinary people who speak out as activists. The trends are inseparably intertwined: a rise of authoritarianism around the world, increased clamp-downs on civil society, and media systems shuttering access and distribution. And yet, there is hope and power found in the hands of storytellers and activists who marshal a way forward, again and again, to push the status quo toward justice with a story-centered approach, armed with the tools and networks afforded by the participatory media age. This book shares their stories.

Documentary Storytelling for Social Justice:
Functions, Impact, and Motivations

Documentary's potential to provide an investigative spotlight on social issues and public affairs hearkens to the turn of the last century, as the turmoil of the second Industrial Revolution called for a spotlight on injustice of all kinds. Poverty, corruption, child labor, widespread hunger, the dawning Great Depression, rapid immigration, and industrialization were all ripe topics for righteous storytellers and reform-seekers. The earliest forms of documentary thus emerged as watchdog and activist, witness and storyteller. Many decades later, through the voyeuristic vérité movement of the 1950s and 1960s, evolving into the 1990s and early 2000s as cable TV and theatrical documentary feature films showed promise in the marketplace, entertainment value began to matter more than it had in artistic documentary's somewhat didactic formative years.[8] Since then, a cinematic approach to telling stories has steadily taken hold in the contemporary age of nonfiction storytelling. Today, artful investigative documentary films—largely developed and produced outside the confines of formal journalistic or entertainment organizations by independent filmmakers who license their work for distribution—are found across a broader range of media outlets than ever before, from PBS to MSNBC and CNN to Netflix, Hulu, and Amazon.[9] We can also see them on local public channels, commercial outlets, and in large and small theaters, community centers, houses of faith, and beyond.

Documentary storytelling is, of course, not new, and a rich history points to its value in social reform human rights and social justice, from the dawn of the moving picture camera through the digital age of media. The desire and motivation of documentary storytellers to use cameras and real life to agitate politics to push for social reform, and indeed, to advance overt social change—acting often as voices of dissent—can be found in important junctures over more than a century of evolution.[10] Documentary, given these origin stories, "has always been driven by engagement, either political or social," wrote scholar Michael Chanan.[11] Well before the stories and filmmakers in this book employed their craft, documentary history reveals powerful undercurrents of movements and nonfiction storytellers' endeavors to make change by showcasing lives, problems, and injustices.[12] Having evolved well past such rich roots, documentary traditions and collaborations exist all around the world, still motivated quite often by ideals of reform and social change.[13]

What precisely *is* and *isn't* a documentary? It's a fascinating question that preoccupies scholars and filmmakers from one generation to the next. This volume doesn't aim to agitate or claim mastery of this particular debate, given our respect for a flexible and wide-ranging journalistic, cinematic art form that evolves across a range of artistic brains and spirits. Several articulations bear mentioning, though. In the 1930s, an early formative time in nonfiction storytelling, the Scottish sociologist and documentary forefather John Grierson supplied perhaps documentary's most enduring broad definition: "a creative treatment of actuality."[14] His approach to this genre emphasized a social reform aspect,[15] which endures in the films and filmmakers we spotlight in this book. Many decades later, documentary historian Patricia Aufderheide complicated and built on this elegant simplicity in ways that signal nonfiction storytellers' inherent challenges alongside

8 RADICAL REALITY

audiences' basic expectations about what they are watching: "A documentary film tells a story about real life, with claims to truthfulness. How to do that honestly, in good faith is a never-ending discussion, with many answers. Documentary is defined and redefined over the course of time, both by makers and by viewers ... we do expect that a documentary will be a fair and honest representation of somebody's experience of reality."[16] As to documentary functions more broadly, theorist Michael Renov described four nonfiction storytelling "modes": "1. to record, reveal, or preserve; 2. to persuade or promote; 3. to analyze or interrogate; and 4. to express."[17]

Building on these ideas, in this book, we are singularly focused on a particular documentary form and motivation, and thus, we use this definition of social-issue documentary as a practice, originally conceived and articulated in *Story Movements: How Documentaries Empower People and Inspire Social Change*, crafted by the first author of this book:

> Contemporary documentary that engages social issues is a creative, entertaining, often investigative narrative mechanism—a process and a product—by which storytellers interrogate and reveal the human complexity of social challenges, thus contributing to the revitalized public sphere, the cultural place where social problems are negotiated and challenged by motivated publics. In such a civic function and practice, the public's access to information is key, and its ability to act is central.[18]

In this context, as agents of—and contributors to—social change, according to this foundation,

> documentaries have incited national and local conversations, set media agendas, provided intimate new lenses with which to see social problems and people, and sometimes contributed to changing laws and corporate policies.... Fueled by the possibilities of the participatory networked media age, the contemporary role and function of social-issue documentaries in the public sphere is embodied also in parallel community engagement practices—the active role of civil society groups, communities, and individual people speaking truth to power.[19]

This sort of documentary, while varied in artistic sensibility—that is, the creative decisions that manifest in editing, music cues, camera angles, narrative structure, and choice of protagonists—generally shares a set of traits and motivations that are meaningful, also reflected in this volume's progenitor book, *Story Movements*. Contemporary social-issue documentaries broadly exhibit the following values and traits through the practices of their makers and output of their work: *editorial independence, commitment to truth and ethics, civic motivation*, and *entertainment value*. These themes will appear throughout the pages that follow and deserve a little unpacking. First, *editorial independence* in the documentary craft leaves the "primary creative decision-making in the hands of independent directors and producers who are not employees of media institutions that commission or distribute their work"—that is, "authorial" documentaries are produced largely by auteurs who are not formally employed by a media institution.[20] To tell stories that move beyond status quos enforced by institutions of power—from governments to corporate actors—editorial independence is vitally important. So, too, is a responsible, rigorous, *ethical approach to reflecting truth* in documentary practice and output, "even if the meaning of truth in creative nonfiction storytelling—an artistic rendering of life and events—will always remain imprecise and not fully resolved, not because creative nonfictions films are not truthful, but at least partially because our cultural understanding of media 'truth' may be inseparably intertwined with journalistic conceptions of 'objectivity' and a neutral, detached view."[21] Artful storytelling does not mean an abandonment of truth, and striving for accuracy is essential. And what of artists' inclinations and intentions, beyond art? *Civic motivation* is the idea that, for social-issue films, filmmakers are motivated—alongside creative impulses, of course—by "the desire to share an injustice or unseen narrative or lens, fueled by the underlying belief in collective wellbeing or the public's right to know and perhaps even intervene."[22] Investigative creative documentary filmmakers are powerfully inspired, also, by the potential for reform on behalf of a common good, even as their stories are rendered artfully.[23] And finally, creativity and *entertainment value* are essential ingredients; after all, audiences should be compelled to watch for more than altruistic reasons, and capturing attention is requisite.[24]

Beyond cultural effects and motivations of the makers, how do audiences play an active role here? What happens to us when we watch evocative, well-crafted documentaries? How we feel and learn from cinematically rendered true stories is meaningful in the overall portrait of how and why documentaries do and can lead to positive social impact. For viewers, the perceived realism of documentaries matters; if and when we perceive we are watching something real and truthful, we are moved and often persuaded by

10 RADICAL REALITY

the story.[25] When we watch an artistic documentary about social issues, our cognitive *and* emotional selves react; we are absorbed into the story world in a way that captures us emotionally and mentally, a process known as narrative transportation, and we experience empathy and parasocial connections with protagonists.[26] This process helps to persuade us because we are thinking and feeling deeply as we watch.[27] Nonfiction storytelling is, in this way, a precise and distinct experience for audiences.

Within this context, investigative nonfiction artistic stories are culturally essential. Documentary is a journalistic, cinematic form of narrative that helps shape our collective understanding about, and emotional connections to, lived experiences in places we may never encounter in our physical lives, or in places we know well but hardly recognize in media portrayals that can range from neglectful and naive to incomplete and dehumanizing, depending on who we are. In this conceptualization, we position contemporary social-issue documentary storytelling around the globe both as a *public good* and as *public interest media*, regardless of how the stories may be distributed (via grassroots means, public broadcasters, or commercial media companies) or experienced by audiences (in faith community gatherings, theaters, or individual bedrooms and living rooms).

To borrow from scholar Victor Pickard's similar reflection about the contemporary state of journalism, "public goods are non-rivalrous (one person's consumption of the good does not detract from another's) and nonexcludable (it is difficult to exclude free riders from consuming the good)," but they are also socially beneficial, in that the "value to society transcends the revenue that it generates."[28] While we might certainly make an obvious economic argument about commercial media documentary distribution, which requires subscription or internet connectivity fees of some kind, the broader point applies to documentaries that delve into public affairs and social issues, often in an investigative capacity. The "positive externalities" generated by such documentaries, to use Pickard's framing of journalism,[29] manifest in such public goods as clean air, justice served to vulnerable populations, upholding human rights, and providing a corrective narrative to offer a lens beyond problematic news framing that can emerge around particular communities and their lived realities. In our view, fighting for basic human rights and dignity—often denied or constrained based on race, class, ethnicity, race, religion, region of birth, and so forth—is a positive externality that benefits all members of a civilized society. Documentaries are often uniquely equipped to provide this kind of view, and thus, the public good framing rings true.

The stakes are high, given that "an independent public interest media system is critical to democratic self-determination and to economic development" around the world.[30] If information systems are solely shaped by the whims of the market, how will communities learn and understand power dynamics that determine nearly every aspect of their lives? How will they know—and *feel*—enough to dissent? It's a wicked, perennial worldwide quandary, regardless of a country's wealth or freedoms (but felt most acutely by countries with less of both). Media output that operates in the public interest is a bedrock to the very idea of democracy, human rights, and freedom. Responding to grave concern about the global state of independent media, the newly formed International Fund for Public Interest Media defines "public interest media" in contemporary terms as:

> media that is free and independent, that exists to inform publics on the issues that shape their lives in ways which serve the public's rather than any political, commercial or factional interest, to enable public debate and dialogue across society, and to hold those in power to account on behalf of the public interest. It implies a focus on ethical and credible media working in the interests of all people across all of society, not just those who have the power or money to pay for or influence media. Public interest media can be commercial, public service or community media and distributed online, broadcast, through print or other channels.[31]

High-quality social-issue documentary storytelling, given civic motivations and other traits, fits within the confines of public interest media—in part because documentary functions as a form of civic storytelling: *transmitting counternarratives* that agitate and complicate a hegemonic dominant narrative that may serve powerful interests; *monitoring* and acting in a watchdog capacity to alert publics to nascent or missing issues of importance; *artistically interpreting* events and realities to provide deeper understanding beyond facts afforded by news media alone; *organizing and mobilizing* public participation in a social challenge or a state of injustice; and *strengthening civil society* by helping human rights organizations to leverage evocative, emotional, artistic stories that allow a distinctly human portal with which to see lived experiences and problems.[32]

Documentaries are powerful, in other words. But when it comes to the possibility of fueling social change, filmmakers don't do it alone. An increasingly connected global network of storytellers, activists, and movement

12   RADICAL REALITY

builders is growing. It's shaped by an activist ethos in a participatory media culture that inspires independent voices and community-building.

A Global Ecology of Documentary Changemakers

As the early days of the social media age revealed some fresh promise for grassroots power, nonfiction film people weren't about to be left out. Digital technology of the early 2000s had already opened doors to accessible media-making gear, not to mention the organizing possibilities of internet-driven communication. All eyes turned to the irresistible spectacle of the pioneering digital-media uprisings in the early 2010s, #OccupyWallStreet and the Arab Spring, which galvanized global actions, stunning the world with the network-building capacity of digital and social media tools.[33] Nascent grassroots organizing strategies sprang up in all kinds of political and human rights work, of course owing bedrock practices and norms to analog-age pioneers.

In this fertile time and space—spanning the mid-2000s to mid-2010s—a growing conversation in regional pockets of documentary communities picked up steam: If documentaries fueled and often enabled human rights activism to gain new traction, then how might this power be exponentially expanded if independent artistic and activism voices could come together as local and global networks? And could stories of documentary-driven social impact—often anecdotal—be shared and somewhat codified as real lessons learned, creating templates and approaches that might work in a range of contexts? Cara Mertes, founder/director of the International Resource for Impact and Storytelling (IRIS) and long-established global leader and funder in nonfiction film and social justice, reflected on that critical juncture:

> [In that time] you've got a tremendous amount of interconnectedness now that people have phones, they have internet, everybody's watching everybody else's stories. So there's this new age of travel and exchange, but also an impulse to choose documentary as the method of telling contemporary stories, stories about what's happening to me or to my community or to my country, and more investigative approaches. There was a now a greater ability to reach a more international conversation and spotlight with your issue. In other words, there was incentive to tell your story, because there were audiences listening.[34]

A global documentary community seemed increasingly possible, beyond the bounds of commerce and festivals. How and why world-spanning documentary network power-building matters for social justice is hard to overstate, particularly when we center reformist ideals of muckraking nonfiction cinema. Individual filmmakers and strategists are the ultimate Davids to the behemoth Goliaths of structural power systems—governments, mega-corporate money and control, deep-pocketed financial interests—that have much to lose when inconvenient truths are exposed and people are informed and moved by human rights abuses. Complex social problems are, of course, intertwined among dominant systems that gain and hold control through propaganda dressed up as advertising, state-censored media systems, and commercial media systems' business models that focus on profit and wide audience appeal, not necessarily the public interest or human rights. How can one filmmaker and one film, left to the whims of marketplace-driven entertainment media distribution, possibly amass the cultural attention and public engagement necessary to help make change? Power through network-based learning, resources, and validation is essential. This is the core idea.

Enter "impact producers," a term derived from generations of community engagement work in and beyond the field of documentary, and more recently codified in part from the UK-based nonprofit Doc Society's (formerly BRITDoc) Good Pitch program, which "invites selected documentary storytellers to showcase their work and 'pitch' assembled aligned civil society actors—nonprofit organizations and community groups, issue advocates, government agencies, philanthropists—to create community engagement and financing partnerships to expand the potential of their films to act as change agents."[35] Notably, while the moniker "impact producer" is relatively young, the practice of developing intentional community engagement with documentary storytelling is many decades old, hearkening back to social movement practices and community engagement through public and independent media in the middle and latter part of the 20th century. Over time, throughout the 1970s and well beyond, efforts of human-rights-focused documentary filmmakers helped to codify intentional community engagement practices and tactics.[36] The dawn of internet-based organizing tools built on established ideas and expanded what was previously possible.

In the early 2010s, a few years after regional hubs of social-justice documentary activities began stirring to life, a series of invited "documentary

14   RADICAL REALITY

community" meetings hosted by Doc Society and others began to assemble a motley mix of documentary storytellers and the impact strategists who worked alongside them, philanthropies, and civil society organizations. Justice-aimed grassroots organizing around documentaries was not a fledgling idea, given powerful roots and evolution in earlier social movement and community media cultures,[37] but the potentially new ease of building network power around the world was exciting. Energy was high. Filmmakers, activists, and marketing strategy professionals shared case studies, philanthropies pledged their support, and alliances began. The "impact producer"—as moniker and framework to describe intentional social movement activism work that happens in collaboration with a documentary film and its creative team—caught on, at least partially empowered by the digital media age, built on a longer legacy of documentary- and community-centered activism, work, experimentation, and history.[38]

Momentum picked up. In 2015 at the International Documentary Festival Amsterdam (IDFA), Doc Society hosted the first-ever invite-only global convening of impact producers and documentary filmmakers (the first author of this book was there) to get serious about building a multinational grassroots network.[39] Based on years of traction and a spark from the gathering, the Global Impact Producers Assembly (GIPA) launched with members from around the world, powered by a busy invite-only listserve and calls for community gatherings at international film festivals and other opportune times to bring folks together. Among others, new global nonfestival convenings of documentary people like the International Documentary Association's pathbreaking Getting Real conferences fostered unprecedented network-building spaces for impact strategists and filmmakers to come together. In 2018, IDA hosted one of the first major such gatherings, informally titled "Building Networks Across Borders," with 56 representatives of documentary organizations around the world, spanning Indonesia, Turkey, Australia, Israel, France, Japan, the United States, Serbia, Chile, and more.[40] Mertes, who played a central role in cultivating and supporting this network, referred to this juncture as

> a simultaneous blossoming of regional nonfiction hubs around the world led by, interestingly, two different types. One was entrepreneurs who had money and wanted to choose this as their way to improve the world. And the second was filmmakers who didn't have any kind of community around them when they were coming up, and they didn't want to repeat that for the

FIGHTING THE GOOD FIGHT AROUND THE WORLD   15

next generation. They were and are artist leaders who wanted to actually build a field for the kind of work that they do.[41]

Communities and networks emerged anew.

Agitation by individual nonfiction storytellers and activists is exponentially more potent when grassroots networks support one another—and when new networks emerge to cultivate solid communities of practice that share resources, shape norms and ways of doing business, lend knowledge, and amplify messages and public engagement tactics.[42] Media makers who investigate, expose injustice, serve as watchdogs, and create counternarratives are often solo acts fighting against seemingly impossible odds that span from funding to legal protection to physical risk. But the story changes when they create allegiances with civil society organizations, philanthropies, local community networks, and social-media-fueled digital activism. Leaning on disparate levers of transnational grassroots power and networks dramatically ups their odds for success, adds needed financial and legal support, and creates vital support networks. It's a synergistic mutual value proposition: Investigative nonfiction storytellers gain muscle by leveraging the expertise, advocacy know-how, and constituencies of civil society organizations, and for their part, NGOs have evocative visual media storytelling to help engage publics in social issues that can be too complex for ready understanding.[43]

A revolutionary era of global network power among documentary filmmakers and collaborative activists, sparked in the nascent and fertile early-to-mid-2000s, is expanding, despite—or perhaps because of—a confluence of both opportunities and challenges, from authoritarianism to the entertainment-ization of documentary storytelling in the streaming media age. Over the past decades, local and regional documentary networks have enabled social impact through nonfiction storytelling, but also to share best practices in their work.

To be sure, this flourishing did not happen by happenstance. Identifying individual regional organizations and bringing them together was an intentional effort—the long game and vision of leaders like Cara Mertes, who went on to leverage her successive posts as director of the Sundance Institute's Documentary Film Program and the Ford Foundation's JustFilms program, alongside fierce fellow visionaries like Jess Search of Doc Society, to provide support and resources to coalesce and strengthen a powerful global network. Through an effort called the JustFilmsBUILD Network, Mertes directed

16   RADICAL REALITY

millions in multiyear funding to eight original documentary organizations focused on human rights—DocEdge, CNEX, AFAC, InDocs, DocuBox, Ambulante, DocSociety, APAN in Brazil, and Beirut DC—unquestionably proving philanthropy's vital role in, as Mertes puts it, "establishing and strengthening this vision of a globally-connected, regionally-rooted independent non-fiction social justice network. . . . Jess, I and others believed that it was time for a global independent documentary network to be formed which prioritized bold, creative non-fiction in the public good."[44]

Among others, there are organizations including Ambulante (Mexico and Central America), In-Docs and DocuBox (Kenya), Doc Sao Paolo (Brazil), Arab Fund for Arts and Culture (AFAC, formerly Beirut DC), DocedgeKolkata Asian Forum for Documentary (India), AFLAMUNA (Lebanon), Engage Media (Indonesia), Unquiet Collective (Australia), Film & Campaign (Scotland), Together Films (United Kingdom), Brown Girls Doc Mafia (United States), Documentary Filmmakers With Disabilities/ FWD-DOC (United States), among others, and international festivals that serve as gathering and network-strengthening hubs for documentary makers speaking truth to power, like DocEdge in New Zealand and International Documentary Festival Amsterdam in the Netherlands. Together, these groups have funded films, resourced and supported filmmakers, developed and implemented human rights campaigns to support their impact, and otherwise enabled thousands of local nonfiction stories to emerge from their countries and regions. It's a staggering impact that's almost impossible to quantify, nearly all of it within the past few decades.

Beyond the business aspects of international documentary markets and festivals, social justice is a persistent theme and value, even as media systems have undergone radical transformation at the hands of commercial streaming-native platforms. Dynamic local and regional hubs of activity in the context of documentary for social change—individual specialized documentary and justice-focused production companies, associations, civil society groups, impact producer and strategy firms, and philanthropies—now exist across disparate regions of the world, including South America, Central America, North America, the Middle East and North Africa, the United Kingdom, Europe, Africa, Asia and Southeast Asia, and the Asia Pacific region. They come together in selective, tight-knit international fora to showcase films, train filmmakers, and collaborate and amplify work across borders. And as a backdrop of networked global and local challenges evolve, their work is cut out for them.

Challenges and Opportunities for Documentary Storytellers Around the World

For documentarians and other independent media makers across the globe, a particular stew of political and economic structural constraints makes for shaky ground. To be sure, documentary work has never blossomed in a stable and predictable environment, but late capitalism in the information society pushes the boundaries of what is possible for an independent-minded nonfiction storytelling field, and its ability to even exist, much less thrive. Among the twists in the veritable maze: Freedom of expression and a free press is under threat across a full range of country contexts; populism and authoritarianism is a new breed, aided by misinformation and echo chambers supported by the same digital information systems that support grassroots engagement for good; digital-native streaming entertainment networks have radically shifted the political economy of the documentary field across platforms; and media consolidation continues at a rapid pace. Documentary storytellers' work is not nearly just the business of researching and artistically crafting the stories. It's a complicated backdrop that requires makers to navigate a shifting morass of finances, distribution, culture, and security risks, each one seemingly unique and yet remarkably consistent from one story to the next. Paradox is—and always has been—engineered into an art form that is equal parts journalistic investigation and cinematic entertainment fare, so it makes sense that contemporary challenges (and opportunities) for muckraking documentary storytellers span a wild range of political and economic contexts—a different set of constraints than either pure journalism or entertainment media alone. Documentary makers weave in and out of both systems *and* their associated hurdles.

On the one hand, the journalistic part of the equation means that documentary makers contend with the same risks that reporters face around the world, particularly those who speak truth to institutions of power. Globally, democracy is under threat even in places where it might have once seemed impossible, and freedom is on the decline, according to the Freedom House annual *Freedom in the World Report*, which concludes: "The struggle for democracy may be approaching a turning point. The gap between the number of countries that registered overall improvements in political rights and civil liberties and those that registered overall declines for 2022 was the narrowest it has ever been through 17 years of global deterioration."[45] A well-known byproduct of authoritarian or even semiauthoritarian contexts, of course, is

18   RADICAL REALITY

a clamp-down on freedom of expression. Both journalistic craft and cinematic storytelling with similar missions are threatened by leaders who infuse the culture with a steady drip of opposition to free speech. In Brazil, for example, former President Jair Bolsonaro, known for intimidating his country's Supreme Court and his critics,[46] targeted journalists during his years in office, culminating in an environment in which Brazilian journalists were harassed online every three seconds during his final election.[47] His own calls to boycott his country's most popular printed news outlet, along with violent threats toward the press in general, most certainly exacerbated the threats in an already inherently risky job.[48] Similarly, in the United States, President Donald Trump called the free press an "enemy of the American people" almost immediately after assuming office.[49]

Documentary storytellers report similar, and increasing, risks in their work—intensified and enabled by surveillance technology and lack of access to financial and legal resources available to traditional newsrooms.[50] The ripple effect manifests in another way when the overseers of government-supported arts funds either directly block or quietly support a message that critical political films won't receive desperately needed financial support, a trend reported by documentary filmmakers in various country contexts.[51] Meanwhile, journalism jobs continue a steady loss around the world, exacerbating an industry "crisis."[52] Every chapter of this book (and particularly Chapter 4) illuminates this set of structural challenges in greater depth, and while the contours of threat from institutional powers are not new—speaking truth to power and pushing for reform has always been risky for journalists and storytellers and artists—they are expansive, particularly considering how the entertainment marketplace is shifting for documentary makers motivated by human rights missions.

On the entertainment side of the documentary formula, the ride has been wild. No consistent guide points exist for independent documentary makers amid the rise of streaming media's radical disruption of both business models and audience behaviors. The shifts are dramatic for the contemporary political economy of the documentary industry that's been called a "golden era" or a "commercialized" era for nonfiction,[53] both alternately true depending on the lens and perspective. As UK-based Netflix nonfiction commissioning team leader Kate Townsend reflected, "What is wrong with wanting documentaries to be widely watched, and what is wrong with wanting beyond a *New York Times* reader? [Is it wrong] to want a broader audience to films? We all came in [to documentary work] to shine a light on issues and social issues. And if you can bring it to an audience beyond the audience that's inherently and already interested in that subject, that's a great opportunity."[54]As usual, a clean binary view is unwise and unrealistic; a quick review of the trajectory helps locate this juncture for independent documentaries that aim for human rights goals.

In 2014, the streaming era of documentary began when Netflix, by then a full disruptor of the scripted entertainment business, acquired and distributed the film *The Square*, an independent eyewitness accounting of the Egyptian Revolution of 2011 that erupted at Tahrir Square.[55] It was a critical and audience success, and independent documentary makers took notice, particularly as Netflix showed up as a huge new buyer of indie docs at the Sundance Film Festival over the next several years, boasting a nearly unfathomable reach to 190 countries around the world.[56] The executive helm of Netflix's move into nonfiction acquired, licensed, and distributed similarly produced human-rights-focused independent films for the next several years—titles like *Winter on Fire: Ukraine's Fight for Freedom* (2015), *White Helmets* (2017), *American Factory* (2020), and *Crip Camp* (2021)— all of which were nominees and winners of some of the biggest awards in the business, including the Oscar for Best Documentary Feature.[57] Netflix is, of course, only one of the global streaming-native networks, alongside the likes of Amazon and Hulu and others, but it's the behemoth next to its other world-spanning network peers that distribute films across cable and subscription video on demand (SVOD), including HBO. Netflix was a sector-leader in terms of business and consumer behavior shifts. At the time, said Kate Townsend, "there was very much a strategy from 2017 to 2019 that we needed to put Netflix on the map. So, supporting the feature [documentary] was a way of supporting, bringing talent, really best-in-class talented documentary filmmakers, into Netflix and garnering a good reputation so that people got really excited about wanting to come to Netflix."[58] It worked, and so did another trend at the same time: the rise of the multipart documentary series.

The 10-part docuseries *Making a Murderer* was the biggest surprise hit for Netflix in 2015—a "bona fide cultural phenomenon"[59]—and it cemented a two-part nonfiction strategy for the streamer (and thus, for other global companies to follow): leverage new multipart nonfiction series to bring in a wider, nontraditional documentary audience and retain the auteur features from independent makers. As Townsend reflected, "Initially it was really the sense that the features were doing reputation [work] and the series were sort

20 RADICAL REALITY

of trying to do a broader reach to audiences that weren't already documentary fans."[60] The promise of new reach and audience seemed possible with the balance of a public interest media orientation. The streamers' entry was meaningful, not only for commercial reasons in documentary world, but also for human rights work, said Cara Mertes: "Independent documentarians could reach a very, very broad international audience with the streamers. . . . Even [if] they were modest in commercial terms, they weren't modest in social justice and civil society terms."[61] And yet, the multipart series frenzy and increase in commissioned films (and series) unquestionably signaled a contemporary evolution: documentary as a genre of entertainment with a capital "E," alongside scripted formats. *Fyre Fest* in 2019, and the monster hit *Tiger King* during the COVID-19 pandemic, were unequivocal signs of the new era. Would editorial independence and distribution for hard-hitting human rights films survive? As with the running theme of documentary's dual journalism-entertainment paradox, the answer is a "yes," "no," or "maybe," depending on one's view.

Nearly a decade after the streaming entertainment age of documentary began, relationships between the biggest, most well-funded global distributors—streaming-native and cable networks owned by consolidated media companies—and independent makers have shifted toward a dominant model of commissioning nonfiction films rather than acquiring fully produced independent projects. A few years after the upstart networks showed up to Sundance and other global festivals to buy indie docs en masse, several have reorganized to largely commission and coproduce films in-house, including Netflix, CNN (which shuttered its CNN Films independent documentary unit in late 2022), and Showtime (which saw massive layoffs and a dramatic restructuring that removed their head of documentaries during its merger with MTV Entertainment Studios in early 2023); others have started new units for commissioned films (NBC Studios).[62] One trade media article summarized the CNN Films shift in 2022:

> What to expect? Less truth to power; more news-driven, low-cost, fast-turnaround documentary films and series. . . . CNN Films will scale back on original documentaries from outside partners. The strategy shift means more than losing a major buyer; for filmmakers it means the great documentary gold rush had a good run, but it's now over. CNN is far from the only platform to tighten its nonfiction belt; cost cutting measures have also come for Netflix, Amazon, and Peacock. However, CNN was one of the last

FIGHTING THE GOOD FIGHT AROUND THE WORLD   21

bastions for hardcore, capital-d documentaries that aspired to more than true crime or "Tiger King."[63]

What's at stake here, or potentially at stake, when distribution options are increasingly limited for independently produced social justice documentaries? Editorial judgment and creative discretion can and does still largely reside with the filmmakers themselves in commissioning scenarios, and yet, the relationship to subject matter changes when the material is produced with the distributor's notes and funding along the way. Netflix, for instance, is involved on the very early side of development and production for "80 to 90 percent" of its films[64] and HBO, operating in territories around the world, reports the same early cocreation process with filmmakers.[65] The marketplace, in this context, becomes the central guidepost. And even then, it's messy, as corporate consolidation continues to decimate media industries, intensifying the challenges for those who are left behind—and increasing risk-averse decision-making.[66] Why take a risk on a human rights film, or a politically critical one, when a music documentary is a predictable audience hit?

At the same time, across Europe and other territories, funding available from public broadcasters—once central for producing and distributing independent social-justice documentaries—is scant, not nearly enough to finance a full network of nonfiction makers. It's increasingly difficult to produce a full film and make money back, much less a living, with dwindling resources on the noncommercial side. The result, according to Townsend, is an unfortunate kind of "two-tiered system" for documentary makers: either work on largely commissioned and funded films from large global networks, or risk not being able to finish a film for many years in the public broadcasting space. And as Mertes puts it, while "there's a tremendous hunger to see these stories, there's also a tremendous hunger to tell and find better modes of distribution."[67]

In sum, the challenges are great, clearly. But it would be simple and reductive to solely rely on a deficit model to unpack and explain global documentary storytellers and their fights for social justice around the world. It's true that they need so much more to do the work properly—financial support, distribution, security—and this book relentlessly interrogates the obstacles in each story. And yet, the ingenuity and enterprise of this network and its individual artists and activists is where power and learning emerge, and thus, this is the centerpiece and throughline of these pages. Opportunities are also

22 RADICAL REALITY

always present—that is, if norms and rules could be made accessible and learned consistently from filmmaker to filmmaker, and if resources could be readily available. Still, the threats are immense. How, exactly, are documentary storytellers and their networks finding ways to tell and share the impossible stories—and to spark the kind of public will and action that can make change? These are the stories that follow.

The Journey of the Book

Radical Reality: Documentary Storytelling and the Global Fight for Social Justice invites readers to learn about documentary films and storytellers around the world who are speaking truth to power, agitating the status quo, bearing witness, exposing corruption, pushing for human rights reform, emboldening activism, correcting false narratives, and creating spaces for healing and repair—all while centering cinematic artistry, entertainment value, and a commitment to accuracy and truth. The book's journey comes from many places and vantage points, and it centers the perspectives of documentary makers and leaders, with whom we spend a great deal of time. Their direct voices—via dozens of in-depth interviews and deep dives into their film and activism stories—are the feature attraction here. And rather than painting merely a tight portrait of a single moment, or even one narrow slice in time, the voices, case studies, and arguments we advance in this book are positioned to illuminate big themes, patterns, and future trajectories that should continue to be studied—and agitated. The topic lives and breathes.

As authors, we bring combined expertise not only in documentary, entertainment media, and journalism scholarship but also professional careers that include producing all of the above, plus social change communication research and strategy, grassroots social justice work, and cultural/narrative change through entertainment storytelling. Our composite lenses are thus hopefully meaningful in obvious ways, but it's worth noting how much our direct conversations and collaborations with documentary makers and leaders have helped shape this book. Among other experiences, through a large-scale, multiyear initiative called the Documentary Power Research Institute (hosted, with a global advisory group, at the Center for Media & Social Impact in the United States), we recently directed and cocreated several years-long global studies with a wide range of documentary filmmakers, impact producers, and organizational leaders who live and work in wildly

FIGHTING THE GOOD FIGHT AROUND THE WORLD   23

disparate corners of the world.[68] Together, we examined how documentary makers are weathering the storms of a radically changing network of global and local distribution systems, how they think about and create social change strategy in political and economic climates that increasingly deem human rights material to be risky (either politically or financially), and what they are thinking and planning for the future of this work—and how they will continue to adapt.[69] Their views are inseparably intertwined with our framing and core questions that guide this book, and their candor opens new doors for readers to contemplate.

It's also important to note what *Radical Reality* is *not* about. While our book covers many stories, motivations, and experiences of filmmakers and grassroots organizers around the world, all rooted in the cultural context of the stories that they tell and the truth that they reveal, it does not focus on a kind of right-wing ideological propaganda that calls itself "documentary." We might think of this as a kind of "dark side" that leverages some production language of the documentary form and yet is motivated by, as the first author of this book wrote elsewhere, "an attempt to manipulate with an arguably blatant disregard for truth. . . . we might call this a visual essay rather than a documentary" if we care about defining characteristics of truth and ethics.[70] That said, this topic is overdue for research attention, and it would make for a valuable and courageous book for a future scholar, although beyond our scope here. Similarly, while *Radical Reality* is preoccupied with social-issue documentary, we notably do not write about the kind of usual suspects—often filmmakers from the United States—who are often listed as the dominant storytellers engaged in these pursuits. With reverence and respect, we see and understand the contributions of folks like Laura Poitras, Davis Guggenheim, Josh Oppenheimer, and others, even while we designed this particular book to shine a much-needed spotlight elsewhere, privileging the stories of many other inspiring documentarians across the globe (far away from, but yes, often including, the United States), especially women-identifying, people of color, and others often marginalized in the industry.[71]

Finally, while this book does not offer a full historical accounting of documentary in any one specific global region, or indeed, around the world, we gladly point readers in the direction of many outstanding, meticulous works that examine rich and varied documentary history, including roots and earlier junctures in social reform efforts, politics, and social change. Many such volumes are cited here, but we spotlight particular scholars whose works provide a full wealth of the histories of the documentary

24 RADICAL REALITY

tradition and chronologies for those who would seek them, including Angela Aguayo, Patricia Aufderheide, Erik Barnouw, Michael Chanan, John Corner, Michael Curtin, Craig Hight, Jonathan Kahana, Betsy McLane, Kate Nash, Bill Nichols, Steve Presence, Michael Renov, William Stott, Thomas Waugh, Brian Winston, and Patricia Zimmermann, among others around the world. In addition, Chapter 2 ("Evolving Documentaries and Social Change: Historical Highlights") of *Story Movements: How Documentaries Empower People and Inspire Social Change*, the precursor to this book in several ways, also delves into analog era history and documentary's early roots, albeit more heavily focused on the United States.[72]

Where will this book take its readers? Picking up from the foundation established in this introduction, each chapter spotlights specific themes that help reveal how documentary storytellers are fighting for human rights in their home countries, even as their stories illustrate broader global struggles. From here, we travel to Chapter 2 ("Confronting Government Power"), which showcases social-issue documentaries around the world that speak often inconvenient truths to systems of power, from government to corporate. Across the globe, contemporary populism may seemingly facilitate political order through repression and control of publics and media, posing threats even in democratic forms of government. Through observational, intimate, expansive storytelling, the documentary stories in this chapter showcase and push back on repressive institutions of power, offering cautionary historical lessons and warning bells for a range of contests, including *All In: The Fight for Democracy* (United States) and *The Silence of Others* (Spain).

In Chapter 3 ("Witnessing Conflict and Resilience"), we explore exponential risk and motivations for documentary filmmakers who endeavor to expose the harsh complicities and realities of war, provide a cultural memory of atrocities in the context of conflict, and offer a deeply intimate lens into lived experiences. To bring this theme to life and explore challenges, practices, and motivations of documentary filmmakers whose work seeks to ensure present-day awareness and long-term cultural memorializing, alongside testimony about human resilience, the case studies of this chapter include *The Cave* (Syria), *For Sama* (Syria), *Peace for Nina* (Ukraine), and *No Simple Way Home* (South Sudan).

In Chapter 4 ("Upholding Freedom of Expression"), we probe films that exemplify freedom of expression, a hallmark of an open, pluralistic society, for centuries threatened by political suppression as a form of social control.

Over the past decade, artistic and media freedoms have declined around the world—in both authoritarian regimes and liberal democracies. In this context, how are independent documentaries telling stories that push hard against censorship and media repression? Chapter 4 explores this topic with profiled films that include *A Thousand Cuts* (Philippines), *Writing with Fire* (India), and *The First Step* (United States).

Chapter 5 ("Demanding Human Rights") delves into the activities of documentary films, collaborative civil society networks, and community groups that are advocating for human rights around the world. A fundamental ideal media function remains its ability to expose violations of human rights atrocities that take place in the shadows. Civil society organizations and activists come together in this pursuit to challenge institutions that are subverting these processes and voices (and who pose a direct threat to justice and human rights in doing so). In 2019, Amnesty International's groundbreaking report revealed the mechanisms and uptick in actions by which civil society and human rights defenders are harassed, surveilled, attacked, and arrested—a global trend, not reserved for dictatorships alone.[73] In this increasingly hostile climate, this chapter presents several documentary projects and teams working to uphold human rights and to cast a bright light on the long-term implications wrought when these rights are abused, though films that include *Hooligan Sparrow* (China), *One Child Nation* (China), *Welcome to Chechnya* (Russia), *Uýra: The Rising Forest* (Brazil), and *He Named Me Malala* (United States).

Chapter 6 ("Demonstrating Activism") lifts up the work of activists—individual people who find themselves in extraordinary times, called or forced to stand up against injustice and fight for their families and communities. In nearly every juncture in global history where justice and equity are expanded, we see the work of activists as they create networks and inspire others, often shifting political systems along the way, for better or worse. This chapter examines why activism matters in regional and global contexts, and it unpackages the inside machinations and influence of documentaries that show activism at work, through films that include *Thank You for the Rain* (Kenya), *Delikado* (Philippines), *The Territory* (Brazil), *And She Could Be Next* (United States), and *I Am Samuel* (Kenya).

Chapter 7 ("Creating Spaces for Reconciliation and Healing") explores the role of documentaries to provide a space for community healing and interrogation, and to recognize underrepresented histories and communities in the governments, institutions, societies, and media systems that have

26 RADICAL REALITY

historically exploited, traumatized, overlooked, and taken advantage of them. While these films might aim for reform related to specific outcome goals (like addressing institutional racism and mistreatment), many of their makers are primarily motivated to create safe spaces and to correct—not simply challenge—historical and dominant narratives for impacted communities. They are, in this way, educating external audiences as a secondary goal, choosing instead to center the lived experiences of oppressed communities and provide a space for healing and recognition and legitimacy to an underrepresented community or issue. Films profiled in this chapter include *Always in Season* (United States), *The Murder of Emmett Till* (United States), *In My Blood It Runs* (Australia), *Pray Away* (United States), and *Quipu Project* (Peru).

Finally, Chapter 8 ("Building a Future for Global Independent Documentary Storytelling to Survive and Thrive") presents final themes and a roadmap for the continuing trajectory of global documentary storytelling in struggles for social justice. Beyond the film stories and networks introduced in the preceding chapters, opportunities and constraints are inherent in this work. This chapter considers possibilities and challenges now and evolving into the future—informed by the stories, voices, and lessons reflected throughout the book—delineated as themes that include surveillance afforded by digital technology, privacy and security concerns, funding and resource support for creative nonfiction storytellers and journalists and supportive civil society, grassroots engagement strategies, and more.

Most importantly, as illustrated by the stories that follow, the tenacity and enterprising spirits of individual filmmakers is the big idea, as has always been the case for documentary artists and the true tales they endeavor to tell.

2
Confronting Government Power

"If democracy had its own doomsday clock, it would be at two minutes to midnight. . . . For the first time in more than two decades, there are more authoritarian regimes than liberal democracies—and we are not doing enough to address this threat," wrote Nobel Prize–winning journalist Maria Ressa and International Fund for Public Interest Media president Nishant Lalwani in a 2023 op-ed.[1] They're not exaggerating—and they're not alone in trying desperately to ring a global alarm bell.

"Democracy itself," according to historian Robert Kuttner, "is under siege. . . . This upheaval is occurring not just in nations with weak democratic roots such as Turkey, Hungary, Egypt, and the Philippines, but in the democratic heartland—Western Europe and the United States. Autocrats are using the forms of democracy to destroy the substance."[2] The number of democracies around the world has fallen to dismal 1986 levels, a time marked by Cold War fear and simmering culture wars. Nearly three-quarters of the world's population (5.7 billion people, 72% of the global population) now live in autocracies, and "advances in global levels of democracy made over the last 35 years have been wiped out," according to the 2023 Democracy Report.[3] Declines over the past decade have been precipitous: rapid deterioration of freedom of expression, increased government censorship of media and suppression of the work of civil society organizations, systematic attacks on academic freedom and open thought, and a dramatic decrease in fair election protocols.[4] A bleak situation worsened in the 2020 pandemic shutdown, leading the long-running Democracy Index report to declare 2022 "a new low for global democracy."[5] Freedom House's *Freedom in the World* 2023 study reports the same level of decline—and the dramatic implications for well-being around the world.[6]

Contemporary authoritarianism is a global movement that has taken off—loosed and spreading around the world. Democracy is disintegrating in many ways, piece by piece, sometimes explicitly, and sometimes in gradual quiet, given the silencing of dissent from scholars, journalists, media makers, and civil society actors. The impulse toward dictatorship is an ancient one,

Radical Reality. Caty Borum and David Conrad-Pérez, Oxford University Press. © Oxford University Press 2025.
DOI: 10.1093/9780197604298.003.0002

28   RADICAL REALITY

of course, but the new threats are insidiously wielded by would-be autocrats under cover of law—"stealth authoritarianism"—on the upswing:

> Although laws have always been valuable tools in an autocrat's arsenal, modern authoritarians began to deploy, to a much greater extent than their historical predecessors, the same laws and legal institutions that exist in democratic regimes for anti-democratic purposes. In so doing, the new generation of authoritarians cloak repressive measures under the mask of law, imbue them with the veneer of legitimacy, and render authoritarian practices much more difficult to detect and eliminate. In the modern era, authoritarian wolves rarely appear as wolves. They are now clad, at least in part, in sheep's clothing.[7]

Nearly all basic human freedoms are at risk when autocracy is on the march: speech, expression, assembly and protest, labor strikes, civil liberties, and basic human rights. Freedoms, after all, are a direct threat to power. State repression is an explicit tool practiced even in open liberal democracies to shut down critique and challenges to entrenched power—a deterrence strategy made visible by doling out costs and punishments to those who step out of line.[8] Progress is the enemy. Absolute power justifies itself under the guise of care for the well-being of the people, who are meant—under this line of thought—to acquiesce and seek safety and security under the all-knowing protection of a benevolent leader.

How did we arrive at this place? A full historical accounting and analysis is beyond the bounds or aims of this chapter, or even this full book, but a few patterns are glaringly clear. Economic disarray and realignment, ultranationalism, and immigration fears and resentments in a global economy with fewer boundary borders than the past: all are contributing factors, driven by what Kuttner calls a "resurrection of heedless, globalized capitalism that serves the few, damages the many, and breeds antisystem politics," stoked by simmering anger in the course of global change.[9] As one structural factor, global capitalism, unleashed and increasingly unregulated in the digital age, doesn't necessarily serve democracy optimally:

> In some idealized world, capitalism may enhance democracy, but in the history of the West, democracy has expanded by *limiting* the power of capitalists. When that project fails, dark forces are often unleashed. In the twentieth century, capitalism coexisted nicely with dictatorships, which

conveniently create friendly business climates and repress independent worker organizations.[10]

Fear—of change, of perceived enemies—and desire to place blame in the face of uncertainty, shifting economies, and social realities constitute a breeding ground for a particular flavor of authoritarianism that thrives through populism, also clearly on display across the global map. Populism is not the causal element, but it may help explain, at least in part, how authoritarian tendencies can seemingly thrive around the world. Populism, writes scholar Michael Kazin, is a kind of "language" that pits "ordinary people" against elites, a style and rhetoric rather than an ideology: "The power of populism lies in its adaptable nature . . . effective at blasting 'elites' or 'the establishment' for harming the interests and betraying the ideals of 'the people'—proud in their ordinariness—in nations which are committed, at least officially, to democratic principles."[11] But populist leaders don't emerge without context: trends toward populism often appear as signs of political unease, as a response to unresolved, percolating resentment; in such a climate, leaders who seemingly champion "the people"—against elite former or current leaders who don't understand their needs because they are too far removed from them—are a kind of savior. They become someone to believe in. Populism often emerges in the wake of financial crises and change, the depression of the 1930s and the recession of 2008 among them.[12]

In the case of right-wing populism—given that populism itself, as a concept and style, does not belong solely to one side of the political spectrum—another perceived "enemy" to blame (for fear, uncertainty, change, economic concern) is offered up by autocratic leaders: not only disconnected "elites" but also immigrants and people of color.[13] In the context of repressive governments and how they are nurtured by the will of the people, populism is both a response to and a sign of political and social systems in a kind of breakdown or crisis.[14] We should rightfully view populist leaders, then, as a warning, not only a reaction.

The global roster of recent and current populist leaders, including those taking firm root in liberal democracies, is remarkably similar, as Turkish scholar Ece Temelkuran writes in her book *How to Lose a Country: The 7 Steps from Democracy to Dictatorship*: "It doesn't matter if Trump or Erdogan is brought down tomorrow, or if Nigel Farage had never become a leader of public opinion. The millions of people fired up by their message will still be there, and will still be ready to act upon the orders of a similar figure."[15]

30   RADICAL REALITY

Populism and repressive government patterns—albeit along a spectrum of severity—are alive and well in United States, Brazil, and other countries in Latin America, Turkey, Great Britain, Hungary, and around the world.[16] And when populist leaders actually succeed and assume elected office, the stakes are dangerously high: power is concentrated, critics are silenced through regulatory and legal means, and the conditions for authoritarianism are thus established.[17]

Back to democracy: Even when government repression and abuse of power is not a consequence or function of populist trends—although the contemporary pattern here seems to suggest populism is a contributing factor in many regions of the world—authoritarian-like climates endanger freedom, human rights, progress toward equity and justice, and environments that value a plurality of voices, viewpoints, and lived experiences. Without democracy, in scenarios with weak or broken democratic institutions and norms—including voting, protest, boycott—even freedom of speech is not safe or useful, but instead devolves into fruitless protest and cycles of repeated repression.[18] Conflict can emerge here.

If we believe in values, norms, and practices of free media as crucial to human rights—and the breakdown in those systems when democracy starts to crumble—it's not hard to imagine why independent, artistic documentaries matter so much. Independent documentaries, through their ability to provide both deep historical context and intimate, emotional access to contemporary human stories, function as a force to reveal—and to resist—authoritarianism and abusive government tactics. Often, due to their artistic emotional resonance, they are able to circumvent usual political divides that can cloak the dangers of repressive government power. Creative and artistic nonfiction storytelling is witness and warning, translator and historical record, and, sometimes, the spark for mobilizing people. Laying bare and making sense of government dysfunction and abuse, calling for witness, and redress, are among the crucial roles of documentaries that speak truth to power, particularly at times when democracy's future seems precarious.

All In: The Fight for Democracy (United States)

On the evening of March 7, 1965, nearly 50 million Americans settled in front of their TVs for the ABC broadcast premiere of *Judgment at Nuremberg*, the Academy Award–winning film about Nazi Germany.[19] By any viewing standards, the audience number was staggering. ABC News interrupted with an urgent report and fresh footage from Selma, Alabama: state troopers and local sheriff deputies beating hundreds of peaceful Black citizens as they crossed over the Edmund Pettus bridge on their way to the state capital of Montgomery, protesting decades of disenfranchisement in the Jim Crow South. The events, given the carnage, became known as "Bloody Sunday."[20] The news coverage and its fortuitous timing—juxtaposed images in the scheduled film and the audience size in peak Sunday night entertainment prime time—helped galvanize a crucial next phase in the US civil rights movement.[21]

Five months later, on August 6, 1965, President Lyndon Johnson signed the Voting Rights Act of 1965, a historic expansion of civil rights and democratic functioning—albeit a violent, traumatic victory.[22] Recognizing a legacy of bigotry, the Act prohibits "any voting standard, practice, or procedure that results in the denial or abridgement of the right of any citizen to vote on account of race, color, or membership in a language minority group."[23] Racially discriminatory voter suppression tactics were well-worn by the time the Voting Act of 1965 was enacted: literacy tests, closing polling places in areas inhabited primarily by communities of color, purging voter registration rolls, redistricting, and other means to make voting more difficult for members of racial minority groups.[24] The Act, wrote the US Department of Justice years later, "would prove to be transformative, enfranchising millions of Americans for the first time and empowering many minority voters to elect candidates of their choice to public office."[25] Voting in the United States was now functionally possible for millions more people as a consequence of dogged, painful activism and a national portal into brutality from within. Had multiracial democracy arrived in America?

Nearly 50 years later, the US Supreme Court weakened a crucial element of the Voting Rights Act in the *Shelby v. Holder* case. The 1965 Act had created an oversight system to ensure particular state and local voting system changes—in states known for racially discriminatory practices—would not harm minority group voters, but the 2013 *Shelby* decision decimated a key provision that powers its enforcement capabilities.[26] As the nonprofit, nonpartisan Brennan Center for Justice wrote:

> The 2013 Supreme Court decision swung open the door for states to enact restrictive voting laws, making it harder for people of color to

32 RADICAL REALITY

vote. . . . The effects of the ruling were immediate. The same day, Texas officials announced that they would implement the nation's most restrictive voter ID law, which had previously been blocked in the preclearance process. That law, which a court later ruled to be racially discriminatory, was the first of a massive wave of restrictive voting policies implemented in jurisdictions previously subject to preclearance. And it turned out that the Shelby County decision was only the first of a series of Supreme Court decisions that would roll back protections for voting rights.[27]

Since the *Shelby v. Holder* decision, in the midst of what the Brennan Center calls a "revival" of restrictive practices that predominantly affect communities of color, jurisdictions across the United States have enacted nearly 100 laws that impede voting—including local decisions about polling places, voter registration rosters, photo ID requirements, and more.[28] Many of the retro tactics returned, sanctioned in ways that would have been impermissible under the original intact Voting Rights Act of 1965. Democracy in the United States, always a tenuous proposition based on its founding structures of inequality, took a step backward. The fragility of the American voting system, which cracked wide open in the post-Shelby years, is the subject of *All In: The Fight for Democracy*, a 2020 documentary distributed by Amazon Prime in the midst of the federal election season and an unprecedented pandemic.[29] Directors Liz Garbus and Lisa Cortés were motivated by the lessons of history and the power of activism—but also by the need for citizen vigilance when democracy is threatened, as Garbus said in an interview with the Southern Poverty Law Center:

> William Faulkner wrote, "The past isn't dead. It's not even past." We see that so clearly when we look at the history of the struggle for voting rights. At every turn, when progress is made, there is a retrenchment—new laws or tactics to limit the franchise. After the Voting Rights Act, we saw another great expansion of the franchise, with a similar retrenchment after the *Shelby v. Holder* decision in 2013. And what we see today: voter ID laws with a narrow set of eligible IDs (for instance, in Texas, your gun license is a permitted ID but not your student ID), poll closures, purges—along with recent threats by President Trump to have a police presence at polls. These are current tactics to suppress the vote. And no surprise, they disproportionately affect Black, Brown, poor, Indigenous, Latinx and young voters.[30]

CONFRONTING GOVERNMENT POWER   33

They found their centerpiece story in the 2018 gubernatorial election in Georgia, between the state's secretary of state, Brian Kemp, and former state legislator Stacey Abrams, a "great-great-granddaughter of slaves," as she reminded would-be voters at a rally captured in the film.[31] When Abrams, wildly popular among Democratic voters in the state, lost to Kemp by approximately 50,000 votes, she addressed her supporters with an admonishment and a warning about voter suppression: "Silence is a weapon for those who would quiet the voices of the people. And I will not concede because the erosion of our democracy is not right."[32] What she meant—and maintained in the ensuing months and years—was the circumstance of her own race against a sitting secretary of state who had, by the time of the election, closed more than 200 polling places in the state (in neighborhoods predominantly inhabited by people of color)[33] and canceled more than 1 million voter registrations, most of whom were people of color or low-income residents.[34] Voter empowerment, as she makes clear in the film, is democracy's cornerstone: "The fundamental power of democracy lies in the right to vote. If you protect that right, you create possibilities for everything else."[35]

Garbus and Cortés were motivated by civic responsibility as much as artistic impulses. By interspersing the historic pattern of systemic voter suppression with a contemporary story, they found a cinematic way to punctuate immediate threats to American democracy, but also the parallel power of activism and citizen engagement. They wanted the American people to get involved—to see, and to resist, a looming menace of government-sanctioned voter constraints. Codirector Cortés explained in an interview:

> Oftentimes, people get discouraged because they think when they've been denied the right to vote, that it's just them. That they did something wrong. Our film showed that historically a playbook was created that made people feel that way and also targeted certain communities. But we also showed the power of organization and gave opportunities and a call to action: If you want to do something more, here's where you go. Here are the resources, here's what you can tap into.[36]

They met with the leading civic engagement cultural leaders around the country to learn and devise a plan. With a team of impact strategists—Ben O'Keefe from Garbus's production company, Story Syndicate, and Lindsay Guetschow from the Raben Group—they shaped a multifaceted public engagement campaign designed to register new voters and encourage them to vote, despite rampant misinformation gaining traction in social media platforms, and in spite of a historic pandemic that had shuttered the country.[37] The Perspective Fund and Chicago Media Project contributed funds to support the impact campaign.

#AllInForVoting launched 100 days before the 2020 presidential election as a full-scale nonpartisan voter empowerment campaign with state-by-state actions, ambassador leaders on the ground, and an ambitious scale—with the full support of the film's distributor, Amazon.[38] Abrams herself, by then a notable voter-empowerment leader in Georgia, reminded Americans of the high stakes:

> Today, we are 100 days out from Election Day—a pivotal moment in our mission to protect our democracy—and we need to come together as a country and make sure every voice and vote is counted. The title *All In: The Fight for Democracy* speaks to the importance and necessity that every American has the right to have their voice be heard and their vote counted. We know that if our votes were not important, so many folks wouldn't be working so hard to take our right to vote away.[39]

Image 2.1 Description: *All In*: AllInForVoting campaign bus. Image courtesy of Amazon Content Services LLC.

The campaign was everywhere: cultural leaders on social media, a 48-city Rally the Vote bus tour in 18 states, voter registration website, pop-up screenings in dozens of communities, "Grow a Voter" resource guide and curriculum program for new young voters and their teachers, 150 local community events and screenings, and donations to support organizations in 10 states with particularly acute voter repression challenges.[40] Altogether, the campaign reached more than 5 million people, and grantee local voter engagement groups reached millions and registered more than 200,000 first-time voters.[41] People power, the directors maintained, is the only way to uphold democracy, but the requirement to engage is a perennial pursuit, not a one-time moment. The work is never truly complete, if history is any guide. Cortés reflected:

> What the film shows is cyclically this historical push and pull of expansion and retrenchment. But it also shows that there is a moment when the arc of justice meets with the arc of progress. And that moment cannot happen by sitting on the sidelines . . . you have to actually find a way to connect with others who are like-minded. And not only get yourself out there, but find ways to engage your own community.[42]

Given its structural design, the United States isn't immune to efforts to chip away at the country's potential to function as a true multiracial democracy—nor is it alone among nations in this particular quandary. The stealthy damage of disenfranchisement is insidious. Limiting and restricting voting is hardly the only tactic of state repression—the list includes limiting speech, the right to protest, and the use of regulatory powers to silence critics and change policies. Without cultural witness and mobilizing forms of media and artistic expression that remind us of the democratic stakes, can we resist? History answers many of those questions.

The Silence of Others (Spain)

In 2002, when novelist Dulce Chacón published her new book, *La Voz Dormida* (*The Sleeping Voice*), it struck a deep nerve across her native Spain. Lauded for a combination of "dramatic intensity and historical authenticity," it was an immediate bestseller, later voted Spain's "Book of the Year."[43] From one devastating story to the next, Chacón weaves a painful tapestry—the

36 RADICAL REALITY

voices of fictional women awaiting torturous fates in a 1939 Madrid prison, sentenced for siding with the prodemocracy faction against dictatorship in the Spanish Civil War. One faces execution after delivering her baby, another will see her husband and four children killed in front of her. The atrocities are unbearable—more so knowing Chacón's characters and stories are based on testimonies from real women, still afraid to share their trauma decades later. Some incidents are so horrific that details are blurred, lest they be too difficult for readers to bear.[44] To some who understand the complex history of the war and its aftermath, Chacón might be regarded as an unlikely narrator. She was raised within a conservative upper-class family, and yet, she said in a media interview, "I grew up hearing only one version of the war. I knew there was another side to the story."[45] Her novel, creative nonfiction inspired and shaped by real events and people, tells the different side. Chacón passed away in 2003 and did not live to see her book transformed onto the big screen in a successful 2011 Spanish film of the same title, wrought in devastating emotional detail at a pivotal time in the country's reawakening about its recent history.[46] The stories of the dictatorship and repression that followed, whispered for generations, were not widely known—by design.

From 1936 to 1939, prodemocracy Republicans fought to support the democratically elected government of Spain against overthrow from Nazi-backed Nationalists—a bloody civil war that resulted in victory for the ultra-right Nationalists and the appointment of General Francisco Franco Bahamonde (known as "Franco") as dictator until his death in 1975.[47] Authoritarianism was immediate: "The political system established in 1939 by Francisco Franco was, along with the Salazar regime in neighboring Portugal, one of the longest-lasting dictatorships in Western Europe. It was the quintessential 'authoritarian' regime (Linz 1975)characterized by limited and non-responsible political pluralism, political demobilization, a leader who exercised power within formally undefined but clearly recognizable limits, and the absence of an elaborated ideology."[48] The repression and human rights atrocities continued during and after the war.

Upward of 300,000 people died in the war or a combination of the formal conflict and imprisonment, torture, kidnapping, and murder of civilians as retribution in the years that followed; and more than 400,000 were sentenced to execution or forced labor, or were sent to concentration camps.[49] The human destruction was vindictive in motivation and practice, as human rights scholar Madeleine Davis writes: "In victory, Franco visited deliberate and systematic revenge upon the defeated Republicans, his 1939 Law of Political Responsibilities providing blanket justification and a number of specially created tribunals furnishing the barest of legal procedures."[50] Thousands of prodemocracy civilians were executed and brutalized with full state support under Franco.[51]

Franco was known as a charismatic "absolute dictator"—many believed anointed by God for his post—and his system, based on his self-appointed "power for life," followed a deeply nationalistic set of values that restricted freedom of speech, expression, criticism, and movement, particularly weaponized against those who opposed him during and after the war.[52] Speaking out against the Franco regime was dangerous and legally impossible. The Press Law of 1938 in Spain, among other policies enacted and enforced by the dictatorship, required state authorities to review and approve news publications' stories, and other topics and critiques—or interpretations of current affairs—were outlawed, including in radio and television in later decades.[53] For nearly 40 years, silence and obedience were the state mandates for both media and citizens.

Franco's rule ended with his death in 1975, and the business of rebuilding a lost democracy began. Letting bygones be bygones, or "forgetting," was the path chosen by legislators across Spain's dominant political parties. Their "Pact of Forgetting" released political prisoners on the left and right but also mandated silence about the atrocities of the nationalist Franco regime and granted legal impunity to those responsible for the regime's crimes.[54] As historian José Álvarez Junco explained, "Both sides were weak and so they were forced to reach an agreement."[55] Talking about what happened was not permitted in any circumstance—a necessary act, some said and believed, for effectively moving forward with the business of creating a fresh democracy that wasn't mired in the past. Not everyone agreed.

The so-called pact of forgetting effectively meant "the progressive elimination of any public disruptive and vindictive reference to 'the former head of state' in order not to hamper . . . transition and further democratic consolidation."[56] While the pain of the past was whispered privately by thousands who mourned murdered or disappeared loved ones, this was Spain's path toward rebuilding, albeit without restorative justice. There would be no "truth commissions," no investigating crimes against humanity—a mandated amnesia in every way, culturally, legally, politically.[57] But in 2007, Spain's Congress passed the Law of Historical Memory, which declared the Franco dictatorship illegitimate and opened the door for Spaniards to begin to understand the silent legacy of their country's recent past.[58] And yet, lack of

38 RADICAL REALITY

accountability was still real, writes scholar Omar Encarnancion: "Major human rights organizations including Amnesty International, Human Rights Watch, and the International Commission of Jurists have criticized the 2007 Law of Historical Memory for failing to conform to international justice standards."[59] Still, a small crack had opened, and stories began to leak through the complicated web of official erasure.

Three years later, not long after giving birth to her daughter with her husband and fellow filmmaker Robert Bahar, Spanish documentary filmmaker Almudena Carracedo could not stop crying one day as she perused her usual daily newspapers: "It was the moment when the stories of stolen children in Spain [during the Franco dictatorship] had just started to really hit the news. There had been rumors, but suddenly it broke in this bigger way. . . . [years earlier] when I read Dulce Chacon's quote, 'we are a part of a generation of silence of others,' I told Robert, 'one day I'll make a film that's called 'The Silence of Others.'"[60] Carracedo and Bahar started the long journey to make their 2018 critically acclaimed film, *The Silence of Others*, the first contemporary documentary exploration about the lessons of state repression and atrocity in Spain, a film, as Bahar described it, "about transitional justice" that asks, also in an international context outside of Spain, "How do we go from dictatorship to democracy?"[61]

In the documentary, the legacy of the Franco dictatorship story picks up in live time with an explosive inciting moment: In 2008, Spanish judge Baltazar Garzon began an official state investigation into the human rights atrocities of the Franco dictatorship, challenging the long-established amnesty that allowed its perpetrators to remain unscathed.[62] The Spanish National Court stopped Garzon's efforts, but the news coverage was prolific, reaching thousands of others who demanded justice. Two years later, several family members of the victims, along with a team of international human rights attorneys, filed an official criminal complaint in Argentina to seek justice for alleged crimes against humanity committed by the Spanish government— that is, crimes by the state subject to global jurisdiction. The unfolding story becomes the film's igniting spark, as Carracedo and Bahar describe in the official synopsis:

> *The Silence of Others* reveals the epic struggle of victims of Spain's 40-year dictatorship under General Franco, who continue to seek justice to this day. Filmed over six years, the film follows victims and survivors as

they organize the groundbreaking "Argentine Lawsuit" and fight a state-imposed amnesia of crimes against humanity, in a country still divided four decades into democracy.[63]

Weaving intimate stories of long-ago murdered victims alongside those who remembered their own torture first-hand, *The Silence of Others* follows the astonishing progress of the "Argentine Lawsuit" overseen by investigating Judge María Servini—an international criminal investigation into human rights violations committed during the Spanish Civil War and through the full expanse of the Franco dictatorship. The stories come together as families start to share their trauma, some for the first time, while they gather courage and stamina to join the international effort for justice. As the film ends, the plaintiffs celebrate progress and momentum, even as they acknowledge how difficult their journey will be. It's not a tidy ending, but instead an awakening and a reckoning—and a reminder of the stakes when democracy falls to authoritarianism and a government grants itself full repressive powers, not only in Spain, but around the world.

Image 2.2 Description: *The Silence of Others:* María Martín sits by the road that covers the mass grave containing her mother's remains.
Photo Credit: Almudena Carracedo. © Semilla Verde Productions.

40 RADICAL REALITY

Image 2.3 Description: *The Silence of Others*: Jose Maria "Chato" Galante in the jail where, as a 24-year-old, he was imprisoned for fighting against the dictatorship. Photo Credit: Almudena Carracedo. © Semilla Verde Productions.

Image 2.4 Description: *The Silence of Others*: The statues featured in *The Silence of Others*, on a mountaintop in the Valley of Jerte, by sculptor Francisco Cedenilla. Photo Credit: Almudena Carracedo. © Semilla Verde Productions.

Seven years after Carracedo and Bahar began filming, while they planned a widespread social impact campaign as part of Good Pitch Europe, *The Silence of Others* premiered at the international 2018 Berlin Film Festival, where it won the two most prestigious awards: the Peace Film Prize and the prestigious Panorama Audience Award. Press coverage emphasized the deeper democratic and human rights themes, and the premiere festival honors, as Bahar reflected in an interview, were catalytic:

> They helped to show that the film was working as a cinematic, emotional and intellectual experience, and could also be a tool for human rights advocates and the human rights community. But also, at that moment, some Spanish journalists and Spaniards in the diaspora who were in Berlin started to see the film and write about it. And we started to see that what we really set out to do with the film was working: to make it very human and to put these human stories at the forefront.[64]

The documentary took off, screening in 80 international film festivals and attracting media coverage across the globe, including leading Spanish news outlet *El Pais*, TTT (Germany), *The Guardian* (United Kingdom), *Le Monde* (France), and *The New Yorker* and *The New York Times* (United States).[65] In Spain, the impact of the film was immediate and far-reaching: it trended on social media on the day of its first theatrical screening[66] and ran for a record four months in theaters, including a particularly resonant screening in Seville that took the filmmakers somewhat by surprise:

> [Robert]: During the standing ovation, after the film, just spontaneously, there was a group of victims who had brought photographs of their loved ones who are still buried in mass graves to this day.

> [Almudena]: They raised their photos and we were all crying. It was an incredibly beautiful moment. The film was serving as an amazing and beautiful representation for the victims themselves, as a visibility tool. And at the same time it was reaching those who had not known about it, and among those were the youth. This came as a surprise for us: we first thought only old people would be coming to the screenings, and what we saw in all of our screenings was in fact a huge variety of ages: it was helping to create an intergenerational conversation.[67]

Image 2.5 Description: *The Silence of Others*: Seville Screening—November 2018 Pre-Premiere of *The Silence of Others* in Seville. Photo Credit: Beatriz Macias.

In 2019, emerging out of Spanish theaters, *The Silence of Others* won the Goya—Spain's "Oscar Award"—and the media-saturated success of the moment opened the door to their deepest hope for the film: a television premiere on RTVE, Spain's public broadcasting network. On the broadcast premiere day, the cultural chatter across Spain was frenzied, trending across social media and culminating in a public post from Spain's prime minister that would have been unthinkable even a decade earlier; translated into English, it says: "The families are still seeking truth and reparation. And it's also the future, the future of a whole country. Only with memory and awareness can we look forward and continue advancing in democracy and freedom. Tonight, watch the movie on TV."[68]

Across Spain, more than two million people have seen *The Silence of Others*, the film that Fotogramas, the Spanish cinema publication, called "The most necessary documentary of the last 80 years."[69] And around the world, millions more have watched across platforms and environments: a PBS broadcast in the United States in 2019, a United Nations event in New York, and global video on demand through Netflix.[70] The film won more than 40 international awards, including high-prestige Peabody and Emmy Awards, and it was shortlisted for the Best Documentary Feature Award in the Academy Awards in the United States.[71]

The Silence of Others was a critical darling that catalyzed a much broader cultural reckoning and conversation about democracy and restorative justice in the face of state repression. As a kind of movement, the film's creative execution and influence illustrate more than one function of independent documentary storytelling in service of upholding democracy and holding government power to account. But how and why—what explanatory elements can spotlight its impact and influence, beyond the filmmakers' ability to produce critically lauded artistic work?

First and foremost, editorial independence, say the filmmakers, was absolutely essential, as was their choice of eventual TV broadcast partners to fit their public service mission: RTVE, Spain's free public TV system, and PBS in the United States. Carracedo and Bahar said they couldn't envision crafting such a bold, unflinching film within the confines of a media company if it opted for a less explicit prodemocracy message, and they emphasized the importance of being able to trust their own instincts and to sculpt the discourse of the film to speak to a particular cultural moment and potential for change. Bahar noted, "A film like *The Silence of Others* is a film where you challenge accepted political discourse of the day—a film that almost by definition has to be made on the outside of the systems. And I think that is a traditional role of public television."[72] The public service values helped the filmmakers to create an opportune way for audiences to access their film at no cost, with a timing strategy that was meaningful and intentional, as Carracedo explained:

> The traditional structure is that usually you first go to paid TV and then you go to free, broadcast TV. But we didn't want to do that. We wanted the film to be accessible to everyone for free. We gave Spanish national public television the exclusive right to show the film in prime time and we asked them to broadcast it in April, which is the month of memory. They agreed to broadcast the film on April 4th, 10 days before the anniversary of the Spanish Republic [April 14th].[73]

Amplifying media coverage and the passionate fervor of grassroots engagement about the film was crucial. In Spain, starting from the film's earliest festival circuit days, widespread news coverage framed the film as essential viewing and a historical mapping with clear overtures to dangerous repressive government trends around the world. In leading Spanish news outlets—*La Razon, Cultura, El Confidencial,* for instance—*The Silence of*

44   RADICAL REALITY

Others is positioned as a necessary vehicle to help atone for the past while clearly understanding what is at stake and what is possible, now and in future junctures.[74] By the time the film made it to a theatrical release in Spain, media coverage was sweeping—millions already knew about it. A galvanizing spark came organically when the filmmakers and RTVE announced the Spanish TV premiere date, and Carracedo and Bahar created a new public engagement effort to expand the cultural conversation. They launched a grassroots WhatsApp campaign that went viral in Spain, and media coverage on the day of the broadcast premiere was extensive, featuring several of the film's protagonists on leading TV and radio programs. As Carracedo recalled in an interview with the journal *Violence*:

> For the morning of the broadcast, we had created a hashtag called "It's time for memory": #EsTiempoDeMemoria. And to our surprise the hashtag actually caught on, it became viral. . . . When we woke up the next morning, we got the news of how many people had seen the film—and this is a relatively new program on the second channel, which normally has an audience of say 300,000 people average: the film had been seen by 1 million people, besides likely 200,000 people that saw it online. It was actually the highest rated documentary of this channel since 2014. And—again—it was a human rights documentary, in Spain. But of course it's a long continuum: thousands and thousands of people have been fighting for this. So our contribution to this super long struggle is this small moment or big moment—however you want to call it—to help create that cultural conversation, that cultural moment in Spain.[75]

The filmmakers were also intentional in the tone and presentation of the story as living reality—a past seamlessly attached to the current moment and the future. Rather than telling the story of Spanish dictatorship as a history account alone (although powerful in itself), they chose to carefully craft and steep their film in the present. It's not a historical documentary told solely through black-and-white archival footage and imagery: Past and present are linked visually, moving around and within individual stories of pain and survival. "[Died] defending democracy and freedom," reads a translated sign at one mass grave as depicted on screen, even as Chato, one of the lead protagonists and a plaintiff in the humanitarian crimes case, says, "This is not about looking at the past. We're fighting for the future."[76] As Carracedo said,

CONFRONTING GOVERNMENT POWER 45

"The film started truly with this goal in mind, to create, rather to catalyze the conversation. Not about the past, rather, but about the present. And that's why we reframe the film in present tense, and we reframe the film as a human rights service struggle." Indeed, according to one review of the film: "With the global rise of authoritarian regimes and ultra-right parties, *The Silence of Others* offers a cautionary tale about fascism's long shadows, and the dangers of forgetting the past."[77] Carracedo and Bahar explicitly wanted to show the ongoing legacy of life under repressive, violent government power:

> [Robert]: Part of what the film helped achieve was that many people who were progressive activists, who didn't conceptualize of these issues being part of the current urgent struggles of the progressive left, which might be focusing a lot on income inequality, and environmental issues, and supporting refugees, and all of these issues that are incredibly important to champion, suddenly these issues also were being framed as present day issues. I think that the film played a role in helping people see them as these are our [current] issues too.[78]

From a creative standpoint, as artistic cinema is able to do, by focusing on the human stories across many walks of life, from mothers mourning their lost babies to children of long-lost murdered parents to those who remember the violence inflicted on them personally, the documentary cut through expected partisan divides. This is a unique quality of intimate independent documentary, and a meaningful one—and in this case, intentional on the part of the artists. As Bahar reflected: "Because the film led with the humanity of the struggle, I think it was able to penetrate that [the political divide]. And in some cases, maybe convert. At the Goya Awards, in her acceptance speech, Almudena said, 'We dedicate this and we honor victims of the Civil War and of the dictatorship,' and almost everyone in the room applauded." Given the fraught history and political passions and resentments, cutting through to the humanity and powerlessness of government repression was a revolutionary act.

The Silence of Others acted as a witness and crucial lesson for resisting government repression of the future, resonating widely perhaps due to the universal themes of democratic struggle, far beyond Spain's borders. Creating a film that would translate to other country contexts with some urgency was part of the filmmakers' hopes, and still, as Carracedo shared, the response

46 RADICAL REALITY

around the world astounded them in terms of the broad appeal and under-standing of shared challenges:

> We had not anticipated the kind of impact that the film would have inter-nationally. We thought people internationally would actually look at the film and realize what had happened in Spain. But we didn't understand that it was actually also going to catalyze a conversation about these issues in other countries. But, for example, in Turkey, you could totally see the Q&A [after a screening there] was about their own country. . . . The film is a warning and a case study of what not to do. It ends on a bittersweet note, but it gives them hope for what can be done, if you organize, if you fight. Which is something that for us was very important, not to end on a dark note. Because at the end, there's always been moments of going back and moments of going forward. . . . I feel strongly that you cannot think of the future, and you cannot think of your present, and you cannot build a strong democracy if you don't understand what's come before you.[79]

* * *

As bookends, *All In: The Fight for Democracy* and *The Silence of Others* exist along a spectrum, from the warnings and quietly creeping signs of repres-sive government power to the long struggle of transitional justice and a re-minder of the violent destruction wrought when democracy is lost. There are steps in between and along the journey from democracy to authoritarianism, often under the seemingly benevolent intent of a strongman populist leader. Before it is too late, spotlighting historical warnings and patterns in acces-sible and unflinching detail, crafted by artists who can connect with the real human stories and living legacies at their core, is significant in both fostering a fuller collective memory of events from the past and informing the actions of the present.

Independent documentaries are connecting the dots, shedding light on democratic dismantling that can be hard to detect by regular people going about their lives. They come from all corners of the world, shaped in a wide range of storytelling styles: *The Fight* (United States), *Last Men in Alleppo* (Syria), *Kingdom of Silence* (Saudi Arabia), *China Undercover* (United States), *Hungary: Viktor Orban's Illiberal Democracy* (France), *The Edge of Democracy* (Brazil), and *The Hungarian Playbook* (Germany), among others. Some—like *Boycott*, Julia Bacha's 2021 independent documentary that chronicles the rise of state-level antiboycott legislation in the United States—are actively agitating against government repression in live time with active public engagement and mobilization campaigns to halt the slow chipping away at democratic functioning.[80] In this way, says Bacha, "documentaries are trying to turn on the lights before it's too late."[81]

Democratic progress and retrenchment—one step forward and three back—is a familiar pattern around the globe. Insidiously, creeping authoritarian tactics can be difficult to detect when they are gradual, and when they are increasingly carried out from inside the walls of legitimate institutions. Military coups from recent history are rare today, but the underlying threats are not. "Democracies still die, but by different means," wrote Steven Levitsky and Daniel Ziblatt in their book, *How Democracies Die*. "Since the end of the Cold War, most democratic breakdowns have been caused not by generals and soldiers but by elected governments themselves. . . . People still vote. Elected autocrats maintain a veneer of democracy while eviscerating its substance."[82] In *How to Lose a Country: The 7 Steps from Democracy to Dictatorship*, Ece Temelkuran's contemporary playbook from her native Turkey, she offers a framework from which to also locate the value of independent cinematic storytelling. The "seven steps" are the warning signs: creating a movement of believers who will stand behind any strong man, no matter how flagrant the violation of democratic norms; criminalize and clamp down on public dissent while disrupting rational language and using language that terrorizes; remove shame; dismantle judicial and political institutions and mechanisms; "design your own citizen"; break habits of empathy and encourage people to "laugh at the horror" taking place in their society; and "build your own county."[83] At the same time, public dissent that calls out government repression can be a true deterrence.[84] And this is where independent documentaries come in: they can shine a glaring, unflattering spotlight on the patterns and nudges, at times covert in their design, of encroaching or expanding tactics of repression. Evocative nonfiction storytelling can render broader realities through the lens of intimate, nuanced, human stories that spark an emotional response in an audience—often more palpable than a purely intellectual debate. And in so doing, documentaries can implore and inspire audiences to see and resist, and, as filmmaker Lisa Cortés says, "to connect the past with the present as a means of activating and motivating people."[85]

3

Witnessing Conflict and Resilience

After enduring multiple arrests and torture at the direction of a Syrian regime bent on silencing his work, director Feras Fayyad persevered because he believed that documentaries could bring truth and justice to a conflict that was grossly misunderstood.[1] Two years after the release of his acclaimed 2017 film *The Last Men in Aleppo*, Fayyad completed arguably the most powerful documentary of his career. In the 2019 film *The Cave*, Fayyad provides an unflinching look at the life-saving work of Dr. Amani Ballour, a 30-year-old Syrian doctor who has been recognized as the country's first woman hospital administrator, as she endures inconceivable risks, discrimination, and hardship to treat victims of airstrikes and chemical attacks during the height of the country's ongoing war. The deadly armed conflict in Syria is generally understood to have started after a peaceful demonstration calling for the removal of Syrian President Bashar al-Assad was violently suppressed by the government, but it had continued for years with constant bombings and unrest, largely driven by the former president's desire to stay in power and through intersecting proxy wars by outside powers, especially between the United States and Russia and between Iran and Saudi Arabia. The film grounds the story of the war in its everyday impact on the lives of the people struggling to survive in the middle of it, and it reveals the extraordinary risk and work of Syrians like Ballour, as she is forced to relocate her hospital underground, just outside of the country's capital city of Damascus, after it had become the target of strikes by the Syrian regime.

In addition to making a compelling film that audiences would want to see, the film team endeavored to document the horrific war crimes and atrocities taking place around the hospital in order to provide unflinching depictions of reality at a time of heavy political speculation, bring justice against those responsible, and ultimately help the people at the center of the film—so their work could be better recognized, understood, and supported. In other words, the risks they took were justified by a mission that transcended entertainment: they wanted to use their film to make a positive intervention in the lives of the people in the film, and in the narratives that surrounded them.

Radical Reality. Caty Borum and David Conrad-Pérez, Oxford University Press. © Oxford University Press 2025.
DOI: 10.1093/9780197604298.003.0003

The Cave was sold to National Geographic just before the company merged with The Walt Disney Company (Disney) in 2019. And with the combined might of the two commercial giants, the film was translated into more than 40 languages and became accessible to millions of people through multiple channels and platforms (including Hulu, Disney +, and the two national broadcast networks of SWR/Germany and TV2/Denmark) in countries around the world. Placement of the film on these global platforms played a critical role in helping the film team to achieve many of its objectives, since finding a global viewership was particularly important to the filmmaker's aims around witnessing and bringing the truth and horrific realities of the war to wider audiences.

While the achievements of *The Cave* are numerous, as this chapter will demonstrate, one of the lesser-known examples of its influence came as a direct result of the global reach of the film. More than a year after the film's release, the Organisation for the Prohibition of Chemical Weapons (OPCW) hosted an event centered around the film in April 2021, according to an invitation shared with the authors. OPCW was established in 1997 and it remains one of the world's most powerful implementing bodies in the pursuit of eliminating chemical weapons, with 193 member states granting them enforceable rights to sanction countries that use chemical weapons in war.[2] The invitation informed the film team that the event would include witnessing statements and participation from the film's two main protagonists—Ballour and her colleague Dr. Salim Namour—to address its members on the day before they would be voting on whether or not to reprimand Syria for its use of chemical weapons against its civilians. During the high-level meeting, which was moderated by the ambassadors of Denmark and France, Ballour and Namour offered witnessing testimonies from their work and experiences in Syria and the OPCW considered their statements as part of their deliberations and collection of evidence that al-Assad had used chemical weapons against Syrians, and that Russian forces were involved.

Further illuminating the potentiality and centrality of documentaries in the world today—when Russia learned of the OPCW event, officials moved to invite the same OPCW members to a competing event, which they called "The Use of Chemical Weapons in Syria: Truth and Lies," hosted two hours before the meeting where Ballour and Namour would be speaking. According to the Russian invitation, the Russian side-event was to include speeches from Alexander Shulgin, Russia's ambassador and representative

50   RADICAL REALITY

to the OPCW; Rania Al Rifaiy, a Syrian diplomat; and Maxim Grigoriev, a Russian national and president of a curiously named organization called "the Foundation for the Study of Democracy." Their invitation noted that the event would "disclose facts supported by related photo and video materials collected at the sites of alleged use of chemical weapons in Syria; provide evidence of staged provocations by armed opposition groups; expose the real role of some notorious NGOs such as the 'White Helmets' etc, in producing fake information about chemical attacks." To demonstrate their claims, the event also involved a propaganda video called *The Tunnel*, which endeavored to discredit Ballour and Fayyad, through interviews with people who claimed that the film was a hoax and based on made-up events. And, yet, despite the last-minute effort, the OPCW committee voted in favor of condemning Syria's actions and stripping its voting rights and privileges in the watchdog organization.[3]

While the film's distributors were not involved in the OPCW event, it was likely because of their global reach that *The Cave* was first placed on the radar of the OPCW committee, reflecting the potentiality of commercial media distribution today. Some producers say that this points to the importance of major commercial distributors and streamers continuing to acquire and promote important films like *The Cave*, even if—and especially because—they focus on controversial and uncomfortable realities.

As global powers and institutions grow to realize the influence of documentary storytelling, the medium will increasingly become the subject of scrutiny and pressure by powerful figures. As such, this story of *The Cave* points toward many imperatives for understanding the unique dimensions and power of documentary today, especially for stories that witness realities of war, resistance, and conflict; including the development of video as an arena of major global consequence and potential manipulation, and the intersectionality of documentaries with humanitarian and political agenda-setting and influence. Another side to *The Cave*'s extraordinary reach is that when the film was acquired by a major commercial distributor, it instantly meant that they needed to be cautious about the kinds of engagement and activist-related activities that they pursued, balancing the social aspirations of the filmmakers with the business logics of commercial media distribution—whose explicit missions centered around the objectives of entertainment, first and foremost, and perhaps to inform and educate, without significant social expectation of using their stories to promote any sort of specific social change. In other words, Fayyad and his team needed to be cautious about the types of activities and individuals that were associated with their documentary. For instance, they couldn't use the film in rallies; they couldn't use it to mobilize a demonstration in front of a government office; they couldn't organize major screening events in order to raise funding for a particular cause; and they needed to be generally cautious about any type of activist-associated activities. And while the collaboration between *The Cave*'s film team and its commercial distributors is generally considered an industry success story—and, indeed, because of its success—it points to the importance of greater deliberation and consensus around what "activism" means in documentary impact today, and what lines are justifiable for distributors to draw around what's permissible, what's laudable, and what's excessive. In today's environment, some producers have questioned whether a film like *The Cave* could even find distribution, not to mention impact campaign funding support.

As revealed in the stories shared by other film teams throughout this book, there is growing industry concern over perceptions that commercial distributors have significantly tightened their regulations since the time of *The Cave*. For instance, some distributors are increasingly working to bring impact work entirely in-house, limiting community screening events, and enforcing "no activism"-related policies around the films they acquire. Filmmakers say that this level of control has become one of the most underrecognized challenges in the industry today—one that conflicts with the core values and purpose that drive many filmmakers to work under extreme risks to witness stories of conflict, war, and resistance.

These experiences point to an understudied but urgent question: What does it mean when a form of storytelling that is, in many ways, an act of activism in itself—in its pursuit to challenge dominant narratives, interrogate power, and witness events and injustices that powerful figures wish to leave unseen—must be cautious about its alignment with any sort of activism-related objectives after its release? This painful dichotomy reflects the relevance and dilemma of a field at an unprecedented critical juncture. It is a question relevant for every chapter in this book. While it may make business sense to separate the world of filmmaking from the world of film distribution, the reality is that the risks, stakes, and purpose that reside in the former only grow more salient in the latter; to ignore this reality is to underestimate the social influence of documentary and undervalue the safety of its storytellers and protagonists, especially for films that document stories of war, conflict, and resistance. This chapter grapples with this challenge.

The Role of Documentaries in Witnessing Stories of Conflict and Resistance

Witnessing and reporting realities of conflict is a dangerous proposition for storytellers working everywhere. Around the world, journalists are watched and targeted—under attack and threat by government and corporate actors alike. To briefly return to a poll cited in the previous chapter, according to the 2023 World Press Freedom Index, a yearly evaluation of journalism conditions in 180 countries and territories, the environment of press freedom is "very serious" in 31 countries, "difficult" in 42, "problematic" in 55, and "good" or "satisfactory" in 52 countries. In other words, the situation for journalists is "bad" in 7 out of 10 countries.[4] Given the yearly availability of such polls, there has been considerable attention given within the news industry and academic fields of media and journalism studies to better understanding the unique risks that journalists face around the world,[5] including with the rise of new technologies.[6] This heightened scrutiny has helped to push journalistic institutions into providing at least some degree of heightened security and legal resources to make their investigative reporters' work possible, even if this level of protection is often disproportionately dispersed between well-financed news organizations and independent freelancers.[7] The same can be said for documentary filmmakers working in an investigative capacity.

At the same time, there has been insufficient attention—within press freedom, academic, and industry circles alike—on the dangers involved in independent documentary filmmaking, especially around conflict, a likely consequence of general misunderstandings about the importance of this type of work and a relative lack of recognition of documentaries as a distinct practice and community within the professional and academic fields of journalism and media.[8]

As this chapter demonstrates, creatively rendered documentary, told by storytellers inside a community rather than outside, can provide critical evidentiary documentation and cultural memory of atrocities in the context of conflict, challenge dominant narratives that oversimplify or misrepresent stories of conflict, and provide a deeply intimate and unvarnished lens into the lived experiences of its protagonists and the issues it centers. To provide a spotlight on specific instances of how documentaries are doing this work, and to explore some of the challenges, practices, and experiences of the filmmakers behind them, this chapter explores these issues through films from Syria, South Sudan, and Ukraine. In doing so, it highlights two distinct ways through which documentaries use *proximity*—(1) to key moments, events, and atrocities; and (2) to key people, leaders, and communities—as an organizing storytelling tactic in order to document atrocities, disrupt routine news narratives, and help audiences bear witness to, and intervene in, unfolding events of war, conflict, and resistance. In contrast to traditional journalistic ideals of objectivity and neutrality, it reveals how filmmakers—who are often from the countries at the center of their films—use the tenet of proximity as a way to capture intimate realities, perspectives, and angles to stories that are often missing in the larger media ecology. Put simply, this chapter illustrates the ways in which a filmmaker's proximity to the story they are telling should reflect the value—not the controversy—of the storytelling form, especially for the institutions who stand to fund, protect, and distribute such stories. And the longer industry attention fails to recognize this unique characteristic of documentary and its vital role in witnessing and better understanding stories of conflict and resilience, the harder it will be for this important media practice to survive and avoid co-optation.

Proximity to Key Events, Moments, and Atrocities

Every form of storytelling mediates only a partial picture of the reality it reflects. And documentaries are no exception. Filmmakers must alter time in condensing years of events into a 90-minute film, they need to make numerous judgments on where to point the camera, when to start filming, and then there is the range of influence that a camera's presence can have. And yet, still, documentary brings a dimension to stories of war and conflict that is arguably more detailed, encompassing, and humanizing than the traditional newspaper and broadcast traditions that have dominated the attention of scholars and audiences for decades.

In her book *About to Die*,[9] Barbie Zelizer examines the ways in which still news images have been used to siphon complex, disparate events into singular tropes and universal signifiers that are recognized by news organizations and audiences, but which often dislocate the image and news audience from realities on-the-ground. Zelizer describes the images of people about to die, often used in connection to—and to frame—stories of war and events of actual death for news audiences, as being, among other things, more invitational than confrontational. They appeal to the accessibility of categories

54 RADICAL REALITY

over the messiness of details, to the generalizable over the particular, and to the familiar over the unfamiliar. In doing so, the circumstances of the image itself—including who or what caused the suffering being depicted—often receive less attention, because the details of the moment captured in time mean less than the emotion that it causes. Consequently, as long as the emotion, or the thematic behind the image, meets the standards of newsworthy timeliness, the image itself needn't be timely.[10]

In one award-winning image explored by Zelizer, for instance, a dying boy is depicted lying on a hospital bed in Rwanda. The image, taken by photojournalist Martha Rial, was not actually published by a newspaper until a year after it was first taken, long after the boy had died. While this would be inconceivable for the traditional news photo, it is typical for news coverage that witnesses war and conflict. Since the Rwandan civil war was still timely when the photo was published, and the image was merely used to stand-in as representative of the many lives lost during the conflict, the date of the actual individual's death and the particularities of his plight meant even less.[11] Thus, Zelizer writes, the "photo functioned like other images of impending death—it was emblematic of the event, not the individual, making the boy's death important to Rial's proclaimed aim of demonstrating the fragility of Rwandan refugees."[12] Zelizer says that Rial's photography also used anonymity—the boy was also depicted in the newspaper image without a name—to "draw attention to the larger issues the images raised," such as the universal plight of children and genocide.[13] As a result, the images were exhibited for over a decade and were even used to raise funds for the International Rescue Committee and their work with Rwandan refugees. In her book, Zelizer points to this phenomenon, through the famine image, in order to make a larger case about why images of people about to die appear so often in the news: they serve journalists with a persuasive tool, she argues, to better engage news audiences and allow them "to engage with public events as much with hearts and guts as with their brains."[14]

By contrast, while the news image often surrenders an event in time and asks readers to fill in the details, documentaries of war and conflict are almost always deeply personal, even if the story appeals to broader themes such as family, humanity, and global conflict. Documentaries linger in the moments frozen by news images and can reveal the unflinching details, multidimensional emotions, and, ultimately, what happens in the moments before, during, and after war. To expand on the foundational work of Zelizer, if news images are invitational, accessible, generalized, and familiar, documentaries of war are often the opposite: they are confrontational rather than comfortable, they appeal to the messiness of details and realities over the accessibility of categories, and they center the particular over the generalizable. In doing so, documentaries often provide a distinct—and increasingly more definitive—type of witnessing than traditional journalistic forms of storytelling, even though documentary has received far less attention than traditional forms of journalism by scholars interested in forms of witnessing. One major exception to this is the work of media scholar Sandra Ristovska. In her examination of how video has been used by human rights committees and courts to verify and discern war crimes and abuses,[15] Ristovska argues that the unparalleled ability of documentaries—even those produced by strategic organizations—to serve as vehicles for bearing witness to the atrocities and consequences of conflict, as much if not more so than a testimonial, has led documentary to serving as legitimate tools of legal witnessing and social justice. Observing a series of videos that documented war crimes and explored horrific outcomes from the war as human rights violations, Ristovska interrogates the role that producing and screening documentaries served in advancing the legal and justice work of The International Criminal Tribunal for the former Yugoslavia (ICTY), a United Nations court of law that that was established to prosecute war crimes that had been committed during conflicts in the Balkans:

> The perceived importance of video to the ICTY's mandate is also implicated in the Outreach Programme's mission "to put into practice the principle of open justice: for justice to be truly done, it must be seen to be done." Bearing witness to the legal process through the act of seeing is considered central to the administration of international human rights justice. By producing documentaries, the ICTY Outreach Office seeks to create a lasting witnessing record of its work and accomplishments in addition to triggering a meaningful engagement with the stories of human rights abuses. In other words, the ICTY places video at the heart of the witnessing work it deems necessary for its contribution towards transitional justice in the region.[16]

The specificity of documentary film is why researchers have acutely pointed to the use of video and documentary as a powerful mobilizer of public attitudes and response,[17] just like news narratives and images, *and* as an increasingly relevant tool for government committees and social justice

56 RADICAL REALITY

and human rights–motivated institutions in corroborating testimonies, mediating witnessing, and pursuing human rights goals.[18] This is to say that documentaries are often personal and detailed by design. In doing so, to borrow once more from Zelizer's framing,[19] documentaries of conflict stand to appeal to both emotions and the brain without needing to hide the messy details of agonism, contradiction, complicity, and pain that the incomplete news image and narratives can obscure. In fact, it's the ability of the filmmaker's artistic license in bringing other human elements and details to the story that can compel a lens capable of disrupting stereotypical narratives and tired patterns of reporting.[20] And the documentaries investigated in this chapter achieve this not through testimonials or retrospective interviews, but through their real-time and prolonged proximity to the unfolding events they cover.

In the context of an ongoing war in Syria, this has proven especially true for the documentaries *For Sama*, which follows the life of a single family for five years during the uprising in Aleppo, and *The Cave*—both of which were released in 2019, nominated for Best Documentary Feature honors at the Academy Awards, and functioned to tell a fuller story of the Syrian conflict than was being depicted in mainstream press. In *For Sama*, Syrian filmmaker Waad al-Kateab documents her own life as a journalist and mother at the front lines of the war, along with the experiences of her husband, a doctor, providing audiences with a look into both the horrific realities of war for those who can't leave and for those who choose to stay, including the intimate and harrowing moments of life that reside within it, including the birth of her daughter. Due to the risk involved in making the film, Waad al-Kateab is not her real name, rather it's the one she created to protect her identity and that of her family from Syrian security forces. Similarly, leaving little to ambiguity, *The Cave* centers the story of the heroic doctor, Amani Ballour, and illuminates the use of chemical weapons against the Syrian people and how Russian aircraft were reportedly among those used. The filmmakers for both documentaries aimed to disrupt global narratives and approaches to the crisis and to bring a positive change to their country.

The proximity of the filmmaker and protagonists to the horrific realities of conflict puts audiences in a position of witnessing the emotion and pain of specific moments of war in ways entirely unique to documentary film. In the first scene of *For Sama*, for instance, we see the face of the filmmaker's newborn daughter, Sama, seconds before she is separated from her mother as their hospital is bombed. The mother, filmmaker Waad al-Kateab, quickly picks up her camera and moves through the hallway outside her room as it fills with smoke. There is a moment of hesitation and then al-Kateab says, "Quick, we've got to go downstairs," as the shaking camera moves through the smoke and to the level below. Realizing that she's been separated from her baby, the filmmaker starts yelling for Sama in the darkness of a hallway that's lost electricity, as bombings continue to rock the building and people rush everywhere around her. In another scene not long after, a woman dressed in all-black enters the hospital and asks for her son Muhammad. The camera finds the woman immediately and follows her closely and she finds his dead body wrapped in a blue tarp. The mother can be seen immediately recognizing the face of her son as she resists the hospital staff and scoops up his body. "This is my son, don't take him away from me," she says, crying, leaving the hospital with his corpse in her arms, fighting off requests from the hospital staff to return the body. At this moment, Al-Kateab intervenes and tells the doctors to leave the mother alone (though this is spoken in Arabic, and is not translated into English), as the camera follows her outside, still carrying the body, documenting the tears, pain, confusion, and numbness of the moment in which this anonymous woman realizes she has lost her son. There is no broader context about the geopolitical nature of the conflict, no description from the filmmaker about how she interpreted the pain of the mother, no testimonial or second-hand account of how someone remembers it; there is no room for subjective assumption or interpretation, there is simply the raw footage of the moment as it happened in real time. This is because the filmmaker was there and the camera was rolling, in the middle of the war, in the middle of the hospital, when the moment occurred.

There is nothing impartial or impersonal about the horror of the conflict that audiences witness through the film, since the audience is immediately aware—from the opening moments of the documentary—of the human behind the camera and her relation to the people and events in front of it. As such, the desire of the filmmaker to use the documentary to support a positive intervention in the war, to do more than simply raise awareness of the conflict, shouldn't be surprising. And, for the most part, the film team's efforts to use the film to advance the goals of its main protagonist and creator, Waad Al-Kateab, was not overtly blocked by their distributors, which included Channel 4 (in the United Kingdom), PBS Frontline (in the United

58 RADICAL REALITY

States), and Autlook Filmsales (as the international sales agency). And, yet, it did quickly become clear to the filmmakers and impact producer team that organizing screenings and securing financial support for any type of advocacy-like effort would need to be sourced independently of the distributor's P&A spend. Sarah Mosses, an impact producer who worked with Al-Kateab in identifying funding and creating a screening strategy around her film, recalled the importance of ensuring that the campaign Waad led—which included lobbying politicians in the UK parliament and other global governing bodies, raising donations for a UK nonprofit that could distribute funds in Syria, changing narratives around the crisis, and using social media channels and demonstrations to bring awareness to the conflict and the bombing of hospitals in Syria—was distanced from the film itself.[21] This meant creating separate websites for the film (forsamafilm.com) and the campaign (actionforsama.com), occasionally tweaking how certain marketing messages and appeals were framed, and ensuring that the distributors would be distanced from the direct impact-related activity that the film team organized. "It was very much a part of the strategy that we had to be mindful of the fact that the broadcasters had particular editorial guidelines that they had to abide to; whereas the campaign could be more vocal about certain topics," said Mosses.[22]

However, what happens when the content of a film itself, and the events it witnesses, are highly controversial? While the film *For Sama* documented horrific acts of violence, it did not go as far as *The Cave* did in directing attention to the perpetrators of the war crimes seen on screen—a critical detail that was also largely missing in mainstream news narratives and reporting about the conflict at the time. As introduced at the beginning of this chapter, *The Cave* directly calls attention to the role that Russia played in perpetuating atrocities and crimes against Syrian civilians and hospitals, which was a reality not widely reported on by news outlets when the film was being made. Early news coverage of the conflict primarily framed it as an internal civil war; though, today, the role that Russia and other global powers played—and continue to play—in the war is widely known.

While National Geographic and Disney didn't interfere with the final cut of *The Cave*, members on the film team said they were questioned about the inclusion of details that directly implicated Russia. However, the filmmakers felt that omitting details about some of the atrocities being committed by Russia would have been to leave out an important reality of the film. In addition to the video evidence, they hired fact checkers and worked with a journalist to help compile pages of investigation that verified and corroborated the evidence in their film with even greater certainty.

Beyond the ultimate hope of stopping the bombing of hospitals and ending the war in Syria,[23] the impact objectives of *The Cave* included two goals: to help create more supportive policies for those implicated by the crisis in Syria, and to directly help the people at the center of the film who had welcomed the filmmakers into their space and lives.[24] If the film team did nothing, then the consequences would likely have been tragic and put the lives of the main protagonists in serious jeopardy. Consequently, the filmmakers looked to build alliances with organizations that could help them bridge entertainment and humanitarian activities, while documenting a brutal reality. To help in this endeavor, the film team brought in Danielle Turkov, an impact producer who worked in politics and social policy before starting her company Think Film, a multi-award-winning impact media company operating at the intersection of art and social change.

Once Turkov joined the team, one of the first things she did was to arrange a conversation with Ballour: it was a moment she will never forget. It was three months before the film team would lock the final cut of the documentary, and about six months before its premiere.

> She was trapped in a refugee camp between Syria and Turkey. She wasn't allowed to leave. She didn't have any paperwork to leave. And we'd get on calls and she'd say: "I'm just going to go back to Syria, because if I can't help anyone here, I'm just going to go back. What's the point in me living and sitting in a camp when I've saved 50,000 people's lives in a hospital and people are still dying in my country, and all you keep doing is telling me a film's gonna be released."[25]

Ballour had dedicated her career to helping people and she had opened up years of her life to the filmmakers at an immense risk to her own personal safety in order to support the film. To learn that she was now stuck in a refugee camp, unable to continue her practice and help people who were still dying back in her home country, and starting to question the value of a documentary, set off alarm bells and an imperative to do more.

In a series of calls, Turkov and the film team worked with Ballour to help her build a platform so that they could raise the profile of her story in order both to help increase her chances of securing asylum in another country and to position her to lobby for change and assistance for other

60   RADICAL REALITY

Syrians.[26] They also submitted Ballour's work for consideration by international human rights awards, including the Raoul Wallenberg Prize and at the Council of Europe in Strasbourg. She won the former and was on the shortlist for the latter. And that is when things started to gain momentum. Without the award or recognition of the film, being able to bring Ballour out of Turkey might have been impossible. However, by winning the prestigious Raoul Wallenberg Prize, which is awarded by the Council of Europe every two years in recognition of extraordinary humanitarian work done by an individual, Ballour had good reason to expect an invitation to another country—giving the film team a window of opportunity. After the award was announced, they successfully requested the European Union to invite her to Germany to receive it. Think-Film coordinated with the French ambassador to leverage an agreement with Turkey to get her out of the country, and then they started the process of pressuring diplomats and pushing for her application for political asylum in Germany. And with Ballour able to freely travel, the film's distributor funded an international tour and festival campaign to promote the film.

Turkov and the film team also worked with Ballour to create her own foundation, which could accept donations from audiences who wanted to help. Ballour now works with the Syrian American Medical Society in the United States and sits on a United Nations committee dedicated to the future of democracy in Syria. With support from the film team, Namour and some of the other doctors and nurses in the film were also able to get travel documents to leave Syria and neighboring countries. In this way, *The Cave* team worked within the parameters of a competitive commercial media landscape, leveraging the interests that govern it (especially in awards and high-profile activities) in order to pursue positive outcomes for the communities at the heart of the film, long after it had been completed.

The type of relationships and practices that are essential to exposing the radical realities of the world today, and to gaining access to experiences in ways that only documentaries can provide, often require an intimate partnership and level of trust with the people at the center of the events being witnessed. And this means that the role of safeguarding the participants at the center of the film is not a commitment that ends when the filming stops. Because, to put it another way, social justice and activism—the desire to use stories to push for both greater understanding and political or social change—is not simply a quality of documentaries that witness conflict and resistance, it is often the lifeblood that creates them.

Proximity to People, Key Figures, and Communities

In addition to documenting atrocities, war crimes, and the horrific realities of war, documentaries are also uniquely capable of featuring the lasting implications of conflict by centering stories of people seeking peace, justice, and new lives after war. And this reflects another distinct way that documentaries are moving beyond other forms of storytelling to foster greater understanding, more nuanced narratives, and advancing social justice work. One of the primary reasons documentaries are often so well positioned to tell these types of stories is because they usually come from filmmakers who operate outside of the push-and-pull of current headlines and who have been filming, investigating, and developing relationships long before the topic of their film becomes—if it ever becomes—popular among mainstream media interests.

To better understand the role that personal proximity plays in documentaries that witness the violence and consequences of conflict, it is important to briefly consider the history and tradition of investigative journalism, as it runs deep in the field of documentary, albeit under the radar of many media observers and with slight, but meaningful, differences in approach. In some ways, the investigative tactics, techniques, and reform-based motives of documentary work veer strikingly close to the long tradition of undercover journalism work chronicled by journalism scholar Brooke Kroeger,[27] as documentary filmmaking frequently involves blending into environments in order to reveal deeper details and truths that are often left unexplained by traditional, deadline-based reporting. However, the methods that the filmmakers of this chapter use to capture these moments of truth often compel a unique type of transparency, in order to gain the level of access required to capture intimate details on camera. At times, this meant drawing on family and community members as sources, or spending years developing personal relationships with the film's main protagonists. And this can also include a need for the filmmaker to center themselves and their lived experiences as a focal point of their storytelling.[28]

Given the centrality that the personal stakes and relationships of the filmmaker serve in informing the entry point for the story that is witnessed, documentaries often present the filmmaker's point of view, and embrace the use of creative and artistic storytelling techniques (including the use of added sound, lighting, and editing) to accentuate certain features and moments of a story, even while following similar reporting protocols as traditional

62 RADICAL REALITY

investigative journalists. As a result, a canon of documentary theory has established—and wrestled with—the tensions inherent in a "creative" treatment of "reality," recognizing that documentary filmmakers' approach to witnessing and telling a story is not necessarily synonymous with reflecting a sole unvarnished "truth."[29] And yet, as film scholar Stella Bruzzi posits, "[i]t can legitimately be argued that filmmakers themselves (and their audiences) have, much more readily than theorists, accepted documentary's inability to give an undistorted, purely reflective picture of reality."[30]

In other words, for many documentaries it is the unique point of view, stakes, and proximity that the filmmaker has to the people that audiences witness on screen that constitute the heart of the film. To give a few examples, this is especially true for Yance Ford's film *Strong Island*, an investigation into the killing of his brother and the injustice that followed it. It is the case for *When the Guns Go Silent*, a detailed and personal investigation into peace negotiations in Colombia by journalist Natalia Orozco, who is granted unprecedented access to the negotiation teams of each side. And this certainly is the case for the film *No Simple Way Home*, a documentary about one of the most influential families in South Sudan, filmed by a member of that family, and the focus of this section.

The history of South Sudan and the decades-long civil war that preceded the new nation is one of the most misunderstood stories of the last few decades—a story that has largely been told by reporters, institutions, and governments outside of the country itself. But in the film *No Simple Way Home* audiences are taken to the heart of a family at the center of the past, present, and future of the country. The film, released in 2022, is the first documentary written and directed by Akuol de Mabior, whose father, John Garang de Mabior, is remembered as a revolutionary leader and national hero of South Sudan. He joined and later became the leader of the Sudan People's Liberation Movement/Army (SPLM/SPLA), and the liberation movement it advanced, for more than two decades. In January 2005, Garang supported a peace agreement that ended a decades-long civil war between the Sudanese government and the SPLM/SPLA, of which Garang was chief. But six months later, Garang died in a helicopter crash that continues to raise questions and conspiracy theories; following 21 years of conflict, he died just 21 days after becoming president of the newly autonomous Southern Sudan region, the film notes, as Akuol watches old VHS recordings of him in her family's living room. After his death, the legacy of her father continued to serve as a galvanizing force behind a move toward independence and the eventual founding of South Sudan as an independent country, in 2011; he is still remembered as a founding father of the young nation.

The complexity of South Sudan's history is incapsulated in the complex story of her father and his role in the country's founding. At the risk of oversimplifying a nuanced history, the 2005 peace agreement stipulated a referendum that would give the people of the south a choice: to remain one country (Sudan) or secede. And Garang had given speeches which suggested that he wanted the people of the south to be self-determining, but that he didn't necessarily want secession.[31] He spoke of wanting people to make an informed decision and he advocated for what he hoped would be a "New Sudan."[32] But he died before any such vote took place. As a result, Garang is at the center of a very complicated history, as his vision wasn't necessarily for secession; but he did argue that it was important for the people to decide. As such, he is regarded as both an advocate for a united "New Sudan" and as a founding father of the new nation of "South Sudan." Through the film, Akuol provides both further detail and nuance to this layered history.

After growing up in exile, the film follows Akuol de Mabior as she moves to South Sudan with her sister and family in order to document her mother, Rebecca Nyandeng De Mabior, and her efforts to safeguard her late husband's vision for the country. The camera stays close to Akuol's mother, who many also consider to be the "mother of the country," as she is called out of exile, and becomes vice president of the country in early 2020.

The film opens with Akuol sharing her personal feelings and insight into her own struggle for identity and all the complexities that come with returning to a country that is also trying to find its own identity: "My family's story is inseparable from the story of my country, even though I've never really lived there." With this, the film immediately provides a unique perspective and level of intimacy to the story of South Sudan, and the long journey toward peace and self-discovery that follows war and conflict. Throughout the film, Akuol shares her own personal struggle of feeling a sense of duty to South Sudan, alongside fears and confusion around her and its future, identity, and purpose. She spotlights the trauma that her family and the people of South Sudan are still healing from, after years of conflict, even though it's not something that is widely talked about or acknowledged in public. She notes how courageous and "sure-footed" her sister seems to be in the face of the challenges, and how she doesn't feel as courageous at times. In other words, rather than telling a single story of hope and determination,

64 RADICAL REALITY

Image 3.1 Description: *No Simple Way Home*: Family portrait. From left to right: Standing: Mabior Garang de Mabior, Chol Garang de Mabior. Seated: Gak Garang de Mabior, Akuol Garang de Mabior, John Garang de Mabior, Rebecca Nyandeng de Mabior, Nyankuir Garang de Mabior. Image provided by: Akuol Garang de Mabior.

Image 3.2 Description: *No Simple Way Home*: Rebecca Nyandeng de Mabior arriving in South Sudan. Image provided by: Akuol Garang de Mabior.

WITNESSING CONFLICT AND RESILIENCE 65

Image 3.3 Description: *No Simple Way Home*: Akuol and Nyankuir. From left to right: Nyankuir Garang de Mabior, Akuol Garang de Mabior. Image provided by: Akuol Garang de Mabior.

Image 3.4 Description: *No Simple Way Home*: Main film poster. Photo Credit: Thomas Morley. Image provided by: Akuol Garang de Mabior.

or of war and trauma, Akuol points the camera to the intimate complexities and uncomfortable realities of the current situation, as she experiences it, which includes the trauma, struggle, uncertainty, agonism, worry, questions without answers, nuance, and promise.

66 RADICAL REALITY

As the city teeters on a renewed war and economic crisis, Akuol works to overcome clichés, stereotypes, and oversimplified news narratives of her country by keeping the camera focused on the day-to-day events and conversations—rather than the geopolitical headlines—to provide a glimpse of what life is really like from where she stands, providing a new dimension to the traditional newspaper headline or nonprofit appeal that has related the conflict for most international audiences to this point. The documentary also provides a level of proximity, candidness, and intimacy to one of the country's most influential figures in a way that only a daughter could provide. "Soon after we lost my father, my mother started sharing her dreams and fears with me, always in the early hours of the morning," Akuol says in a narration, about five minutes into the documentary, as she films an intimate moment of her mother climbing out of bed. "I decided to start filming our morning conversations."

In an interview for this book,[33] Akuol said that her initial motivation to make the film was to tell the story of her mother. While she was in film school, she read an article about an influential figure who had just passed away; her name was Pauline Opango, an important Congolese activist and the wife of the late Patrice Lumumba, the first prime minister of the Democratic Republic of Congo. In all the news coverage, she couldn't find an image of her, only of the former prime minister, who had been killed more than 50 years earlier. "I feared that [my mother] would also be forgotten or her contribution would be forgotten," she said. "So I wanted to make a film in appreciation of her contribution to the movement and in appreciation of what I saw growing up, all that she sacrificed and that she did."[34] However, as her family moved back to South Sudan, Akuol realized both how vivid her father's legacy remained in South Sudan and how much of her mother's contributions and influence were still actively shaping the country. So instead of a biographical film that primarily looked backward, she decided to center the story and experiences on her family's experience in the moment. "I decided to shift focus to where we are and where we're going," she said. "Both as a family and as a country."

Akuol said that she always saw South Sudanese people, in the country and in the diaspora, as the target audience for the film. Rather than simply trying to educate outsiders, she said that one of her biggest hopes for the film was that it would "open up spaces for conversations that we don't tend to have."[35] Akuol says that it can be difficult to find instances of intergenerational dialogue and uncomfortable conversations in the country—especially around issues of power, trauma, tradition, and stigma—but she has been surprised just how effective documentaries have been in creating a space for those conversations to happen. The film has been screened in various communities in the country's capital city of Juba, and she has seen the film spark a range of emotions and debates from audiences. One of the most relatable struggles of the film, especially for South Sudanese people living in the diaspora, she said, is the feeling that everyone should feel a sense of "duty" and "patriotic responsibility" in their hearts to return to the new country and help processes of peace and nation-building; when, in reality, people can feel many conflicting emotions about what they should do or what they want to do.[36] People have approached Akuol in tears after screenings, expressing how her film helped them to name many of the struggles and feelings they have had for a long time and it has helped start larger conversations on similar topics, as well.

One of the greatest lessons Akuol said she learned in making the film was the importance of local support networks for filmmakers. While nonprofit funding has made several positive contributions and is a vital stream of support that Akuol says she hopes will continue, a danger of primarily having global organizations and international NGOs providing substantial funding for films in the region is that their association can dislocate filmmakers from developing relationships with local communities and audiences. But this doesn't mean that one approach should replace another, she said, as there is value in (and a need for) both funding models. This is why, Akuol says, regional and local filmmaking networks and funders are so vital for films like hers to be able to continue to be made. If funding comes primarily from global institutions, it can influence the type of audiences that filmmakers have in mind when they are making their film, said Akuol, and it can also influence how audiences perceive a film or screening event.[37] Regional and local film networks and organizations, on the other hand, can help filmmakers create content with local audiences in mind, help them explore alternative funding and marketing opportunities in their country, and improve their relationships with audiences in the region. In making *No Simple Way Home*, Akuol said she worked with producer Sam Soko, who directed the acclaimed film *Softie*, and his production company LightBox Africa, which provided support in several areas, especially in supporting critical fundraising activities that allowed the film to be made.

During our conversation, Akuol frequently noted that, while she has close proximity to key leaders and people in the country, she is not and doesn't

68 RADICAL REALITY

ever claim to be "an authority of South Sudan" and said, "my experience is not representative." At the same time, that is the value of documentary, she says. While it can't capture everyone's reality, it can at least come very close to capturing her reality, and, in doing so, it can itself serve as a recognition that everyone's lived experience is unique and important:

> I feel like our experiences are so different that expectations of the "representative experience" should be dropped, because each experience is unique. And in our case, in South Sudan, we are coming back to South Sudan from so many different places. And then also you have people who never left. So there's a fractured sense of what South Sudan is. So this expectation for "representative experience," doesn't make sense. So that's the access point, or my unique position, is from my limited perspective and my experience and relationship to my parents and my relationship to the country. But from a personal and limited perspective.[38]

Shifting attention to eastern Europe, recent films from Ukraine also illustrate the salience of personal proximity to documentary storytelling. In the months that followed Russia's deadly invasion in February of 2022, there was an immediate and insatiable appetite for news stories out of the region. News organizations and distributors across media industries distributed scores of frontline broadcast news reports, investigative features, and eyewitness videos that provided a glimpse into the horrific happenings of war for interested audiences. Films like *When Spring Came to Bucha*, *We Will Not Fade Away*, and *Iron Butterflies* reflect just some of the dozens of short films featured in events by Human Rights Watch, and other human rights groups, from filmmakers documenting Ukrainians' fight for survival, alongside documentaries commissioned by news organizations (*I Did Not Want to Make a War Film*, released by *The New Yorker*; *20 Days in Mariupol*, released by the Associated Press and PBS *Frontline*; and *Occupied*, released by the BBC) and other films distributed through festivals and various platforms in 2022 and 2023 alone (including *Freedom on Fire, Eastern Front, Slava Ukraini, Ukraine'22: Diaries of War*, and *Ukraine from Above*, to name just a few), all of which received international media attention for their harrowing stories and frontline footage. At the same time, there were also documentaries released that had been in production years before the escalation of the war in Ukraine had caught the media's eye again. Beyond the important role of eyewitness video, these other films demonstrate the

WITNESSING CONFLICT AND RESILIENCE 69

unique contribution that documentaries also provide when they focus on deeply personal stories, even for issues that might seem oversaturated in the media landscape, allowing audiences to engage with the complicated truths and emotions beneath the headlines.

One such film is *A House Made of Splinters*, nominated for the 2022 Best Documentary Feature Film Academy Award, which shares the story of three displaced children who live for about a year in a shelter that temporarily houses children who have been taken from their homes by the state of Ukraine because their parents are unable to take care of them. The shelter is based in eastern Ukraine, an area impacted by the ongoing conflict, and exemplifies both the long-term consequences of war, especially for communities and families who live near the frontlines, and the struggles social workers are having to provide care in a country that lacks adequate infrastructure investment to care for displaced children. And while marketing for the film situated the story within an urgent political moment, the film was not made "in the moment" by a parachuting storyteller with a video camera; as with all of the documentaries featured in the book, the filmmaker's camera was rolling long before an international appetite for stories about the conflict in Ukraine had developed. Similarly, the 2023 documentary *We Will Not Fade Away* focuses on the lives of five teenagers living through bombings and ongoing conflict in the Donbas region of Ukraine in the four years leading up to the 2022 invasion, providing a glimpse into the emotions and daily challenges experienced by young people in the lead-up to the escalation.

In another documentary, *Peace for Nina*, audiences are given intimate access to the struggle of a Ukrainian woman, Nina Branovytska, whose son was captured and executed by Russian mercenaries after he had volunteered for the Ukrainian Army and tried to defend the Donetsk airport in 2015. The film follows Nina as she pieces together the final days of her son's life by collecting evidence of his extrajudicial execution, including engaging with lawyers, former war prisoners, witnesses of war crimes, and Ukrainian army members who served with her son. By centering Nina's pursuit of justice and her fight to see the recognition of her son's killing as a war crime in Ukrainian and International Courts, *Peace for Nina* witnesses the years of grief, pain, and enduring struggle that follow war. Nina learns that many of the men who executed her son were killed and so they will never face a trial, leaving her to question what justice and reconciliation can and should look like. With war crime trials already beginning in Ukraine, producers of the film's impact efforts say they hope Nina's story will help shape existing movements toward

70 RADICAL REALITY

justice and accountability by informing future legal efforts so that they can operate effectively and that by helping families imagine what can be achieved for victims when criminal prosecution is not possible.[39]

The Ukrainian director of the film, Zhanna Maksymenko-Dovhych, was a close family friend of Nina for many years before the tragedy. Because of this history and trust, Nina allowed Zhanna to follow her every day for five years as part of the filmmaking process, bringing a level of intimate proximity that could only come from the development of extraordinary trust. Zhanna began filming in 2015, around the time that Crimea was annexed, but she struggled to get anyone interested in financing or backing the film. This all changed once Russia's invasion of Ukraine became a mainstream news story, and there was a sudden appetite for conflict films from the region swept through the film industry.

The Site of the Struggle

The proximity of the filmmakers spotlighted in this chapter to the stories, events, and people they feature illustrates one of the fundamental ways that documentary is capable of differentiating itself as a trusted vehicle for witnessing stories of conflict and resistance, and of reaching beyond the conventions and limits of traditional journalism to provide detail, perspective, and nuance that is often missing in dominant media narratives. The films highlighted in this chapter reveal how the capabilities of documentary as a tool for witnessing do not stem from the technological value of video alone; instead, it's often the unique connections that filmmakers bring to unfolding events that makes documentary such an effective medium for revealing the realities of war.

Put another way, the films spotlighted in this chapter are all personal, not simply because they center personal stories, but because the filmmakers behind the cameras have personal stakes in the events that unfold. And it was often this level of connection that allowed them to get intimate access and details. To assume that someone with such close personal ties to the events and people they film would not also have personal stakes in the safety of the film's participants, or in how their documentary is used, is to misunderstand the essence and authenticity of the craft. To presume that these filmmaker's work is done after their film is completed is to neglect the humanity at the center of the documentaries featured here, through which filmmakers spend years with people—who are rarely paid or financially compensated in any way—as they open up their lives to a camera, often because of at least a small belief that it could bring a helpful impact to their lives or that of their community. While the word "witness" may bring a connotation of neutrality for some, especially those who study traditional tenets of American journalism, the word "witness" compels the opposite for many of the film teams engaged in this chapter; for them, witnessing compels responsibility, complicity, influence, and a need to recognize their part in the events that unfold during and after the filmmaking process.

The stakes of misunderstanding this fundamental reality are consequential. More than a theoretical quagmire over the boundaries of journalistic practice or the lines between creativity and objectivity, discussions over the role of proximity in documentaries of conflict and resistance are often about the role of filmmakers, funders, and distributors in matters of life and death for the people they feature. They are about the influence that a film has in tipping the scales of justice and accountability, in changing a country or governing body's perception of a war, and even in influencing the course of global conflict—all of which are outcomes of the films highlighted in this chapter, regardless of whether their distributors or audiences see them purely through the lens of entertainment or not.

Consequently, the longer distributors refuse to acknowledge the personal stakes of documentary, the less prepared they will be for addressing existing and new challenges posed by other actors who do recognize the potential and influence of documentary, especially authoritarian governments and forces that are already using video to obscure or bury truths that challenge their power. There has long been great debate around the lines of truthfulness and authenticity in documentary,[40] with scholars like John Ellis[41] recently charting what he sees as an industry shift in how documentaries are made, moving from their observational roots, marked by a purposeful lack of overt editing choices, to a more evidential-based approach to storytelling that uses narrative devices, sound, and stylistic choices in order to build a more transportive experience for audiences into a past moment in reality. And these debates have only grown more salient as the development and circulation of fake content has reached new levels. Headlining the 2023 World Press Index report, the survey found that in 118 countries, two-thirds of all countries surveyed, most of the respondents "reported that political actors in their countries were often or systematically involved in massive disinformation or propaganda campaigns."[42] Of particular concern, the report

72 RADICAL REALITY

notes, is the permeation of fake photos and video by AI programs, used by governments and citizens alike, to spread false information or propaganda that is increasingly difficult to verify.

As such, the growing prevalence and power of documentary film at a time when video can be easily manipulated has prompted fresh challenges and concerns for the field.[43] In a warning that adeptly predicted the type of ploy attempted by the Russian propaganda film *The Tunnel*, media scholar Sandra Ristovska notes, "As video increasingly provides the main mode of accessing ongoing conflicts, and as institutions and public's trust the knowledge provided by video, the visual field will grow as a site of struggle and manipulation."[44] It is precisely this level of power and importance—to the individual in a refugee camp, to the NGO working at the intersection of the issue, to the human rights committee deciding sanctions, to the mother pursuing justice and accountability, to the survivors of war and injustice who are piecing together new identities and ways forward, to the individuals holding oppressive government's accountable—that points to the importance of better recognizing, understanding and harnessing the witnessing potential of documentaries today.

4

Upholding Freedom of Expression

When Maria Ressa accepted the Nobel Peace Prize in 2021 alongside Russian reporter Dmitry Andreyevich Muratov—the first working journalists to receive the honor in 85 years—she paid homage to a peer who missed the same opportunity. In 1936, the Nobel Peace Prize went to Carl von Ossietzky, whose dogged reporting and critique of Germany's political trouble sounded alarm bells during the rise of the Third Reich. Adolph Hitler, infuriated about the award, ensured that von Ossietzky didn't make it out to Oslo to accept it; a few years later, von Ossietzky passed away in a Nazi concentration camp.[1] But, as Ressa said in her speech, "hopefully we're a step ahead because we're actually here!"[2] In this contemporary global climate, independent journalism and media, she explained, are in trouble. The stakes in a worldwide digital information economy could not be higher, nor the urgency more desperate:

> I stand before you, a representative of every journalist around the world who is forced to sacrifice so much to hold the line, to stay true to our values and mission: to bring you the truth and hold power to account.... We need information ecosystems that live and die by facts. We do this by shifting social priorities to rebuild journalism for the 21st century while regulating and outlawing the surveillance economics that profit from hate and lies.... we need to help independent journalism survive.[3]

As Ressa said in her Nobel talk, the global challenges exist beyond her work in the Philippines. Ten years earlier, following an illustrious media career including a stint as Southeast Asia CNN reporter, she cofounded the independent investigative journalism start-up Rappler, based in the Philippines, which she described as

> our attempt to put together two sides of a coin that shows everything wrong with our world today: an absence of law and democratic vision

Radical Reality. Caty Borum and David Conrad-Pérez, Oxford University Press. © Oxford University Press 2025. DOI: 10.1093/9780197604298.003.0004 for the 21st century. That coin represents our information ecosystem, which determines everything else about our world. Journalists, the old gatekeepers, are one side of the coin. The other is technology, with its god-like power that has allowed a virus of lies to infect each of us, pitting us against each other, bringing out our fears, anger and hate, and setting the stage for the rise of authoritarians and dictators around the world.[4]

The trouble began quickly for Ressa and the Rappler investigative re-porting team. In 2016, populist Rodrigo Duterte assumed the presidency of the Philippines and promised a swift crackdown on illegal drugs to al-legedly address the country's crushing poverty. During his years in office—but dating back five years to his stint as Davao City's mayor—thousands of killings, primarily of urban poor, took place in a concerted campaign that Human Rights Watch deems a possible crime against humanity.[5] Rappler covered Duterte's every move, even as he systematically dismantled the free press in the Philippines, shutting down critical print and TV outlets and om-inously threatening news media by publicly stating that "just because you're a journalist doesn't mean you are exempted from assassination."[6]

In 2020, Duterte's administration passed a new law designed to curtail press freedom in the country. Soon after, a Filipino court found Ressa, and a former colleague of hers at Rappler, guilty of cyber libel in connection to their reporting.[7] Many pointed to the controversial charge as a clear example of Duterte's abuse of power and the blatant political motivation behind the ver-dict to silence the press.[8] But the problem is more complex: As Ressa tracked online responses to Rappler's reporting, it was increasingly clear that a vast network of disinformation, carried and amplified by social media platforms and opposition voices, makes free and factual reporting nearly impossible. Social media is weaponized by actual and would-be dictators, crushing dis-sent and critical freedom of speech and expression—and the stakes are dire for democratic functioning, she said:

> Social media is a deadly game for power and money, what Shoshana Zuboff calls surveillance capitalism, extracting our private lives for outsized cor-porate gain. . . . Facebook is the world's largest distributor of news, and yet studies have shown that lies laced with anger and hate spread faster and further than facts on social media. These American companies controlling our global information ecosystem are biased against facts, biased against journalists. They are—by design—dividing us and radicalizing us.[9]

While Ressa and her unflinching stance were attracting critics, trolls, and admirers around the world, documentary filmmaker Ramona S. Diaz entered the picture. A renowned, celebrated documentarian—Guggenheim fellow, member of the Academy of Motion Picture Arts & Sciences—Diaz's body of work focuses on the experiences of Filipino and Filipino-American people. "I felt very compelled to tell her [Maria's] story," she said in a media interview. "It's both *of* the moment and yet timeless because you are speaking truth to power. This is a David and Goliath story, which is timeless and also timely, because she is talking about misinformation and press freedom."[10] Years of following Ressa, aided in part by funding from the International Documentary Association's prestigious Enterprise Documentary grant for investigative documentary storytelling, came together in Diaz's independent feature documentary, *A Thousand Cuts*, which premiered at the Sundance Film Festival in 2020 and on PBS *Frontline* in 2021, winning Emmy and Peabody Awards the next year.[11] With meticulous attention to intimate detail, the film tracks Ressa and the Rappler news team along with two pro-Duterte leaders, revealing, as Ressa says in the film, "death by a thousand cuts . . . little cuts of Filipino democracy."[12] Predictably, the film and Ressa were targets of violent online trolls—including the kind of sexualized, gendered threats that increasingly confront women journalists[13]—and yet, as Ressa said in a press interview with Diaz, "We have to hold the line, because if we don't, our democracy will die before our eyes . . . we have to uphold our rights."[14] In 2023, the International Criminal Court (ICC) judicial panel announced its continuing investigation of Duterte and his administration for alleged crimes against humanity,[15] a story known to Filipino people and others around the world, at least in part, because of Rappler, Ressa, Diaz, and independent documentary filmmakers and journalists speaking truth to power, often at great personal and professional risk.

Freedom of expression, a hallmark of an open, pluralistic society, has for centuries been threatened by political regulation and suppression as a form of social control.[16] But over the past decade, freedom of expression and media freedom have declined around the world—in both authoritarian regimes and liberal democracies alike.[17] And yet, this scenario is not a consequence of government systems alone; it's aided and abetted by increased commercial consolidation in media more broadly, which leaves the marketplace to determine which stories are seen and distributed widely.

In this context, how are independent documentaries telling stories that push hard against censorship and stand up to media repression? In the

76   RADICAL REALITY

fraught misinformation era, documentary films like *A Thousand Cuts* are doing a kind of double duty to uphold the line. Not only do these kinds of independent films illustrate and exercise their own right to free speech and freedom of expression but also they serve as witness to document the precarious nature and heroics of independent journalists and storytellers around the world. And there are many, with frighteningly similar parallel themes: *While We Watched* (India), *Lyra* (Ireland), *The Killing of a Journalist* (Slovakia), *Etilaat Roz* (Afghanistan), *The Dissident* and *Endangered* (United States), *Radio Silence* (Mexico), and *Je Suis Charlie* (France), among others. As they—and the films in this chapter—make clear, editorial independence is the vital ingredient, and yet, the structural factors that quell independence are immense. The challenges are always, as Ressa says, "about power and money."[18]

Freedom of Expression and Media Freedom Under Duress

Individuals' right to speak freely, and the ability of a free press to disseminate news and information, are bedrock ideals to functioning democracies. Intuitively simple and straightforward in theory, the existence of these freedoms manifests in living, breathing practice. Likewise, their precarity is seen in the invisible (and often shockingly public) ways they are endangered by institutions and individuals in power. Threats to freedom of expression and media freedom exist along a continuum, and herein lies the need to understand how and why they happen—and the implications for democracy and citizens when they do. Independent documentaries and their makers find themselves in this complicated maze in myriad ways—made insufferably complex in the era of digital media, surveillance technology, the global capitalistic system, and increased commercial media consolidation.

To begin with a refresher on the fundamentals, the right of expression is, as human rights scholars affirm, a "basic and unalienable right . . . Article 19 of the Universal Declaration of Human Rights establishes that 'everyone has the right to freedom of opinion and expression; this right includes freedom to hold opinions without interference and to seek, receive and impart information and ideas through any media and regardless of frontiers."[19] In the United States, as only one example, free speech is enshrined as the First Amendment of the United States Constitution.[20] Freedom of expression is, therefore, a "bulwark of liberty ... a source of inspiration for religious liberals and proponents of democratic self-rule."[21] Free speech, writ large, is threatening to institutional bodies and leaders interested in exerting high legal or social command and control. In response, curtailing freedom of expression has long been a tool of social repression wielded by governments, corporate entities, and individuals with some degree of power (financial or station or renown)—working through political regulation, threats, forcing de facto self-censorship, and other forms of suppression.[22]

Media freedom evolves from freedom of expression, and likewise, its meaning is precise in practice—and only understood when we consider the fullest context in which media systems operate. We use scholar Jennifer Whitten-Woodring's framework to define "media freedom," taking into account underlying legal, political, economic, and professional environments:

At its deepest level, free media:
1. Operate in a legal environment that: a. provides and enforces constitutional protection of media freedom; b. is free from laws which restrict reporting.
2. Operate in a political environment that: a. is free from government censorship; b. allows open access to multiple competing sources; c. is free from intimidation and physical violence against journalists;
3. Operate in an economic environment that: a. is free from financial manipulation by government or other actors (including restrictions on production and/or distribution and reliance on advertising and/or subsidies); b. encourages a plurality of ownership that facilitates competition among media outlets; c. facilitates the dissemination of information to citizens;
4. Operate in a professional environment that: a. encourages journalists to serve as watchdogs, monitoring and reporting on government; b. encourages the coverage of contentious stories; c. encourages news media to serve as a voice for the marginalized; d. discourages self-censorship.[23]

Media freedom is not a negotiable reality when it comes to functioning democracies; it serves as a watchdog on government and other forms of power—and as a vital protection against human rights abuses. Beyond its role in providing a reliable and consistent way for publics, governments, and

78 RADICAL REALITY

elite institutions to share information, media freedom is also an essential peacekeeping and peacebuilding force, as Whitten-Woodring writes:

> Freedom of the press in particular, has long been considered crucial to democracy because the news media provide a fundamental informational linkage between mass publics, elites, and governments. . . . Further, countries with free media are also less likely to engage in conflict and war with another, given that their open media systems allow an "exchange of trusted information" and therefore, free media also helps to facilitate and ensure peace.[24]

And here is where an alarming pattern is spreading around the world, albeit with some exceptional outliers here and there. Only 13 percent of the global population is currently able to consume free media.[25] Threats to freedom of expression and media freedom—from all manner of actors, from corporate to government—are well underway and have endured (and in some regions, increased) for decades. Independent documentary storytellers and journalists working as watchdogs, human rights witnesses, and investigators are impacted directly. The *Columbia Journalism Review* calls it a "worldwide crisis" for journalism, an escalating downhill spiral exacerbated by the pandemic, job cuts and losses, media consolidation, furloughs, and outright shutdowns of independent media outlets, including countries across Europe, plus India, Australia, and others.[26] And this set of structural dilemmas doesn't even include the explicit (or attempted) suppression of media voices, an insidious danger facing documentary storytellers (and journalists) who bring inconvenient or controversial topics into the light.

How bad is it? According to the most recent iteration of the World Press Freedom Index published annually by Reporters Without Borders, "the environment for journalism is 'bad' in seven out of ten countries, and satisfactory in only three out of ten."[27] Similarly, the 2023 Freedom in the World report from nonprofit Freedom House found that "global freedom declined for the 17th consecutive year," since 2006.[28] According to lead author Yana Gorokhovskaia, of all "freedom indicators" composing the "global freedom" portrait, the greatest decline is in media freedom:

> In general, what we're seeing is that the number of countries and territories where there's what we would consider absolutely no media freedom at all has increased. These are countries that score a zero out of four. In 2005,

there were 14 countries and territories that had a zero out of four, and last year [2022] there were 33, so it's more than doubled.[29]

The problems facing creative investigative documentary storytellers and journalists alike are uniquely acute for *independent* media—that is, work like Rappler's, designed to remain free of editorial or creative interference by institutions or financial interests that may prevent exposure of wrong-doing or bring troubling realities to light. This is an alarm-bell-worthy global quandary, says Nishant Lalwani, CEO of the International Fund for Public Interest Media (IFPIM) (for which Maria Ressa is a cochair with Mark Thompson), which "aims to enable global media markets to work for democracy," focusing specifically on public interest media.[30] The Fund's founding report is grave in its problem statement: "Independent media, acknowledged for generations as a fundamental pillar for the functioning of democratic societies, is under unprecedented and, in some settings, existential threat. That threat is both political and economic."[31]And yet, despite evidence of serious danger when independent media freedom is threatened—peace, fair governance, basic democracy, human rights are all at risk—global and regional bodies are not yet responding with appropriate urgency. As Lalwani said in an interview for this book: "If you talk to the major political leaders of our time, disinformation, election integrity, fake news as many people call it, is a huge priority to try and deal with this. And yet the amount of resourcing that they're putting towards it is minuscule, it's just 0.3% of foreign aid."[32] Business models to support independent media, which have never existed consistently in the first place, are difficult to create and maintain. Funding models for independent media are similarly elusive and ad revenue is down by the billions around the world, which means that, according to IFPIM, "the strategies available to public interest media to sustain themselves are extremely limited, especially in resource poor settings."[33]

Taken together, the repercussions of declining media freedom are grave in virtually all regions of the world. Without reliable, trustworthy, and high-quality independent media, the essential check and balance of a democratic system totally erodes. Power can be wielded without fallout. As the International Fund for Public Interest Media warns: "The consequences of this decline for the prospects for democracy, development and good governance are dire. There is ample evidence that, as well as weakening electoral and democratic processes, corruption, conflict, violent extremism and man-made disasters like famines and epidemics are more likely."[34] And the damage

80 RADICAL REALITY

can endure indefinitely. While shifting democratic norms seemingly happen in quick spikes, improving damaged democracies is, as Gorokhovskaia says, "a long, arduous process."[35] The long-term impacts of democratic patterns, in other words, can reach far into the future.

While the general patterns are not new, in order to have any hope of understanding and addressing them successfully, it's worth briefly spotlighting precise present-day factors that contribute to, and prop up, clampdowns on freedom of expression and media in symbiotic, reinforcing ways, namely: *political, technological,* and *economic.* Politically, as Chapter 2 explicates in more depth, democracy is in trouble around the world; "autocracies are on the march and their path to power is principally by attacking the media."[36] Silencing media critics, whether independent documentary storytellers or journalists, is a distinctive and consistent power pattern. And on the other end of the repression spectrum, state-funded propaganda works seamlessly in parallel. But the precise machinations are murky and seemingly invisible to regular citizens. As Nishant Lalwani says, "Information ecosystems are a huge lever in the way that authoritarian leaders are exerting their power overtly and covertly on populations."[37] For instance, the Chinese and Russian governments have invested billions of dollars in propaganda outside their own borders, and India's government has made conditions virtually impossible for independent media organizations within the country, he says. Funding, in this context, can easily act as a media repression tool: India, for instance, recently passed a new law to tighten its existing Foreign Contribution Regulation Act (FCRA),[38] bringing new restrictions that make the flow of international resources to support independent documentary storytellers and journalists in the country exceedingly difficult; the new law effectively "starves many really independent, courageous journalists of the ability to raise money and do good work and important work," says Lalwani.[39]

Other state-run regulatory tools can stifle media operations by creating conditions that threaten any kind of financial independence or viability: government licensing, approvals of various forms of funding, threats of legal action, and even halting any form of advertising as funding and revenue source. So, according to Yana Gorokhovskaia, lead author of the Freedom Index report, this kind of government control is not necessarily "criminalizing the media, but it's certainly making operation of independent media difficult . . . there's just a huge stacking up of challenges that independent media face commercially, and then also criminalization and punitive action."[40] Meanwhile, physical threats to journalists continue,[41] some of it advanced by elected leaders themselves.

The second factor, technology, is an undercurrent of nearly every contemporary challenge to media freedom and freedom of expression—again paradoxically, given that digital media also have expanded voices and storytelling opportunities dramatically over recent decades. Several distinct issues are at play here. Rampant misinformation and disinformation spreads dramatically across social media channels, which serve as essential platforms for propaganda and information chaos. As a result, individual media consumers increasingly don't know what or whom to believe or trust. Maria Ressa, as established earlier in this chapter, has taken up this mantle in much of her work. And according to the 2023 Freedom in the World report, the influence of social media platforms (algorithms and reach)—and explicit work from political actors—has taken root very quickly:

> The 2023 Index spotlights the rapid effects that the digital ecosystem's fake content industry has had on press freedom. In 118 countries (two-thirds of the 180 countries evaluated by the Index), most of the Index questionnaire's respondents reported that political actors in their countries were often or systematically involved in massive disinformation or propaganda campaigns.[42]

Additionally, for independent media-makers and journalists, surveillance technology tools—artificial intelligence (AI)—are direct threats to their safety and ability to speak truth to power. Human rights violations are rampant. According to the Carnegie Endowment for International Peace, "a growing number of states are deploying advanced AI surveillance tools to monitor, track, and surveil citizens to accomplish a range of policy objectives—some lawful, others that violate human rights, and many of which fall into a murky middle ground."[43] Advanced spyware is freely and often inexpensively available in the consumer marketplace; even independent documentary storytellers with trained digital hygiene skills (and consequently, their protagonists and sources) aren't immune to the dangers.[44] The result may be an obvious immediate risk for storytelling in the moment, but also self-censorship over time. Digital surveillance tools, says Yana Gorokhovskaia, are threat number-one for media professionals:

82 RADICAL REALITY

> If you are exposed to spyware and people are aware, first of all, that means that your sources are exposed and the fact [is that] you're putting people in danger potentially. But second, over time, it makes your work more difficult.... That has had a huge chilling effect on media and journalists. And the other worrying part of it is that it happens in democratic countries. We've seen journalists in France, we've seen journalists in Greece be hacked, but it also happens beyond a repressive country's borders.... So this spyware has incredibly serious ramifications across the board for human rights, and it has specific professional ramifications for the media.[45]

Political trends toward authoritarianism and technology challenges combine with evolving economic realities facing independent media creators across the globe, including documentary storytellers. Commercial media consolidation and streaming platform dominance together create conditions where the marketplace is increasingly the nearly sole deciding voice in the stories that are financially resourced, supported, and distributed to the widest possible audiences—and thus far, travel, music, murder, and celebrity profiles are the winners.[46] Stories about political turmoil and dissent, along with human rights, are increasingly difficult to sell to consolidated media systems that focus on broad audience appeal and non-controversial fare. For instance, Netflix translates many films into dozens of languages for global distribution—a time-consuming task. As a result, a documentary that works for worldwide streaming economics must be evergreen enough to remain relevant months later, a reality that's hard to achieve for stories that focus on unfolding or fresh political issues and drama.[47] In this way, these economic realities, too, are part of the clampdowns on free media and freedom of expression, even if not intentionally nefarious. As Nishant Lalwani reflected in an interview, "I think it's important to ask ourselves, 'What is a healthy information ecosystem?' And it's one where there is not only truly independent media, but also a plurality of voices. It's frankly extremely difficult for any one media organization to be representative of all the diversity of society."[48] As more and more media outlets consolidate into megacorporations (not at all a new reality, albeit alarming in the vast scale and power of information control in the streaming age), independent makers ("freelancers") work in even weaker environments with less opportunity for economic support, and as a result, publics are exposed to fewer and fewer diverse viewpoints and lived experiences.[49] At the same time, distributor interest in new and emerging marketplaces—including in authoritarian countries and places without a free press—is alarming new and seasoned journalists alike, as raised here and in chapters to follow, who worry that even US media companies are increasingly adopting restrictive decision-making processes in the types of films they acquire—including a disinterest in films that challenge institutional power—in order to seemingly ensure that they don't risk losing access to those markets. Institutional power dynamics can intertwine in insidious fashion when fewer media outlets exist, as content that pushes against status quos—or is simply perceived as disruptive—is seen as risky to contemporary media outlets hungry to conquer expanding markets, as the next stories reveal.

Writing with Fire

In Uttar Pradesh, the most populous state in India, temperatures can spike well above 105 degrees Fahrenheit at the height of the warmest season. It's the kind of weather that can melt phone batteries and overheat camera gear—until the monsoon rains arrive. Situated in India's northern region, Uttar Pradesh holds wonders and contrasts: the famous Taj Mahal and many ancient Hindu and Buddhist temples are there, and the massive Ganges River winds through a rural landscape packed with roughly 200 million people in a space that's not quite half the size of California. It's a sacred place to many Hindus and Buddhists—a "quintessential Indian travel experience," says the *Times of India*.[50] The residents of Uttar Pradesh are not a monolith and yet, a portrait exists: more than three-quarters live in rural villages, and the majority identify as members of the lowest caste groups in India,[51] classified today as "Scheduled Castes" and "Scheduled Tribes (Indigenous peoples).[52] Here in this region, as in other parts of India, casteism is alive, even if not officially sanctioned.[53]

For more than 2,000 years, despite being outlawed—first in 1947 with Indian independence and then codified in the 1950 Indian Constitution—manifestations of the country's social hierarchal caste system have held fast, particularly when it comes to the Dalit community, formerly known as the "untouchables," or, in literal translation from Sanskrit to English, "the broken people."[54] Caste-based discrimination and violence falls hardest on this group, positioned in a subterranean rung below the system's ground floor, rooted in a legacy of inequality that remains difficult to fully dismantle. Despite social progress, violence against Scheduled Castes in India

84 RADICAL REALITY

continues, with the greatest number of "atrocities" taking place in Uttar Pradesh: "The Dalit minority in South Asia has endured centuries of prejudice, marginalisation, stigma, and violence. And the phenomenon of prejudice based on ancestry is what causes this violence."[55]

Dehumanization and cruelty facing the Dalit community hit its women and girls—reported as "among the most oppressed in the world"[56]—the hardest. Beatings, rape, sexual assault, lack of economic opportunity, public humiliation and shaming: the violence directed toward Dalit women in Uttar Pradesh is, as scholar Devi Dayal Gautem asserts, a complex intersection of both gender and caste, "located in the links between the two."[57] It's also specific and systemic, notes journalist Murali Krishnan: "The nature and frequency of the violence faced by Dalit women is unique to them as it is backed by economic oppression and socially sanctioned through the continued existence of the caste system."[58]

In such a complicated place and social environment, a thriving system of independent journalism, particularly of the investigative variety, might seem onerous in obvious ways: difficult weather patterns, rural landscape, a teeming population with thousands of stories to be told, tricky financial resources. Add layers of gender- and caste-based risks, and the proposition for locally rooted watchdog journalism seems especially difficult. And yet, the two founders of *Khabar Lahariya* ("News Wave" in English), Kavita Devi and Meera Jatav, were determined to make it work when they launched India's first all-female newspaper in 2002, based in Uttar Pradesh.[59] Years later—as *Khabar Lahariya* evolved from an eight-page printed newspaper to a robust digital news service covering local and rural issues primarily in Uttar Pradesh, Madhya Pradesh, and Bihar—the publication expanded its all-woman team, most from rural and lower caste communities, including Dalit.[60] Their stories—many developed from citizen tips—spotlight realities and news that may otherwise go unreported, crafted by reporters whose lived experiences provide the local nuances that are difficult to access otherwise.[61] The job is always risky.

The *Khabar Lahariya* team's existence and tenacity, extraordinary on its own, is notable for other reasons, given the context of media freedom and decline of independent media in the country more broadly. Independent journalists and media organizations are increasingly endangered in India, which recently fell to position 161 (out of 180) in terms of media freedom in the world, according to the 2022 World Press Freedom report published by Reporters Without Borders, which wrote: "The violence against journalists, the politically partisan media and the concentration of media ownership all demonstrate that press freedom is in crisis in 'the world's largest democracy,' ruled since 2014 by Prime Minister Narendra Modi, the leader of the Bharatiya Janata Party (BJP) and the embodiment of the Hindu nationalist right."[62] Consolidation, mergers, and takeovers of remaining independent media outlets are picking up. A noteworthy example: stalwart New Delhi Television (NDTV) was taken over by a billionaire Modi ally,[63] and the fallout is both precise and sweeping, as media historian Mukul Kesavan said in an interview: "It would be a mistake to look at the takeover of NDTV as a thing in itself. I think it's part of a much larger battering down on basic, fundamental, democratic rights—the right to organize, the right to protest, the right to march, the right to speak and the right to publish."[64] In 2020, Amnesty International, which also reported on hostile targeting of journalists in India, was forced by the Indian government to close its doors in the country, matching a general pattern of increasingly restricted free expression.[65] As political scientist Somdeep Sen said in an interview with NPR, "What's left . . . is a few major [digital] outlets that are independent. If this trend continues, the future is grim for Indian democracy."[66]

All of it—the rural women reporters, their precarious work, the state of Indian independent media and democracy—felt urgent and motivating to filmmakers Rintu Thomas and Sushmit Ghosh, who initially approached the *Khabar Lahariya* leadership with an open-handed request to follow their transition from print to digital. It would be impossible, they said, to separate the journalists' work from the larger themes at play—media freedom, structural and cultural power dynamics, whose stories are told, and by whom—set against undercurrents of gender and caste social strata. Thomas explained:

> We're both interested in the role that women play in a democracy and the different contours of that. What happens when a woman's voice is invisibilized? How does she reclaim that space? And we've always noticed through our decade-long work in India, and a majority of that work has been with rural communities, that it's almost like playing a game of cards. When you're negotiating with systemic inequities, you need to know when to play your cards, when to withdraw, hold back and when to leave the table. And that process of negotiation is of great interest to us. A lot of our earlier films have looked at women leaders who've mostly been in margins of power dynamics. And how they've used the margins to create an alternative structure of power and thrived there.[67]

86 RADICAL REALITY

To construct their documentary, *Writing with Fire*, Thomas and Ghosh followed the women of *Khabar Lahariya* over the course of five years—covering, along the way, rape culture, the evolving dominance of Hindu nationalism, and other political and social issues as the women reported them. The film begins in 2016 as the publication moved from print to digital for the first time, tracking a steady timeline while media systems in India continued a steadily downward freedom trend. Efforts to curtail independent media content and functioning, as Ghosh explained, "really cripples how much a journalist can then really report in the public domain. And when you then contextualize this to the work of women in Uttar Pradesh, it is really, really dangerous work."[68]

Their timing, as it turns out, was both fortuitous and daunting: on the one hand, the film depicts, with harrowing detail, the reporters' obvious professionalism and risk. In scene after scene, the women fight for every scoop and story—every piece of crime evidence, access to a source, community trust, and their own physical safety. On the other hand, making and distributing a film that centers contemporary human rights and politics is a study in the colliding impediments of economic, political, and technological forces that can effectively shutter—or at least dampen—voices perceived as threatening the status quo. The story of the film's critical acclaim, distribution, and grassroots efforts reveals an eye-opening pattern in contemporary challenges to media freedom.

After years of development, production, editing, and pitching, *Writing with Fire* exploded onto the global film stage at the Sundance Film Festival in January 2021—the only Indian film in the documentary competition—immediately winning two of its most prestigious awards: the Audience Award and the Impact for Change Special Jury Award.[69] The movie was a buzzworthy darling: standing ovations from audiences across the globe, glowing critical reviews. Thomas and Ghosh traveled the world that year, screening the film at nearly 100 festivals and winning 19 international awards along the way, including the International Documentary Association's Courage Under Fire Award in 2021.[70] High-level media outlets covered each screening hit and honor, from *The New York Times* to *Time Magazine*, *The Guardian*, *Marie Claire*, *Los Angeles Times*, Al Jazeera, BBC, and others.[71] And so it went, as the codirectors followed the festival circuit and worked with teams of sales agents to find possible regional and global distributors. "Every time the film screened in any part of the world, whether it was Poland or Jordan," said Thomas, "we would get these emails, our Instagram handles would get these messages where people are like, 'I loved the film, thank you for making it.'"[72]

In 2022, *Writing with Fire* made history when it was nominated for the Best Documentary Feature Award in the Academy Awards, a first for an Indian film. In 2023, it won a Peabody Award, also an unprecedented win for Indian cinema and filmmakers.[73] By any standards, Rintu Thomas and Sushmit Ghosh had achieved a series of feats previously unrealized by any Indian documentary filmmakers, not to mention an astonishing level of critical success for any documentary film produced anywhere. And yet, their funding and distribution challenges tell a different story.

Were it not for an international funding network, *Writing with Fire* would not exist, and it's a double-edged blessing, say the filmmakers. The list of funders is staggering in global breadth and scope: Thomas and Ghosh pitched at Good Pitch India, DocedgeKolkata, the United Kingdom's Sheffield Meet Market, and the International Documentary Festival Amsterdam; production funding came from Chicken & Egg Pictures (United States), Doc Society (United Kingdom and United States), IDFA Bertha Fund (United Kingdom), Tribeca (United States), Sundance (United States), Canada's Fondation AlterCine, and the SFFILM Documentary Film Fund (United States).[74] None of the funding came from Indian

Image 4.1 Description: *Writing with Fire*: Codirector and cinematographer Sushmit Ghosh filming Meera Devi on location in Uttar Pradesh. Image Copyright: Black Ticket Films.

sources, but not for lack of trying. At best, said Thomas and Ghosh, the system for funding and producing independent and documentary media in India is "undernourished;" the two possible Indian grants that might have supported their film are now extinct. The filmmakers were self-taught and self-sufficient by necessity—from fundraising to production. Even with international funding, telling their story in their own way was not a given. As Thomas said, "we are always producers on our own films to make sure we have editorial independence," and Ghosh added: "Independent doc filmmakers [in India] are faced with the dilemma of raising resources from international institutions that often—but I would say this is changing—have a preconceived notion of what a story from South Asia should look and feel like. And in that space, we are complete outsiders identified as filmmakers of color who have to really walk the tightrope of fighting for our own artistic independence and visual language."[75] Editorial independence, they said, is essential, and it can be a delicate debate even with well-meaning philanthropic funders who can't fully understand the visual grammar or cultural nuance of countries outside their own.

And how, outside the festival circuit, could people see *Writing with Fire*, a film with evident universal audience appeal? Securing widescale distribution for such a widely lauded independent documentary—particularly one that launched in dazzling fashion at the Sundance Film Festival—might be an obvious assumption. A premiere at Sundance, or a small handful of high-prestige competitive international film festivals, is a known pathway for precisely such a transaction. But it was not to be for this movie. "Our outlook [for the film's distribution] was international, and we brought Submarine on board," said Ghosh. "They were very excited about the prospects of the firm. But a month after Sundance, they were just baffled. They were just like, 'We don't understand what's going on, this is a film that should be picked up, but is not.'"[76] The reason: likely a confluence of events, including the COVID-19 pandemic at the time, but India's prevailing politics and official media regulatory policies also played a central role.

In early February 2021, a few days after *Writing with Fire* received its first global awards, the Indian government published its Information Technology "Intermediary Guidelines and Digital Media Ethics Code Rules 2021," which provides explicit—and also broad, with the potential for sweeping subjective interpretation—rules about permissible material on India's social media accounts and streaming video platforms, including Amazon Prime, Netflix, Disney, and others.[77] On Twitter (now "X"), for example, users who supported a farmers' protest in Delhi were blocked, a new requirement under the rules.[78] Content on streaming video outlets that could be deemed offensive in matters of religion, sexuality, and politics is now legally problematic, according to the guidelines, which also specify "tonal considerations that might have an influence on classification include the extent to which the content presents a view of the world that is anti-life, pessimistic, or despairing"[79] and "[t]he category classification of a content will take into account the potentially offensive impact of a film on matters such as caste, race, gender, religion, disability or sexuality that may arise in a wide range of works."[80] Even a "self-regulation toolkit"—adopted previously by the major global streamers operating in India (Netflix, Amazon, Disney, Viacom, SonyLiv, Discovery Plus, Lionsgate Play, along with Indian media companies)—wasn't enough, because, according to India's Ministry of Information & Broadcasting, the toolkit "failed to list prohibited content."[81] Under the newly tightened censorship environment, Amazon's head of original content in India narrowly escaped arrest after a scripted original series, *Tandav*, which depicted a Muslim actor in the role of a Hindu god, Shiva, attracted the outrage of Hindu nationalists in positions of regulatory power.[82] After the *Tandav* controversy, Ghosh said, everything changed:

> Streamers pulled back, and in India right now, in terms of content, there is no political film or film that is critical of any system that is ever going to be programmed. And everyone's just watching and programming true crime and big celeb docs and these entertainment pieces, which is basically reflective of what's happening in most parts of the West as well, but also in India. And in India, you need a censor certificate [for a film to screen in public] as well. And this film is not going to get a censor certificate. Not without cuts.[83]

"The fact that this is an Oscar-nominated film has not changed the fact that we have no distribution offers," said Thomas.

> That censorship clause, essentially, is what led to the streamers essentially pulling back. If you look at our film, it's not that it is against anyone, against any government, but this is a pro-democracy film. But it can be read as a film that is critical of the times that we are in. Because India's now the biggest market for everybody [the global streamers], and they don't want to mess it up.[84]

90 RADICAL REALITY

The marketplace isn't the only block: showing the film publicly in India requires passing through the Indian government's censorship certification process, a complex proposition for precisely a film like *Writing with Fire*. Ghosh reflected:

> We've gone into the space of thought crimes. . . . Basically what the state is telling you is that you need to have us legitimize your story before you're able to screen it for the public. And if it's a critical story, then you need to censor yourselves.[85]

And yet, the filmmakers had other ideas in mind, despite the obvious obstacles. From the beginning, Thomas and Ghosh identified a social impact mission and set of goals for *Writing with Fire*. In a classic example of the "dual distribution" systems for independent social-justice documentary films,[86] their mission played out in a years-long grassroots engagement campaign for the film, outside of formal marketplace distribution, country by country—in journalism classrooms, college seminars, meetings, community spaces. Determined to leverage the film to raise the profile of *Khabar Lahariya* and encourage global support for their work, while also hoping to inspire meaningful conversations about independent journalism and rural communities, their early forays created a robust ecosystem of community partners and supporters. At Good Pitch India in 2018, hosted by Doc Society, the International Press Institute (IPI) invited Meera, the lead protagonist, and the filmmakers to screen the film and connect with their peer journalists from around the world.[87] Other organizations and entities—from Indian Parliament to global NGOs and journalism groups—invited screenings and outreach collaboration. "A lot of effort went into creating an ecosystem of collaborations with organizations both in India and globally," said Thomas. "Like the Committee to Project Journalists or the International Press Institute. With all of these organizations, *Khabar Lahariya* started to be on their radar. And that makes a huge difference, that makes you counted in the larger cannon, so to speak, of independent news outlets."[88] With global journalism and human rights organizations taking notice, Ghosh added, the *Khabar Lahariya* team would ideally have a greater degree of protection—and avenues for expansion:

> Impact was a clear goal for us because it was deeply built into protection for their work. For 20 years they have existed in one region of the country,

and after the film went out into the world, visibility came with it and the new partnerships that we were able to structure. They have been able to almost double their team size and also expand into three new states in India . . . the more visible they became, the more protected their work in India would be.[89]

More than 200 film festivals and 40 global awards later, alongside dozens of special screenings around the world, the film has generated new funding, gear, and global media attention to support *Khabar Lahariya*, and in March 2022, *Writing with Fire* made its US broadcast premiere on PBS's Independent Lens series.[90] In an interview, the film's lead protagonist and *Khabar Lahariya*'s managing editor, Meera, said: "From a global perspective, we have become a lot more popular since the film came out [in Sundance]. Both personally and professionally, it has really amplified the newspaper and its work. We have witnessed a completely different kind of popularity—and that is really good."[91] For their part, Thomas and Ghosh, alongside independent film contemporaries in India, marshal onward with a wary and determined eye. More than 100 screenings in the country have been organized by civil society, film festivals, colleges, newsrooms, and cultural spaces: "Censorship in its own myriad ways has existed in India, but since 2014, it's just come down full force—basically the laws have been weaponized against citizens. But I think that's the vibrancy of any democracy where people will find ways to tell their stories. Every time we've screened the film, people have left these spaces deeply moved by the essence of the story and the work that's happening on the ground. It just gives us all the more impetus to continue pushing through and find newer ways and pathways."[92]

The First Step

On a brisk evening on March 6, 2023, in an old theater in Milwaukee, Wisconsin, filmmaker Lance Kramer stood on stage and asked a room of about 100 audience members to raise their hand if they had an interest in seeing more documentaries about bipartisan coalition-building, like the one they had just finished watching. Everyone raised their hand. Even if for just a moment, their soaring unanimity served as at least partial vindication for an embattled Kramer, who had been told the exact opposite by more than 40 commercial distributors who passed on his film *The First Step* over the previous three years. But the question, and his desire to ask it, points to an increasingly alarming trend for the state of documentary and public discourse in the United States.

Premiering in June 2020, *The First Step* follows the struggle of long-time activist and political organizer Van Jones, a former advisor to President Barack Obama and founder of Dream.org, among other initiatives, as he forges collaborations across party and ideological lines in pursuit of a landmark criminal justice reform bill. At a moment of escalating polarization, the film provides an intimate look into the struggle that Jones encounters as he tries to facilitate dialogue, between actors within a divisive government administration and those on disparate frontline coalitions, in order to create reform on one of the most entrenched social justice crises in the world.

Mass incarceration is one of the most misunderstood, inhumane, and staggering social crises in the United States. While the country accounts for less than 5% of the world's population, it accounts for nearly 25% of its prisoners, with about 2.3 million of its citizens behind bars, reflecting the highest incarceration rate in the world.[93] And beneath the country's incarceration rate is a history of persistent racial inequities and injustice, with Black Americans facing time in prisons at nearly five times the rate of white Americans.[94] In response to this challenge, years of advocacy by people across the political spectrum led to a bill named The First Step Act being passed by Congress in 2018. The bipartisan criminal justice reform legislation enacted several changes in US federal criminal law, including changing many harsh federal sentences (leading to more than 25,000 people returning home after being released early from federal prison), giving more discretion to judges to give less than mandatory minimum sentences for certain low-level crimes, and reducing the federal prison population, all with the aim of being a "first step" toward additional needed reforms.

The documentary, *The First Step*, provides the most intimate and comprehensive look at the development of the legislation and the efforts that went into getting it passed, including scenes of high-level meetings in the White House and Congress, contentious conversations between Jones and various movement leaders who disagree with his willingness to work across party lines, emotional gatherings between disparate groups of white conservatives from coal country West Virginia and liberals of color from South Los Angeles (who represent communities struggling with different crises—opioid addiction in Appalachia and the criminalization of crack in Los Angeles), and the personal moments and spaces of the legislation's chief advocate Jones.

UPHOLDING FREEDOM OF EXPRESSION 93

Image 4.2 Description: *The First Step*: Van Jones advocating for criminal justice reform in Washington, D.C. Credit: Meridian Hill Pictures.

Image 4.3 Description: *The First Step*: A coalition from West Virginia and Los Angeles come together to discuss criminal justice reform. Credit: Meridian Hill Pictures.

94 RADICAL REALITY

The filmmakers battled through multiple barriers to provide a first-hand look into the spaces of deliberation in action—including active discussions in Congressional offices while the bill was at stake, candid conversations between senior members of Congress and the bill's organizers, strategy conversations between President Trump's son-in-law Jared Kushner and Jones, internal meetings between high-level White House officials and the coalition members from West Virginia and Los Angeles, and contentious grassroots movement discussions. In doing so, the documentary spotlights political egos and agendas that collide in the making of governmental laws, and, especially, how deeply entrenched the divides are across party lines, coalitions, and movements in the United States today. Among other controversial moments, the film reveals politicians and movement leaders proclaiming to be publicly supportive of criminal justice reform, but who resist bipartisan efforts behind the scenes and would rather see no reform happen than to work with someone from an opposing political party or group.

At its center, the film reveals the human journey of what it's like to seek reform that aims to change a system, and the need to work with people who don't agree with one another to do so. During the filmmaking process, this required the filmmakers to go into rooms that were skeptical and unwelcoming to journalists. Beyond their anticipated battle to gain unprecedented access to a White House administration, led by then president Donald Trump, known for its repeated attacks on press freedom and journalists, the filmmakers also needed to develop relationships with grassroots leaders who were equally untrusting of media professionals. When the filmmakers arrived to meet with a sheriff in West Virginia, for instance, they were greeted with a giant white board behind his desk that declared: "The Media Does Not Define Us."[95]

The film followed a Webby Award–winning series, *The Messy Truth*, produced by the Kramer brothers, which followed Jones as he traveled to the homes of supporters of Trump to identify issues of common support and shared interest (including criminal justice reform) in the lead-up to the 2016 election. The film also follows a series of other important documentaries, that explores the history of racial injustice, inequity and family trauma in the criminal justice system in the United States, including *13th*, *Just Mercy*, *The Innocence Files*, and *Time*. But unlike those films, *The First Step*—which spotlights moments that key public figures in power would likely prefer the country not to see—struggled for years to find distribution. Directed by

Lance's brother, Brandon Kramer, the film received overwhelmingly positive audience reception and reviews from the largest newspapers and industry publications in the country, as the most comprehensive film about the country's most substantial criminal justice reform legislation in a generation. The film also had support from Kartemquin Films, the legendary documentary production group behind some of the biggest social-justice-minded films of the last several decades, including *Hoop Dreams*, *The Interrupters*, and *The Trials of Muhammad Ali*. But after nearly 3 years of pitching the film to nearly 50 commercial outlets, everyone had passed. The reason, they heard, was because its focus on bipartisan politics and criminal justice is too controversial.

"There is a lot of momentum to avoid, and not really dive into, controversial politics, and there is a lot of fear from major companies about presenting those narratives," said Brandon. "And that concerns me as a filmmaker and a person [in this country]."[96] The experience of the Kramer brothers is echoed by many other documentary makers who say that it is getting harder to sell films that focus on controversial social issues to North American distributors. Dozens of filmmakers interviewed for this book expressed alarm, but the concern is given distinct expression in the context of *The First Step*, given that studies reveal there is declining interest in cross-sectional dialogue between politically diverse groups in the United States.

Recent studies from the Pew Research Center have found that Americans are engaging less and less with people they disagree with. Nearly half of the country admits to having stopped talking to someone because they disagree with them on a political or social issue,[97] and nearly 6 in 10 Americans say that its "stressful and frustrating" to talk politics with someone who disagrees with their views (markedly higher than in previous years).[98] In another reputable 2022 national poll, 84 percent of adults said that a fear of retaliation or harsh criticism for speaking freely represents a "very serious" or "somewhat serious" problem in the United States.[99] And the same poll found that 46% of adults feel less free to talk about politics compared to a decade ago, while only 21% of people reported feeling freer to talk about politically related issues.[100] In a March 2022 article titled "America Has a Free Speech Problem," the *New York Times* editorial board wrote that the implications of Americans' slipping willingness to share their perspective and engage in discussions with groups and individuals different from them should be a matter of grave concern for the country: "For all the tolerance and enlightenment that modern society claims, Americans are losing hold

96   RADICAL REALITY

of a fundamental right as citizens of a free country: the right to speak their minds and voice their opinions in public without fear of being shamed or shunned."[101]

On the one hand, given this public climate, it might seem unsurprising that commercial distributors would move away from documentaries that feature uncomfortable conversations and messy bipartisan collaborations. However, in early 2023, after being turned down by every major distributor in the country, the Kramer brothers refused to simply move on. Instead, they decided to follow the recipe of bridge-building demonstrated in their film and they sought relationships with any organization or individual who was interested in screening it. Soon after, they discovered that people across the country were desperate for opportunities to come together and talk about issues related to criminal justice reform, addiction, and bipartisan collaboration. As word spread that the filmmakers were willing to share the film with community organizations, hundreds of people across the country came forward with an interest in participating in a screening event. Within weeks, the Kramer brothers started a multi-month tour—organized with 8 Above (led by distribution pioneer Jon Reiss)—of bringing the documentary to rural and urban towns and cities in nearly every corner of the country, without any funding from a distributor.

Perhaps even more surprising than the number of interested organizations, Lance said that the different types of organizations that organized collective efforts around the film surpassed their wildest expectations. In one Arizona event, in February of 2023, the film was jointly screened by the American Civil Liberties Union and the Americans for Prosperity (a libertarian conservative political advocacy group funded by the Koch brothers), two groups rarely associated with one another, but which share an interest in addressing the country's mass incarceration crisis. In another event, in a small Republican-majority county in Indiana, a group of community members and leaders across the political spectrum convened a meeting at the town's single-screen community theater. The discussion included city council members, a local pastor, police officers, probation officers, a YMCA leader, progressive activists, addiction and family medicine workers, neighbors who had children or relatives who recently died from the town's addiction problem, and, as one person referred to herself, "just a community member," to name a few people who participated. In the end, multiple city leaders told the authors that the screening event was among the most productive community conversations the town ever had on its addiction and incarceration crisis. As part of an independent study into the nature of these screenings, the authors witnessed similar experiences in several other cities, including in Chicago; New York City; Washington, DC; Los Angeles; and West Virginia.

In Mississippi, soon after being released under The First Step Act and learning about the documentary, Maurice Clifton got the idea to screen the film in prisons. The First Step Act allowed Clifton to be released about 10 years early, in 2020, after having served 23 years in the federal prison system. Clifton's experience of being unjustly locked up under an inhumane criminal drug law, which led to him receiving a 400-month sentence for a low-level, nonviolent crime, as a first-time offender, is an example of the injustice being perpetrated, primarily against people of color, in the country's criminal justice system, especially in the state of Mississippi, which has the highest incarceration rate in the country.

Soon after being released, Clifton, who continues to work as a chaplain at the Mississippi Department of Corrections, organized a screening of the film in Parchman prison, one of the country's largest maximum-security prisons. In the first screening, he showed the film to a group of incarcerated people who were part of the prison's seminary school. Clifton created and printed an Excel spreadsheet that he handed to them so they could rate the film and talk about it afterward. Clifton said it became immediately clear to him that the documentary was serving as a trusted source of information that could help educate people about important legislative rights and processes, and even help motivate people to become more involved in seeking change themselves.

The First Step Act does not automatically free anyone. People have to prepare and present a motion in order to be considered for early release under it. This means that if people don't know that the new legislation exists then they won't know if they are eligible, said Clifton. In that way, a ticket to *The First Step* documentary can literally be the ticket that leads to their freedom. Following the successful prison screenings by Clifton at Parchman, the Kramer brothers moved to support screenings in prisons across the country—where it received the same favorable response. After seeing the impact of the screenings firsthand, Clifton became interested in supporting more screening events in community settings and colleges across the state. Many people in his community don't typically watch documentaries, he said, because day-to-day life takes precedence; and that is why community events involving films can be so important are powerful.

"Documentary is a good way to get information," said Clifton, who noted that scrolling through an article about *The First Step Act* doesn't come close to providing the same level of knowledge-building and understanding around criminal justice reform as a screening event does. "But the way to get the message out is to have these open-ended, community discussions [after screenings]."[102]

After one screening in Mississippi, Clifton said he was amazed with how many people were moved by the experience. "A lot of people came to watch it, and a lot of people were moved to tears because they didn't know that this was happening in our own federal justice system, and they couldn't believe it."[103] Clifton said that the film has been helpful in coalition building, because people from across state lines are now coming together through the screenings—and initiatives that followed it—to share knowledge and work together. And he says that the film's ability to help educate audiences to the scale of the social problem of mass incarceration has been profound. For Clifton, it's this education component that is the "key" to the film's power.

> It definitely opened a lot of people's eyes about the injustice that's going on.... It changed a lot of people's perspective. A lot of people call me and ask me [about the film], and I share it with a lot of people, and they tell me that they watched it. And I've been getting a lot of good feedback about it. It's not my film, man, but it's the avenue. It's the key. You know, when people are incarcerated, we always talk about keys. That was the key that set me free. *The First Step* was the key that set me free. So I just think that the success of the film, the success of the film was to educate a lot of people and to continue to educate a lot of people. So I think that that's what it's doing. I think it's doing its job, it's just doing it at a slow pace. But change is difficult.[104]

Clifton said the film and the work of Van Jones have also motivated him to work across party lines: if Jones had listened to the people in the film who told him not to collaborate with conservatives or activists who held different views and political stances than him, then Clifton would still be in prison. "[The documentary] opened my eyes," he said. "I can sit at the table with the people that did me wrong. If it's going to make it better for the people that's behind me, in the future, we can sit down and have a discussion about change no matter what you believe in.... The motivation that this film gave me, you know, is to work with other people."[105]

On the other side of the political spectrum, another, perhaps surprising, supporter of the film is Pat Nolan, a prominent conservative voice for criminal justice reform who founded the Nolan Center at the American Conservative Union. Nolan is justice-impacted himself and had been influential in drafting and shepherding the First Step Act from its conception to passage by Congress. He also participated in the bill signing in the Oval Office. While his voter registration would put him on the opposite side of the political spectrum from Clifton, Nolan is among the film's screening partners and even participated on a panel for the film during an event at Arizona State University. He also helped in the background of the film's community screening efforts to help organizers make connections to conservative and faith-based partners. Following the screenings, Nolan reflected that the political division in the United States is so deep that it's difficult for him to see ways that the film—which centers a progressive activist like Van Jones—can be widely useful for organizations on the political right.[106] However, he said the film has important value and has even been useful to advancing his own work around criminal justice reform:

> I have found the film useful in explaining to activists on the left the balance necessary to get the legislation signed into law. Often, those activists oppose "the good" and press for "the perfect" and end with nothing accomplished. The film highlights the critical role Van Jones played in keeping the bill on track for passage. . . . I think the film helps separate those who would rather keep complaining about "the system" from those who actually want to move the ball forward in reforming the criminal justice system. The former offer no actual help to those who are trapped in our failing system, while the latter actually improve conditions for them.[107]

It has been in witnessing the film build connections between unlikely allies, and through the more than 50 independent community screenings (as part of the 2023 release) and more than 100 screenings overall (since the film's 2021 Tribeca Premiere), organized by a myriad of groups across the country, that Lance says the film's greatest service can be found:

> We tried really hard to build allies for the film—both likely allies and people who could have a vested interest in the film, including local, state-level, and national level groups that are working on reform and on justice advocated issues, who saw that narrative in the film and felt seen in that narrative. And

100 RADICAL REALITY

it's amazing to see how they are using the film now to do their work and show people what it is that they are doing and working toward.[108]

The effort of the filmmakers, and their impact team, to build cross-country relationships with interested publics and community organizations reflects one of the ways that filmmakers are working outside of traditional film festival and distribution pathways and platforms in order to engage audiences in meaningful ways around documentaries; the film was also screened in 40+ regional film festivals prior to its theatrical/community release, which the filmmakers say was also a crucial part of their release strategy. However, their experience might also raise alarms for fellow filmmakers. There is never a guarantee that a documentary will find a distributor. But given the film's level of demonstrated audience interest, critical acclaim, unprecedented level of access to the country's corridors of power and deliberation, and the intersectional urgency of the issue at the center of the film (criminal justice), several filmmakers and industry veterans—including those who were not associated with the film—shared concern that it wasn't able to find a single distributor in the formal media marketplace. In June of 2023, nearly two years after it premiered, the film was acquired by Deskpop Entertainment and released on TVOD on Amazon Prime, Apple+, VUDU and Google Play, and acquired by GOOD DOCS for educational distribution, marking the first time it ever became publicly accessible, but this only happened after years of community organizations across the country demonstrating their interest and raising enough noise about it. A crucial reality: the controversial issue at the heart of the film was cited by some of the distributors as a reason to pass on the film.[109]

Consequently, while the filmmakers stress the importance of the community engagements and coalition-building efforts born from the film, Lance said that to focus only on those achievements would be to miss the forest for the trees: "There needs to be more of a conversation about what are the consequences of the commercialization of the field, where certain films are getting blocked-out from major platforms because they address controversial subjects."[110]

The experience of *The First Step* not only reveals the difficulties of creating meaningful reform that changes a system; it also reveals increasing cracks of the media ecosystem and flow of information in a country that nominally holds the right to a free press and freedom of expression. When word of a transformative new law struggles to find its way to the people who would benefit, and an authoritative documentary about the law struggles to find distribution because the film shows real politics at work, a deeper problem exists.

* * *

Quieting media freedom or dissenting expression can happen through a gradual constellation of actions and policies—and it can be harder to fully detect when it's not the explicit singular doing of a single institution.

What, if anything, is optimistic and motivating here, within this context? New global funding models for independent media (detailed in the final chapter of this book) constitute one important source of hope, but there is also something to say about the nature of both democracy and independent nonfiction visual storytelling. Freedom, as democracy scholar Yana Gorokhovskaia says, turns out to be "surprisingly enduring," and democracy itself inspires a kind of self-perpetuating collective desire for people to speak out and protect that system; research has repeatedly shown that, as she asserts, "people, regardless of where they live and regardless of how much experience they've had with democracy, have a demand for freedom and for fundamental rights . . . so that's kind of the starting point."[111] Documentaries—with their command of rich storytelling and entertainment appeal—can provide a cinematic understanding of complex messages and realities that might otherwise be difficult to access or comprehend, particularly when they are independently produced. And yet, if the pipelines for distribution are blocked by wary government bodies, leaders, and corporate outlets, their impact is limited for the foreseeable future, despite how carefully they are made.

5

Demanding Human Rights

In January of 2020, award-winning filmmaker Nanfu Wang wrote an article reflecting on why her film *One Child Nation*—and its Chinese translation (独生子女国度 or 独生之国)—had been scrubbed from news coverage and search engines in China. The film, an investigative documentary she made with fellow filmmaker Jialing Zhang about China's one-child policy, had just been shortlisted for the documentary feature film category of the Academy Awards and it was being covered by news outlets around the world as a result. But searches in many of the major search engines, news sites, and social media platforms in China, the place where she grew up, returned no results. Only the following: *The result of this search cannot be displayed because it violates related laws and regulations.*[1]

"Any person living in China who might be following the Oscars would have no way of knowing that a Chinese film is a contender in this year's documentary category," she wrote.[2] This also meant that few in the country could have had any way of learning from the content of her film, which uncovered the Chinese government's decades-long propaganda campaign and effort—from 1979 to 2015—to brainwash, intimidate, and push its citizens into limiting families to a single child each, and to committing horrific crimes and human rights abuses as a way of preserving the interests of a national agenda that benefited a powerful few over the lives of millions.

Even in news coverage of the awards show, Chinese media, articles and broadcasts mentioned every film shortlisted in the documentary category—except the one that Wang had made. By this time, Wang had come to know well the ways in which China manages and distorts the flow of information and public discourse in the country, but what surprised her most was how many of her old friends and classmates came to question why she was interested in pointing her camera at the human rights violations and struggles in the country, rather than favoring more positive depictions. Government interrogations, threats to her family and loved ones, police harassment, and threats of physical violence, these had become some of the painful challenges she had come to expect. But after the documentary's release, she was

Radical Reality. Caty Borum and David Conrad-Pérez, Oxford University Press. © Oxford University Press 2025.
DOI: 10.1093/9780197604298.003.0005

reminded of just how powerful and deep systems of misinformation can run in a society, and just how important and disruptive the work of documentary can be in challenging it.

> It was never my expectation that I would lose friends because of my work. I didn't expect that lifelong friends would accuse me of lying and trying to damage China's reputation. But when I return to my memories of myself as a teenager—every day, copying down the state's news broadcasts, accepting them as fact, taking pride in my ability to digest and regurgitate them—my friends' reactions become less surprising. If I had never left China, chances are I would be posting the same hashtags as them. I'd be just as skeptical of news reports claiming China is committing human rights violations, and I would probably see in them no motivation beyond embarrassing China as part of an imperialist scheme.
>
> I have no illusions about Western countries' imperviousness to propaganda. Every human mind is vulnerable to it. Chinese people have the particular misfortune of facing punishment for speaking the truth, if they can find it in the first place. On the flip side, I believe people in societies that call themselves free have the particular responsibility of speaking the truth when they find it, of wrestling with each other about what the truth is, of questioning what powerful people tell them to believe is true.[3]

The immersive and carefully investigative films made by Wang, often using first-person narration, have interrogated authoritarian governance, corruption, surveillance, intimidation, and the power of oppressive mandates and a lack of accountability on the lives of individuals and communities, particularly—though not always—under repressive policies in China. In the film *Hooligan Sparrow* (2016), her first major film, she spotlights the life of a women's rights activist, Ye Haiyan, as she protests the sexual abuse of six elementary schoolgirls by their school principal. A few years later, in the 2019 film *One Child Nation*, Wang brings audiences on a personal exploration of the one-child family planning policy in China and the violence and suffering it caused families across the country. The film includes interviews with community and family members she grew up with, along with local officials, doctors, and the families who were forced to abandon or give up their babies under the policy. And then, in the 2021 film, *In the Same Breath*, Wang explores China's attempt to control narrative and cover up truths around the COVID-19 outbreak, and the similarly catastrophic policy failures and

104 RADICAL REALITY

spread of misinformation in the United States. Her films have been distributed by almost every major platform—from Amazon Studios (streamer), to HBO (cable), to PBS and POV (public media)—and have received several industry awards and recognition as some of the most exemplary works of investigative reporting to come out of China.

More recently, however, Wang has begun to question whether films can bring the level of change that she originally envisioned. When we first spoke for this book, in the summer of 2023, Wang said that she was at one of her most pessimistic moments as a filmmaker. Since her earliest film (*Hooligan Sparrow*), Wang has wondered why her documentaries were not having a greater impact:

> After [*Hooligan Sparrow*], I had very specific goals and hopes for the film; that, once released, if it received enough exposure, enough spotlight, then it would do the change that I had hoped for. For example, getting people who were in prison out of prison, or getting a policy changed, or getting the government to do something differently. And none of those things that I had hoped for happened. I waited three months, six months, a year. It made me question, "Wait, why did I make films if it didn't do the things I hoped for?"
>
> And I think in the next year or two when I was making my second and third films, as they came out, and as I toured with them in different parts of the world and met different people, I saw some change when people would come up to me after a film screening. They often cried and would share how the film had changed the way that they see China or the world, or a very specific issue, or learned a specific part of history. And they said that they would never look at the world in the same way that they did before seeing the film. . . . So after having those experiences, I then gained some hope that: maybe the changes that I was hoping for through filmmaking are not necessarily going to happen in a very concrete policy, governmental level. And it might not be able to swing an authoritarian government to amend or to admit to a mistake or to make some big change. But it affects individuals. It raises awareness, and it can change people on the individual level: their consciousness, their worldview, and, with those people, it has a ripple effect. Those people could affect their circles through their words, through their actions, their behavior.[4]

Wang said that she still holds this belief in the potential of film to move individuals to meaningful action, even in authoritarian regimes where

DEMANDING HUMAN RIGHTS   105

human rights are not as easily protected in legal or policymaking terms. But the harsh trends of the media environment today, and the growing difficulty for films like hers—which critique power and expose uncomfortable truths—to be made and distributed, even outside of China, has brought Wang to a new level of concern:

> But, now, I think the world is going in a very different direction since the day I made my first film. Because whether it's my home country, China, or the US, where my adopted homeland is, everything is in decline. The political environment is getting worse. There's less freedom, there is more disinformation, there's more propaganda. I feel like documentaries are fighting against those [forces], and they are trying to be one of the narratives that hopefully will stand as a counternarrative to the mainstream. But [in terms of] how well it can succeed in that direction, how many people will see it, and how it can change people, it's hard to be optimistic.[5]

Wang's concern resonates with many other filmmakers engaged in this book, and it reflects a fundamental characteristic and shared value among many documentary makers: a desire to change the world for the better. While in other forms of journalistic storytelling, the struggle is often over whether intervention, intention, or influence should or should not be within the boundaries and conventions of the craft,[6] the struggle for many of the filmmakers in this book is not whether a film should be an advocate for change, but whether it has done enough to bring that meaningful change. At their core, the documentaries in this chapter do not only document human rights abuses and issues, they demand change. And the filmmakers who make these films also expect change.

At their core, documentaries have a way of telling stories of human rights abuses in painfully personal and galvanizing ways. As *New Yorker* film critic Richard Brody observed after watching one of Wang's films:

> Any investigative journalist could have pursued the story told in "One Child Nation." . . . Indeed, they include one such daring and persistent journalist in the film. But for Wang, who was born in China in 1985 (and immigrated to the United States in 2011, at the age of twenty-six), the one-child policy is also the story of her own childhood, and in her bold, probingly investigative, painfully intimate film, she approaches her subject with regard to its most personal implications. In so doing, she locates the political network

106 RADICAL REALITY

in which lives like hers were caught, and traces the one-child policy's consequences, as well as the attitudes underlying it, into the present day and into her own life, the lives of others, and the world at large.[7]

Wang said that the films she makes are motivated by both the "desperate need to offer a counternarrative to the official narrative" around social and human rights issues at the center of her films, and because she feels a sense of responsibility to reveal realities that she knows are being either misrepresented or hidden from the public eye.

> It's challenging for Chinese filmmakers to make documentaries inside China with the level of surveillance and censorship, let alone to get it seen outside of China. I have the resources and freedom to be working and living in the US. I felt that if I didn't try to make the films while I could then somehow I'm irresponsible. . . . And even though it might not change anything now, even though I would have no way of knowing how many people would see it in China. This is all hard to know. But my hope is that as long as it exists, then it will be discovered. It might be ten years later, when somebody [from China] travels to the US and accidentally has a chance to see it. Or fifty years later, somebody's researching on this topic, and they are going to find it. And even that kind of longevity of hoping that eventually if people are looking, if people are questioning, and the film exists, then there is a way to learn—that is enough to motivate me to continue creating.[8]

When someone does find one of Wang's films, they will learn that much of the content is in English. The voice-over for *One Child Nation* and the script of *Hooligan Sparrow* are both in English, for instance, and she says that this is purposeful. "In China, words like 'democracy' and 'human rights' are given negative undertones. . . . I realized that I couldn't tell this story in Chinese," she once said in an interview with the *New Yorker*, recalling an earlier attempt to create a Chinese version of her film *Hooligan Sparrow*. "I know what the translations are, and I know the expressions. But it feels embarrassing and unnatural. I almost feel as if I don't dare to say these words."[9] Wang's struggle points to the complexities of defining "human rights" in a universal context. For the purposes of this book, human rights can be generally understood as reflecting the rights and freedoms inherent to all human beings, regardless of where they live, who they pray to, who they love, or what they look like. And yet, the mere language of universal rights presumes a political and legal arena beyond borders, in which rights can be identified, realized, and protected, regardless of the interests or interpretations of specific nations or territories. As such, as Hannah Arendt famously puts it, and many human rights organizations and leaders echo, human rights also involve the ideal of an individual's "right to rights," including the right to be part of a political, judicial, and social community that protects such rights.[10]

Among the most irrefutable understandings among human rights groups and scholarship is the position that the media play a vital role in recognizing human rights, exposing and bringing awareness to violations, and empowering people, institutions and governments to take action to protect human rights. To be sure, the persuasive and central role of the media in shaping social understandings and action, politics and policies, institutional norms, and legal reform, among other functions, in the arena of human rights has long been a focus of interest and a relative given among studies of media. As media scholars Howard Tumber and Silvio Waisbord note:

> It is not an exaggeration to say that the way societies come to understand and experience the situation of "human rights" is largely shaped by mediated communication. . . . They underpin the processes by which activists petition authorities to act, and to demand laws, active monitoring, and enforcement; by which governments aim to convince various publics about policies and decisions; and the way publics react to denunciations of human rights violations, develop empathy with victims and the manner in which affected communities tell stories and seek justice.[11]

As such, the work and mission of filmmakers like Nanfu Wang reflect one of the most important functions that documentaries and media can serve today. Even more to the point, it would be a difficult challenge, if not impossible, to find a portfolio of media stories created by a single person that have done more over the last 10 years to galvanize global interest, attention, and debate around the realities of human rights violations in China than the films of Wang.

And yet, within conversations at the intersection of media and human rights scholarship, the role of documentary has received little attention. In one of the landmark books on human rights and the media, *The Routledge Companion to Media and Human Rights*,[12] published in 2017, more than 50 leading media scholars chronicle the many ways in which various forms of media serve to expose human rights struggles. And while many of the critical

108 RADICAL REALITY

theories and important work included in this 500+ page tome informs this book, it is worth noting that only 2 of the 50 essays engage substantively, or even tangentially—in more than two paragraphs—with the role that documentary filmmaking has played in covering and advocating for human rights. Instead, the compendium of essays primarily centers around the work of print and broadcast forms of media. More than reflecting the state of media influence today, this common oversight is emblematic of the relative lack of attention and recognition of the growing influence of documentary in the arena of human rights, even for the most astute scholars of media.

Further, the subject of documentaries is all the more salient given recent research that suggests they are capable of telling stories about human rights without reinforcing neoliberal, hegemonic narratives of passive victims and Western saviors—tired tropes that continue to dominant human rights media and Western news coverage of international conflict and crises. Despite theoretical expectations, when scholar Kate Nash investigated films being used in human rights film festivals in Europe and the United States, for instance, she was surprised to find that they allowed for relatively complex narrative themes and alternate forms of audience solidarity with protagonists, rather than the victim-savior framing that often appear in human rights stories.[13] In an important article published in the journal *Public Culture*, in 2018, she argues that the documentaries she observed are organized around narratives of "self-responsibilisation," a phenomenon that this chapter will further unpack, which forms a substantive way that documentaries are not only observing—but are actively contributing to—transnational human rights culture.[14] Such findings disrupt decades of scholarship about the dangers of media portrayals of human rights issues. There has especially been considerable and important criticism over the use of oversimplified narratives, or what Richard Rorty called—and Nash references as—"sad and sentimental stories,"[15] along with the privileging of the voices and frames of intervening NGOs and international forces over the experiences and histories of affected communities,[16] through which Western news and media has formed problematic arrangements of human rights culture.[17] In the reporting of international news, for instance, particularly on human rights and global crises, one of the most recurring offenses of journalists has been the overdrawn victimization of those they report on. In other words, the investigative prowess, rigor, nuance, and depth that news organizations are capable of, and often afford to areas of domestic reporting, has long gone missing in much coverage of some of the most complicated and globally significant events and issues of the last century. As documented several times over now, news coverage of global crisis and human rights often follows a certain pattern of reproducing generic, decontextualized images and narratives of suffering—be it impoverished children, war-torn villages, or the lurid effects of famine or AIDS—in hopes that this sort of reporting will compel humanitarian giving and action to help those in need, with little consideration given to the longer-term consequences of such portrayals.[18]

There is a stream of important conversations happening among scholars and philosophers, including Luc Boltanski,[19] Susan Moeller,[20] Wazhmah Osman,[21] Slavoj Žižek,[22] and Lilie Chouliaraki,[23] among others, about the mediation and consequences that humanitarian narratives of suffering have on how society sees itself, how it manifests in forms of individual versus collective action, and how news consumers are being conditioned to see and react to suffering "others" and entire "other" countries as a result.[24] In other words, important theoretical work about the implications of such stories on how people relate to one another has continued, and it has built a compelling case that the forms of agency, pity, and spectrum of emotional responses that such stories and frames of suffering produce may not be having the effect that journalists hope for or be as selfless and admirable as news audiences are led to believe. As a result, the potential that documentaries have to disrupt, rather than reinforce, such problematic forms of representation surprises many theoretical and face-value expectations, Nash notes, especially given how vulnerable the transportive medium of film could be to privileging and disseminating "sad sentimental stories."

At the same time, Nash argues, "there is surprisingly little academic work on human rights film."[25] And the work that has been done primarily places the focus of study on audience reception (i.e., on "the viewer") and interpretation—of their degrees of responsibility and capacity for addressing the human rights challenges.[26] Ultimately, Nash finds that the narratives of the human rights films she observed—primarily anchored in an analysis of the films *Sonita* and *The Act of Killing*—incite audiences to "self-responsibilize," through which "viewers are called on to see themselves as world citizens through identification with the journeys of victims and perpetrators toward their own self-realization as individuals with international rights and responsibilities."[27] And, of special relevance to this chapter, Nash also finds that documentaries on human rights are capable of

110 RADICAL REALITY

building action and movement in ways that offer "nuanced, even challenging narratives"[28] and which inspire a broader range of emotional responses:

> We can conclude that the viewers of human rights films are not invariably positioned as enjoying the "humanitarian gaze" of the privileged Westerner called on to rescue pathetic victims.... Human rights films of the kind that are shown at human rights film festivals call on viewers to identify or to experience fellow feeling with protagonists who overcome obstacles at the local and national levels to become world citizens.[29]

This finding by Nash points toward a growing canon of evidence that documentaries can inspire improved understanding and more dynamic forms of engagement around human rights issues; this runs in contrast to ironic acts of solidarity, for instance, as the important work of Lilie Chouliaraki has found in coverage of human rights issues in the contemporary media environment, which often flattens complex stories into commercialized products and arrangements of solidarity while obscuring uncomfortable truths and issues of complicity. The implications of this potentiality of documentary storytelling cannot be understated. The work of Chouliaraki on posthumanitarianism communication tells us that the seemingly ubiquitous media and communication technique of cleaning messages in an effort to spur consumerist impulses (i.e., click to donate, or buy a coffee to save a life, etc.) is likely leading society away from actually being moral.[30] It's not building a form of engagement that is in true solidarity with those who are suffering, in which people are truly helping others; rather, it's reinforcing a dynamic in which news audiences are made to "feel good" about themselves, suppressing the voice and experience of the sufferer in the process. It is directing acts of engagement toward one's self, but not to those whose stories are being told. Yet, stories of distant suffering or crisis, writes Chouliaraki "should not be reduced to the world we comfortably inhabit."[31] Instead, she argues, people should be confronted with "agonistic engagement" that forces them to raise questions, such as whether donating is enough, that challenge their own sense of responsibility, complicity, and positionality.[32]

This is precisely the type of engagement and storytelling that many of the documentaries in this chapter (and book) seek to create, which privilege the experiences and interests of the communities and individuals at the center of the film over the comfort of audiences or the expectations of geopolitics and market logics, even if it's increasingly to the determinant of the filmmaker's ability to sell their work to major distributors. And while there have been remarkably few studies on human rights documentaries, there have been even fewer studies on the processes by which films on human rights issues are made, the experiences of their makers and the people they center, and what they hope documentaries will achieve.

To help change this trend, and to inspire further inquiry, debate, and recognition around the role of documentaries in human rights, this chapter presents documentary projects and teams who are working in increasingly hostile climates to reveal human rights violations and acts of resistance, to cast a bright light on the long-term implications of human rights violations and injustice, and to ultimately bring justice and positive change. This chapter also provides special consideration of the specific ways that documentaries are achieving this, including through personal and intimate stories, working undercover with activist groups and organizations, and centering stories on key figures and movements. In doing so, this chapter argues that documentaries should be of special interest to scholars working in every arena of media and human rights, including those interested in media policy and law, journalism studies and practice, activism and witnessing, media representation, and political communication.

Documentaries are arguably one of the most effective vehicles to raise awareness and advocate for human rights today. To borrow the perspective raised earlier by Nanfu Wang and echoed by one of the world's most famous climate and human rights activists, Greta Thunberg, documentaries do not only spotlight the work of human rights activists, they make activists. "The thing that's made me open my eyes to what was happening to the environment and climate was films and documentaries," said Thunberg. "That was what made me decide to do something about it."[33]

Undercover Reporting and Working with Activist Groups to Expose Human Rights Violations in Hostile Territories

In 2019, an alarming report from Amnesty International revealed the sweeping mechanisms and uptick in actions by which civil society and human rights defenders are harassed, surveilled, attacked, and arrested—a global trend, not reserved for dictatorships alone.[34] This trend has continued since the report's release, with a 2023 Amnesty International study finding that half of the world's countries (49%) arbitrarily detain human

112   RADICAL REALITY

rights defenders.[35] And yet, documentary filmmakers—whose cameras only add to their vulnerability in drawing attention—are continuing to find ways to bring attention to human rights struggles and violations in some of the world's most hostile countries for journalists.

The film *Welcome to Chechnya*, released in 2020, is one such example. The film follows a group of activists as they risk their lives to help people escape their country's effort to detain, torture, and kill them simply because they identify with the LGBTQIA+ community. The film is based in the semiautonomous Russian territory of Chechnya, where its leader, Ramzan Kadyrov, who was installed as the region's president in 2007 by Russian President Vladimir Putin, has been enforcing a devastating campaign to "cleanse the blood" of LGBTQIA+ Chechens. In the words of Kadyrov, during July of 2017: "We don't have any gays. If there are any, take them to Canada. . . . Take them away from us. To purify our blood, if there are any here, take them."[36] At great risk to the film team and the people it centers, the documentary exposes many of the horrific atrocities and human rights abuses suffered under the campaign, alongside activists—primarily based in Russia—who are shown resisting the antigay purge in Chechnya through heroic acts of taking matters into their own hands.

In an interview for this book, the film's producer, Alice Henty[37] said that she learned about the crisis after reading a June 2017 *New Yorker* article[38] by Masha Gessen, titled "The Gay Men Who Fled Chechnya's Purge," which mentioned how more than 40 Chechens were still living in undercover housing arranged by local activists in the country. Henty was shocked at what was happening and then learned that filmmaker David France, who had optioned the article and wanted to produce a documentary that went beyond its current reporting and provide greater details and documentation of the atrocities, had access to the very activists and undercover safe havens she had just read about.

> My first thought was, "Of course I want to work on this film. I want to do everything I can to help stop the abuses." And I thought that a film would help do that. As we got into it, it became clear that regime change is a pretty lofty goal for a film to make . . . but it did seem possible that we could put the story back into people's feeds and consciousnesses. Also if we are documenting something that is being denied, we would have evidence, right? It's actually proof. So they can continue to deny it, but anyone who believes them in theory, once they see the film, would be swayed.[39]

DEMANDING HUMAN RIGHTS   113

In addition to alerting the global community, Henty said that they had an early interest in ensuring that people within Russia—including key politicians and individuals close to Putin and Kadyrov—would see the film too, as a way of helping to bring greater awareness to the atrocities and move individuals who could make a difference and push Putin to intervene.

Henty said that she isn't necessarily someone who came from the school of social justice filmmaking. Rather, she first entered the field of documentary because she loved film and storytelling. As a result, the films she has helped create run the gamut from stories squarely in the social justice bucket to entertainment biopics and music films. But as her career progressed, she came to see just how powerful documentaries can be in helping to expose injustices and change people's minds on critical issues, and how no other form of media or storytelling comes close.

A motivating principle driving Henty and the film team's work, which is included in a higher education resource guide[40] that was created for classrooms and schools to engage with the film, is articulated in Susan Sontag's essay *Regarding the Pain of Others*:

> Someone who is perennially surprised that depravity exists, who continues to feel disillusioned (even incredulous) when confronted with evidence of what humans are capable of inflicting in the way of gruesome, hands-on cruelties upon other humans, has not reached moral or psychological adulthood.
>
> No one after a certain age has the right to this kind of innocence, of superficiality, to this degree of ignorance, or amnesia. There now exists a vast repository of images that make it harder to maintain this kind of moral defectiveness. Let the atrocities images haunt us. Even if they are only tokens and cannot possibly encompass most of the reality to which they refer, they still perform a vital function. The images say: This is what human beings are capable of doing—may volunteer to do, enthusiastically, self-righteously. Don't forget.[41]

As Sontag notes, and Henty emphasizes, it is often imperative for people to see the radical reality of injustice in order to more fully "know" it and to ultimately be compelled to end it.

The decision to work on a film that served to vitally document grave injustices was one thing, actually completing it was another. And Henty said that the safety and security challenges, not to mention the logistics, inherent

114   RADICAL REALITY

in this type of investigation are numerous. In order to allow audiences to see with their own eyes the human rights abuses taking place in Chechnya, through the unfolding events and experiences of people on the ground in the country, the film team needed to embed its efforts with the people at the heart of the struggle. As the film's director, David France, recalled: "We had heard nothing out of the new U.S. administration to try and stop [the abuses] and that, in fact, there was really very little in the way of political pressure on Russia to end this horror and to bring the perpetrators to justice. That meant that it was left to the LGBTQ+ community there to do something about it."[42]

One of the early steps they took was strengthening their relationships and contacts with local organizations, in order to ensure that their film would be aligned with their work, safety, and context. With the support of impact producer Alison Byrne Fields and coproducer Igor Myakotin, the film team did extensive research and connected with about 35 different activists and groups working in Russia, Chechnya, and elsewhere in Europe and in North America, who were able to provide a detailed description of what was needed on the ground, how the film could help their work, and what could potentially be harmful.

This film team's decision to focus on the activists was a purposeful one, said Byrne Fields. "[France] could have made a film about the strong men who are making people's lives miserable. So it could have been about Ramzan [Kadyrov] and Vladimir Putin, but it was a film about the activists that are doing the work to get people out of Chechnya."[43] By putting audiences directly in the struggle on the front lines of the crisis, she said, the hope was that they would be empowered to do more than simply become "aware" of the hate crimes taking place in Chechnya, they could also be shown a pathway to directly supporting the activists buy plane tickets, rent apartments and do the urgently needed work of "getting people on planes so that no one would kill them."[44]

Through their consultations the film team ultimately identified four central objectives for the film: support the evacuation of victims though their support of key activist organization on the ground, amplify international outcry by raising awareness of the film and its story, hold perpetrators accountable by supporting legal efforts that the team highlights on its web page, and better understand the global context of the issue through learning where other countries are criminalizing sexual identity and how to support efforts in those places too. The primary purpose of the documentary was to use the film as an intervention to expose wrongdoing, inspire global action, and ultimately stop the violence against—and bring justice to—the LGBTQ+ community in Chechnya. To help achieve this, France joined the activists in early 2018 and remained embedded with their underground operation for the next 20 months.

One of the greatest priorities and challenges for the film team was ensuring the wellness and safety of the activists at the center of the film, which included a need to safeguard the identities of the participants from the very beginning. This meant that they had to be targeted and extremely cautious about what information they shared outside of their film team at every step of the process—from securing funding, to making the film, to seeking distribution.

When it came to funding, Henty recalls how wary people were to support undercover work in a hostile country, and how they couldn't just do a community pitch or simply send a link or file of the film because of the sensitivities of the subject and participants. Every pitch they did needed to be in person using their own encrypted software. This level of care scared off many of the traditional documentary funding groups.

> Some of the funders we approached were just totally freaked out by it. They were like, "The fact you're going to this level just to tell me about the film, we don't want to take the risk by funding the film."[45]

To help circumvent the hesitations of some funders, especially individual donors, the film team offered individuals and organizations the opportunity to donate anonymously. This allowed some foundations to contribute who wouldn't normally have done so.

During the filmmaking process, to ensure that buzz about the film wouldn't reach beyond funder meetings and interfere with their work in Chechnya, the film team didn't talk to any major network while they were making it. But when it came time for seeking distribution the film team also couldn't just send a link of the film to prospective platforms. They needed to fly someone to whichever network they were pitching so that they could show them the film on an encrypted drive. "And that also freaked people out," said Henty. "We went out to every major network, and HBO was the only one that did not blink about taking the risk."[46]

The process of safeguarding the identities of the participants in the film was not only among the most important challenges faced by the film team; it was also one of the most expensive. During the editing process, the film team followed extremely tight protocols—all editing happened in their office

Image 5.1 Description: *Welcome to Chechnya* BTS VFX SHOOT.
Image credit: Courtesy of the *Welcome to Chechnya* Film Team.

through air gapped computers, which meant that their computers and editing system needed to be isolated so that it could not be accessed via the internet and so that footage could only live on encrypted external hard drives. The team followed the "Safe + Secure" standards set in place by Doc Society, along with their own protocols, which included maintaining a small team, prohibiting the use of cell phones in the edit room or when translating footage, never emailing anyone about the project, and conducting all communication through Signal or by literally passing encrypted thumb drives around if anyone needed to share documents. The team also managed translation by having a small group of vetted translators come to the office for the work, so that no files would be exchanged.

Given the level of courage and trust that the participants at the center of the film showed to the filmmakers, Henty said it was critical that the film team didn't compromise their safety or interests when it came to distribution. This not only meant ensuring that the final cut reflected the shared objectives of the activists but also ensuring that every effort was made to safeguard their identities in the film itself.

The film team worked with the film's participants in several areas of security (including physical and technological security in order to protect the

DEMANDING HUMAN RIGHTS 117

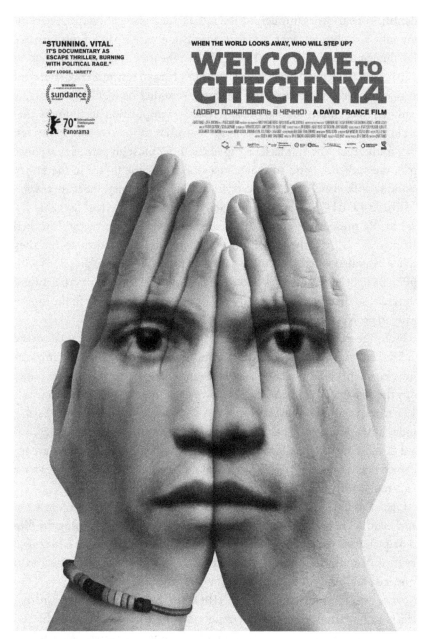

Image 5.2 Description: *Welcome to Chechnya* poster. Image credit: Courtesy of the *Welcome to Chechnya* Film Team.

118 RADICAL REALITY

identities of survivors through confidentiality and encryption training), anonymity, visibility, consent, and power imbalances. As part of this process, the film team also collaborated with Thalia Wheatley and the researchers at Dartmouth College's Social Systems lab in order to test masking strategies so that the faces of activists in Chechnya wouldn't be identifiable.[47] They explored specialized animation and video manipulation techniques that could perform partial and entire face swaps. From the research endeavor, they found that "the full facial swap elicited the most empathetic response from the audience," and so they chose that technique to use in the film.[48] Working with visual effects experts, including Ryan Laney, the team invited US-based LGBTQIA+ community activists who already had a visible social media presence to "lend their faces to replace those of the Chechen survivors."[49] Ultimately, several people volunteered to participate and they sat for extended video shoots that captured their faces and expressions with different lighting and from various angles, along with other verbal sound exercises, so that their faces could replace those of the activists in the film in order to protect their identity.

From the perspective of the director, France, this technique was critical and it distinguishes itself from the harmful use of virtual effects manipulation elsewhere in the media because it doesn't change what people are saying, only the face that says it, and that it allows survivors and vulnerable activists "to narrate their own stories . . . in a way that would not have been possible under other circumstances."[50] The use of the technology is briefly discussed and disclosed for audiences at the beginning of the film, and viewers are informed that a halo effect can be seen around the characters whose faces have been replaced by the protective technique.

Once the film was released by HBO in January of 2020, the film team worked to set in motion many of their early objectives around using the film to help change the situation for the LGBTQIA+ community in Chechnya, trying to "amplify the outcry" of the activists in the film, and to use the film to fundraise and support the work that they were doing.[51]

Since the film's distributor was HBO, the only North American distributor that supported the documentary, the film team knew that its reach might not be as large as some of the other streamers. As a result, the film team worked to secure screening and broadcast partnerships with targeted countries outside of the United States. Interest for the film within Russia, and among Russian audiences, was even greater than the filmmakers initially anticipated, illustrating both the urgency of the issue

DEMANDING HUMAN RIGHTS   119

and the region's appetite for films on important social issues. In late May 2020, a trailer for the film was released on YouTube by HBO. Within days it had generated nearly a million views, primarily from Russian-speaking viewers expressing an interest in seeing the film. And after the film was released by HBO, on June 30, it was quickly pirated across Russia and became one of the most-viewed films in the country even without a distributor there. Soon after, BBC News Russia (part of the BBC World Service) distributed the film, making it their first-ever film acquisition; they made it available (for free) to audiences in Russia, Armenia, Azerbaijan, Belarus, Georgia, Kazakhstan, Kyrgyzstan, Tajikistan, Turkmenistan, Ukraine, and Uzbekistan. In an effort to also break through misinformation bubbles in Russia, the film team engaged with social network platforms, like Hornet, a dating app that's used mostly by gay men in Russia, in order to spread additional word of the film and to provide information for anyone who needed protection or support.[52]

Since the film's release, the film team has continued to push for progress on the issue of human rights in Chechnya. And their achievements are remarkable. They have raised more than $200,000 for key activist groups and partners engaged in Chechnya—including Russian LGBT Network and the Moscow Community Center and Maxim Lapunov, who was tortured and jailed just for being gay and became the first survivor to publicly come forward to share his story and to seek justice.[53]

And while the horrific persecution of the LGBTQIA+ community in Chechnya is still ongoing, global efforts have begun to place pressure on Russian and Chechen officials to stop it. When asked if Vladimir Putin had seen the film, in July 2020, his then spokesman Dmitry Peskov responded by saying "we believe that there are a lot of far more important issues."[54] However, many others have seen the film. The film team has since supported coalition-building efforts, sanctions, and high-level advocacy attempts through screenings and direct engagement of UN officials, along with US and EU politicians, court officials, and Kremlin officials. In the years since the film's release, several leadership groups have referenced the film *Welcome to Chechnya* as serving a vital role in inspiring and advancing their efforts—ranging from new sanctions and legislative actions taken by the US government, the UK government, and the European Union, to new criminal cases being pushed in Europe against key perpetrators of the violence, to new visa/asylum protections in several countries for Chechyns who escape. This means that the film team's push to end violence against the

120   RADICAL REALITY

LGBTQIA+ community in Chechnya has moved meaningful action from US State Department officials, government representatives, and congressional leaders; United Nations officials; human rights leadership in and outside of Russia; European Union representatives; and government leaders and representatives throughout Europe, Canada, and Australia.

In other words, it could be argued that despite years of reporting, such global attention and action to end the violence against LGBTQIA+ people in Chechnya did not substantially advance until the documentary was made and distributed. In the words of Rachel Denber, deputy director of the Europe and Central Asia Division of Human Rights Watch: "There is no better advocacy calling card for Chechnya than this film."

Connecting Audiences with Key Human Rights Figures, Movements, and Organizations

The film *He Named Me Malala* illustrates the role a documentary can play in moving audiences past a moment of awareness to directly advancing the work of a particular organization and activist. The film documents the journey of Nobel Peace Prize Laureate Malala Yousafzai. At just 11 years old, Yousafzai had begun blogging about her difficult experiences living as a girl in the Swat Valley of Pakistan for the BBC, alongside her father, Ziauddin, a school founder and teacher who was outspoken about his belief that girls had a right to an education. But the more they spoke up about the injustices they witnessed and their desire for human rights in the country, the more threats they received from extremists and the Taliban in their country, eventually leading to then-15-year-old Malala being targeted, shot in the head, and nearly killed on her way home from school. The film shows Malala's journey to survival and to leading a global campaign for every girl's right to free, safe, and quality education as cofounder of the Malala Fund.

For the team that worked on it, the film itself was just a starting point for the large human rights objectives and advocacy goals that the film team wanted to achieve. Malala herself pointed to the documentary as a human rights vehicle that she hoped would continue to be "watched by children in developing countries and inspire them to stand up for their rights and fight against the issues that are stopping them from going to school."[55] For this reason, Lindsay Guetschow, who developed the strategy and led impact efforts around the film within the Malala Fund, said that screenings can be just the starting point for the role and work of documentaries around human rights.

> I always say that the film is just the jumping off point. It's a way to convene people to emotionally engage in an issue through a compelling story and piece of art. Screening the film is the very beginning of the impact work. Within any film campaign, my goal is always to center the impacted community to be able to lead these efforts. It can't be people outside the community coming in. However you can cocreate a strategy and establish partnerships to share powerful resources and relationships, build capacity and then get out of the way.[56]

The act of ensuring that all impact efforts and engagement were led by local teams and experts on the ground—not international organizations and Global North "experts"—was crucial for Guetschow and the impact team. In the five countries (Pakistan, Afghanistan, Nigeria, India, and Kenya) where they pursued large-scale national-level advocacy and hyper-local community engagement goals, they worked with local organizations to codevelop strategies targeting areas that had the highest number of girls out of school.

> We did not want to insert ourselves or be leading the impact work from the Global North. We spent a lot of time in the regions that we were focusing on listening to our grantees, policy experts, community leaders, and girl advocates to collectively build the campaign. A big first step was establishing security protocols to keep all of our partners and grantees safe as well as building relationships with local leaders and tribal elders to get their approval. To be able to even show the film, and do the kind of work our community partners and grantees wanted to do, we needed to get their buy-in. We ended up dubbing the film in ten different local languages so it was accessible to the communities we were working with across the five countries we were working in. Many of the people we were hoping to reach were illiterate and could not read captions, so having the film dubbed in local languages and using visual graphics to prompt conversation was paramount. We are extremely grateful that the distributors and filmmakers were on board with this strategy.…
>
> This was the first time I was embedded within an organization running an impact campaign. It absolutely made the most sense for this campaign and I hope more impact strategists and filmmakers consider what it might

122 RADICAL REALITY

look like to have grassroots leaders run impact campaigns within their organizations. These organizers and organizations have longevity and will continue the work long after a traditional campaign window. Through the Stand #withMalala campaign, we trained folks on the communications, programs, and advocacy teams at our nonprofit partners around the world on how they might use storytelling as an additional tool to further their work and amplify their message. Many had never used a film as a way to convene their community or center a human story with policymakers. It sparked something within these organizations, and it's amazing to see how they continue to use the film and other pieces of storytelling to further their work.

These efforts can live inside organizations. It's not just a big moment around a film premiere and all the ancillary releases, and then the campaign just goes away after a set amount of time. In this scenario all of the research and progress we made toward our advocacy goals, the programs we established, the relationships and community that we built within the campaign continues to lives on within the Malala Fund.[57]

In the case of the Stand #withMalala campaign, which was organized around the film, the nonprofit run by the main protagonist, Malala, called the Malala Fund, was the home of the impact campaign effort. Guetschow actually worked at the Malala Fund and led design efforts around the campaign—meaning that the effort was orchestrated and started from within the main protagonist's own organization and nonprofit. And this allowed any global or national level goal or effort to feed back into the local organization and country-level work.

And the reason that we did that was because the film was about her and her efforts as one piece of a global collective effort around securing safe, free, and quality secondary education for every girl, everywhere. How odd would that have been to have a production company, or someone outside the work trying to feed what the advocacy goals should be, or what the programmatic goals should be within a campaign? Those already lived within her organization; her foundation was living and breathing this day in, day out. It was easy for us to build an impact campaign using the film as a tool, to further and build upon the existing organizational and advocacy goals. We worked closely with local partners, experts, and girl advocates to inform our advocacy goals and programs in Pakistan, Afghanistan, Nigeria,

Kenya, and India and had multiple ways for people to plug in from a global perspective to our broader campaign.[58]

At the country and global level, their campaign involved screenings with high-level stakeholders and at meetings (including African Union Summit or at UNGA) with policymakers and movement leaders; convening high-level advocacy meetings, and working on research reports and reporting current data and statistics to aid advocacy work. On the local community level, they engaged in a robust community screening campaign—including mobile screenings in refugee camps in Kenya, hosting leadership and advocacy trainings with young girls across all the countries they worked in who then shared their stories (anonymously) and advocated, via radio programming, and joined local stakeholders at advocacy events, programs specifically targeting fathers and brothers (main deterrents for girls attending school) among other activities, and supporting door-to-door educational and advocacy campaigns, alongside free educational screenings at schools. In total, the Stand #withMalala campaign engaged over 1.3 million young people in screenings and campaign programs around the world, helped shift education policy in Nigeria and Pakistan, raised over $3M to support Malala Fund programs in developing countries, and trained close to 1,000 girls in advocacy and leadership in Pakistan, Afghanistan, Nigeria, India, and Kenya.

However, Guetschow said, the common denominator for their success went beyond the delivery of the screenings and engagement activities and was rooted in the longevity of the conversations they started—and any chance of this happening successfully was through partnerships with local organizations working on these issues, who could keep the work going through the grants the campaign delivered long after the screenings ended.[59]

Using Documentaries to Empower Underrepresented Communities and Tell Stories That Go Beyond Violent Statistics and Traditional Storytelling Conventions

If *He Named Me Malala* reflects one of the more traditional approaches to grassroots engagement, the film *Uýra, The Rising Forest* demonstrates a perhaps less common, but no less powerful, approach to embedding a film with one individual in order to advance a social movement or human rights cause through documentary film.

124 RADICAL REALITY

In the film, Uýra, a nonbinary Indigenous activist and biologist, shares ancestral knowledge with Indigenous youth to confront issues of historical racism, transphobia, and environmental destruction, and works to help bring greater awareness and understanding to the importance of the Amazon at a time when it is under direct threat by Brazil's oppressive political regime and its former president Jair Bolsonaro. The documentary combines elements of music, dance, drag, and performance, to demonstrate the significance of the environment to issues of identity and place for Indigenous communities, and to amplify the film's message that "the root of every social fight, is the preservation of life."[60]

In making the documentary, the filmmaker, Juliana Curi, said she was influenced by the Brazilian Cinema Novo movement and felt compelled to amplify Uýra's story and experience in order to help people to better understand the disproportionate impact of the climate crisis on underrepresented communities.[61] In an interview for this book, Curi said that journalists tend to respect numbers, but that the story of Uýra, and the consequences of climate justice and the destruction of the forests in Brazil, is a story that numbers alone cannot tell. As a result, she used aspects of music and dance to go beyond traditional storytelling conventions of both traditional journalism and documentary itself, especially in crossing into lines of fiction at times. Curi said that her documentary endeavors to "break the false segmentation that we have in our industry that art films and social films are separate products."[62] Instead, the film incorporates the artistic modes of expression and storytelling that are used by Indigenous communities in the Amazon.

> On one hand, we have a very violent story. And we need to address these numbers. Brazil is one of the countries that kills the most transgender people, Indigenous people, and environmentalist activists in the world. So I need to honor this information and address it in the film. But at the same time, when you travel through the Amazon and you meet people and communities, they talk about the spirit of the forest as a living being that is part of their lives. So I couldn't address this story in a linear, Cartesian way. We needed to honor all of this mythology, and we needed to create a film that audiences could both understand intellectually and feel in their hearts.[63]

For more than a decade, Brazil has been one of the most dangerous countries in the world for transgender and queer people, accounting for the most

Image 5.3 Description: *Uýra*: Film national premiere at Nossa Senhora de Fátima, Uýra's neighborhood—Manaus, AM. Image credit: Matheus Belém.

documented killings of transgender and queer people each year. By focusing on Uýra's story, the documentary both spotlights the severity of this issue and goes beyond the boundaries of many documentaries about the environment and climate change by demonstrating the disproportionate impact that the climate crisis is also having on Indigenous and queer communities in the Amazon.[64] "We have always been here," Uýra says in the film. "Groups that are persecuted and denied their earth-given diversity are like plants growing and living in violent and abandoned land, living off the strength of memory."

Ensuring that the film was driven by Uýra, its main protagonist, and rooted in her community, Curi and the film team said it was essential that the film would go to the Amazon first and focus on engagements that directly supported Uýra's ongoing efforts. "Often we see documentary films going through the traditional process—festivals, theatres, streaming—and they never return to the original community," said Curi. "In order to avoid this extractivist type of production, we designed an educational exhibit and program that traveled to important places in the Amazon, democratizing the film's offerings there."[65]

As a result, before the festival circuit or a world premiere, the film team spent about six months developing an impact strategy—with support from a

Image 5.4 Description: *Uýra*: Film national premiere at Nossa Senhora de Fátima, Uýra's neighborhood—Manaus, AM. Image credit: Matheus Belém.

Doc Society climate impact grant—that situated the documentary as "a tool of education for the Amazon youth" through a series of screening events, local partnerships, and community engagements. The first screening of the film in Brazil also took place in Uýra's town. "We brought a street cinema and popcorn. We invited the whole neighborhood," said Curi. "One journalist mentioned that, 'this was the first time in 25 years that the Nossa Senhora de Fátima neighborhood is covered with a cultural event.'"[66]

For Curi and the film team, it is essential that documentaries—especially those which center issues of human rights—keep the interests of the communities they feature at the center of everything they do. "For me, it's super important. If you are going to talk about a specific community, they need to be at the center of your decisions: 'what is good for them, not what is good for me.'"[67] Finally, Curi noted that another important consideration in making the film was ensuring that Uýra and the people in the film were depicted as valuable and powerful. "It was important to create a possibility for this community to see themselves on screen—not as a subject that is asking for something or needing something, as commonly seen in films about social and climate justice, but as characters that are offering us extremely valuable knowledge and worldviews."[68]

DEMANDING HUMAN RIGHTS 127

Image 5.5 Description: *Uýra* film poster. Image courtesy of *Uýra* film team.

Human Rights Films Under Threat?

In one of the most hair-raising moments of *Welcome to Chechnya*, audiences witness a rescue operation involving one of the film's main participants, a woman named Anya (a pseudonym), after she had pleaded for help through a local organization. Anya's uncle had threatened to reveal that she was gay to her father—a high-ranking government official—unless she would have sex with him. Using hidden cameras, the film follows Anya as she works with activists to strategize an escape from the country. It shows her working with the local activists to build a backstory, and it follows her as she navigates tense questioning at roadside security checkpoints. While it's not shown in the film, the filmmaker, David France, was also interrogated by officials during the extraction. France told them that he was a soccer enthusiast and that he was visiting the country as a tourist who was retracing the steps of his favorite team.[69] He even used a decoy phone full of soccer-fan photos and videos to help convince skeptical security officials. Through a geotracker, producer Alice Henty followed the process from her home in New York, watching a dot move across the country for several hours until the rescue was complete.[70] This entire operation was facilitated by the small film team without the support of any major institution, government, or organization; it was driven solely by their motivation to bring a little-known injustice to a wider audience.

The level of risk that went into the relatively short scene reflects the commitment that filmmakers and the participants they center have in revealing human rights abuses around the world. At the same time, filmmakers worry that distributors are becoming increasingly risk-adverse when it comes to funding or distributing such films, since it could influence lucrative commercial agreements and relationships in authoritarian countries. At the risk of anchoring this book's investigation to a potentially unique moment in time, such perspectives merit further discussion, especially if recent hesitation around media content about human rights is only at the beginning of a new and concerning trend, as many filmmakers suspect.

The independence and resoluteness of filmmakers to continue to film human rights struggles and uncomfortable realities as they exist in the world is important to note, but to confuse the process of documentary filmmaking with the world of documentary distribution would be, to borrow a phrase popularized by journalism historian James Carey, to confuse "the fish story with the fish."[71] The worlds of documentary production and distribution are increasingly governed by fundamentally different actors, interests, and motives; and the later field is undergoing swift and dramatic change. Put simply, Henty says that she thinks *Welcome to Chechnya* would not have been able to raise the funds or distribution it needed in today's environment. Only a few years removed from the film's release, she says it feels like everything has changed as streamers have taken a firmer grip on the industry.

> Today we find ourselves in this world where the networks are stating quite clearly that they don't want anything political with a capital "P." Even if they're not saying that outright, that's the message we're hearing through the sales agents and through the reps. It's the same story [from the sales agents and reps]. It goes: "If you could reframe that so it's not political, then we can take it to them." . . . And what does that actually mean? If we were coming out with *Welcome to Chechnya* now, I don't think it would have distribution.[72]

Identifying the reason for a network's hesitation is difficult, but consensus among several filmmakers engaged in this research, and past studies led by the authors, indicate a prevailing belief that it's primarily about maintaining access to new markets. When recalling the level of fear and worry that distributors had about sharing a film that was critical of Russia, Henty put a feeling shared by many filmmakers in this book into some of the clearest terms:

> The fact that some of [the streamers] were opening-up in Russia, I think had a lot do with [the pushback]. We were told that it was for the safety of the people who were working in Russia for the networks. But I think it was more commercially driven. People were more concerned that they wouldn't be able to continue to open in Russia if they had a film that was so anti-Russian. If it was a sports documentary or something, probably not an issue, or a murder. So, it's disturbing, isn't it? Here we are with these huge conglomerates who are, in some ways, more powerful than governments in deciding what can and can't be seen in certain countries. It is a form of censorship . . . when you can't get your film out because it's saying something controversial or political about a country that the network is trying to make money in.[73]

130　RADICAL REALITY

Similarly, Nanfu Wang says she also wonders if her film *One Child Nation* would be able to get distribution in today's media environment. And Wang said that these are the precise conversations she has been having with other filmmakers over the last couple years:

> I think people who are making films around human rights, politically sensitive films are facing challenges from multiple levels and directions. For example, people who are making a film in China that is reflecting the repression, they are not only risking their personal safety within China from the Chinese authority, they also face the challenges of getting it supported and funded outside of China. It forces a lot of people to give up on those stories.[74]

Similar to filmmaker observations shared in Chapter 3, Wang worries about finding funding for documentaries that attempt to show the full complexity of human rights stories, regardless of how controversial and uncomfortable the underlying realities of those stories might be:

> I do worry about it because I also have noticed the trend with streamers and media consolidation. There are less channels and less distributors who are brave enough to touch on issues that are politically sensitive. And in terms of what is considered politically sensitive—it is what affects the interest of their own companies, their own shareholders. And oftentimes it's not explicit and not conveyed; it's not publicized. So you can't even have proof why something isn't funded, something isn't distributed, because of certain political reasons, because you don't get this explicit answer and you can only speculate—even though you might have off-the-record conversations and strong evidence that alludes to that possibility and reason, you still can't be 100% certain. And I worry that it means the public will see less and less films around issues that are challenging, that are questioning, that are radical, that are controversial.[75]

The films explored in this chapter reflect just a few of the many documentaries that have received considerable attention for spotlighting important human rights crises and struggles for greater recognition and engagement, but there are many more, including *Nasrin* (about Iranian human rights lawyer, activist, and political prisoner Nasrin Sotoudeh), *Nowhere to Hide* (about life in central Iraq), *Human Flow* (about refugee camps in more than 20 countries), *Joshua: Teenager vs. Superpower* (about a teenage leader and organizer in Hong Kong), *India: The Modi Question* (about the Indian president's connection to a deadly riot that killed more than 1,000 people, most of them Muslims), *Plan C* (on the fight to expand access to abortion pills across the United States), and *Queendom* (about a young queer Russian person who is forced to leave the country because she doesn't want to participate in the war against Ukraine), to name a few. Most of these films have also faced similar challenges in gaining support from major distributors, and some have yet to find distribution at all.

The hesitation to support films that tackle urgent human rights challenges, especially if those films are based in authoritarian countries and markets, holds for some well-regarded funders, as well. Like other filmmakers, Wang expressed the frustrating reality that many of the major global funders in China—including organizations that are in the country to support human rights issues—also seem to fear being associated with work that is critical of the authoritarian government.

Ultimately, in the field of documentary, the evidence is building that the editorial and acquisition decisions of major distributors are not based on a set of conventions or values over what's a "good story" or what will bring the widest audience; the trends that filmmakers are seeing appear much less complicated. Within the community of filmmakers who have dedicated their lives to documenting stories about human rights, there is growing concern that many of the largest documentary distributors seem to be making film acquisition decisions based on the degree to which the film could endanger their hold over key markets. Over time, the voices of human rights defenders may become increasingly silenced in the name of the marketplace.

6

Demonstrating Activism

At his Agence France-Presse (AFP) office in Hong Kong, around 7:00 am, just before his work day was to begin, Karl Malakunas sat down for our conversation. For the last several years, this has been his routine—squeezing in his documentary filmmaking commitments before and after his day job as the Asia-Pacific deputy-editor-in-chief for one of the world's biggest news organizations. It has been exhausting, he admits, but there has been little other choice. In his capacity as a reporter and editor, Malakunas had tried for years to bring greater attention to the experiences of a small group of land defenders, including members of local Indigenous communities, who have been risking their lives to resist the illegal destruction of their land in the Philippines, until realizing that the only way their story could receive the recognition and attention it deserved was for him to work outside of the confines of the daily journalism world that had dominated his professional life. Their story had to be told, he felt, through a documentary—even though he had never produced one before in his life.[1]

Malakunas had spent almost his entire career in daily journalism. He cut his teeth as a 17-year-old "copy boy," worked for 10 years as a reporter at a daily newspaper, and then spent the next 20 years at a wire agency. He now heads a team of more than 200 reporters covering the Asia-Pacific region for AFP. Much of his reporting over the last several years has focused on covering the escalating challenges wrought by climate change, along with the many other pressing news stories (including around Duterte's deadly drug war) that come with being the bureau chief of the Philippines capital city of Manila for AFP, the position he held before becoming AFP's regional deputy editor-in-chief, the role he had taken by the time of our conversation. In 2011, before he was to leave for an assignment to the dreamy archipelagic land and rainforests of Palawan, a favorite tourist destination, where Malakunas thought he would be doing a light story about ecotourism in one of the Philippines' most beautiful locations, he learned that his contact for the story—an environmental activist—had just been shot in the head and killed. The tragic news prompted Malakunas to travel to Palawan for a

Radical Reality. Caty Borum and David Conrad-Pérez, Oxford University Press. © Oxford University Press 2025.
DOI: 10.1093/9780197604298.003.0006

DEMONSTRATING ACTIVISM   133

new purpose—to investigate the killing. That's when he discovered that "this seemingly idyllic island was being destroyed by the same people in power who were meant to be protecting it."[2] This was also when he discovered a small group of activists who were risking their lives to try to stop the destruction. During the course of his reporting, he formed relationships with Bobby Chan, Tata Balladares, and Nieves Roseto—three land defenders and activists in Palawan—who have been at the frontlines of the battle against climate change in the Philippines for years. Bobby is an environmental lawyer and leader of the group, Tata often leads patrols in the area, and Nieves is the mayor of Palawan's main tourist town.

Land defenders were, and still are, being killed in record numbers around the world. Reports estimate that more than 2,000 environmental defenders have been killed in the last decade, though the total figure is likely much higher, with the Philippines consistently ranking as the most dangerous country in Asia for land defenders. Thus, the struggles that Bobby, Tata, and Nieves face are the same kind of battles being fought in Mexico, Brazil, Colombia, Cambodia, and elsewhere in the world. After meeting with the group, Malakunas wrote an 800-word article for AFP about their struggle; the article helped raise some attention, but then it quickly fell off the radar. Then, a few years later, he turned his reporting into a multimedia story— including a 4-minute video, a 1,200-word article and photos, for AFP, which was distributed to the agency's hundreds of media clients around the world. The four-minute video for AFP helped him to generate some attention, which led to new opportunities to secure some funding and partners to turn what had become more of a "passion project" into a longer-form professional documentary. Up until then, he had filmed dozens of hours of shaky, hand-held footage and interviews, but he said he didn't "have the resources, skills or experience to make a documentary." He believed the story needed a more intimate and up-close approach than wire journalism allows—one that could help audiences to better understand and connect with the stakes and risks of the story, in a way that was more similar to the way he had come to experience and learn from the lives of the activists at the center of the struggle.

> For me, going in depth would be going on a mission somewhere and spending a month in a place where there's a conflict or natural disaster or something like that. So I've done a lot of that over the years, lived in multiple countries around the world. But I've always had an urge to try and do something a bit deeper. Do something that I felt could be more impactful.

134 RADICAL REALITY

> I guess on the bigger picture, I'd hoped that a documentary would have a more meaningful impact than daily journalism; that would be diving deep with these incredible people and that I would be able to really do justice to their heroism. And I really felt that what I was feeling when I was seeing them could be transferred to an international or even a Filipino audience much more powerfully than with an 800-word article or with a four-minute video.... I really felt driven when I met Bobby and Tata and then Nieves. They were very special people. And this was a way for me to be able to do my bit in a more powerful manner.[3]

This endeavor to tell a fuller story of the land defenders in Palawan became the documentary *Delikado*, released in 2022 by POV, the documentary strand on US public television. The film won an Emmy for Outstanding Investigative Documentary, and Malakunas was also awarded with the Walkley Award, Australia's version of a Pulitzer, for Best Documentary. *Delikado* follows the three environmental defenders as they struggle to save their homeland from the illegal destruction of its forests, fisheries, and mountains. At the core of Malakunas's decision to expand his reporting into documentary was the feeling that it would allow him to help audiences understand a story with a level of depth and sensory detail that daily journalism is rarely capable of providing. He felt that by demonstrating the activism at the heart of their struggle—why they cared so much, how it affected them, and how they were resisting—then, as the reasoning went, more people would be able to gain a greater understanding of not only the issues at the heart of the film but also the activist movement that was beneath them, including how they could support it. As the cultural historian and American media and communications scholar James Carey once put it: daily journalism can deliver the "whos" and "whats" of the world, but it often leaves much to be desired when it comes to the "hows" and "whys" of culture and the issues beneath the headlines.[4] It was precisely this disconnect that prompted Malakunas to turn to documentary.

Just months after its release, Malakunas said that the film's impact has already manifested in several ways, including in breaking through the stereotypes that people in the Philippines and region hold about Palawan. When people in the Philippines want to go on a vacation, they often think of Palawan, reiterated Malakunas, with its limestone cliffs and blue waters. But *Delikado* is helping people to see what is happening behind the idyllic curtain, and to form greater understandings of their complicity and the

Image 6.1 Description: *Delikado*: Tata Balladares rests on a fallen tree while searching for illegal loggers in forests of southern Palawan, Rizal, Palawan—April 2018. Photo Credit: Karl Malakunas.

Image 6.2 Description: *Delikado*: Tata Balladares and other PNNI para-enforcers walk through a patch of destroyed forest. *Delikado*: Photo Credit: Delikado LLC.

136 RADICAL REALITY

oppressive, violent actions their money and silence is supporting, so that they can make more informed decisions. Perhaps of even greater significance, by demonstrating the activism of these land defenders, Malakunas said that he is witnessing coalition building in real time as audiences express feeling emboldened, after community screenings, by seeing others in their country successfully fighting for change.

> It's happening in almost every community in the Philippines. Anyone who's taking on powerful interests, whether it's those that are plundering the land or engaging in other corrupt activities, people are getting killed for taking on those powerful interests. It's one of the most dangerous countries in the world to be a land defender, one of the most dangerous countries in the world to be a journalist, one of the most dangerous countries in the world to be a judge. And when we are showing this film, one of the most incredible things we hear is: "Oh wow, we're not alone. It's not just us."[5]

In a small community screening with Indigenous land defenders in the Malaysian island of Borneo, Malakunas said that people expressed overwhelming emotional responses from seeing activists like them being represented as heroines: "That's my fight. This is exactly what I'm doing," people said to him. The *Delikado* film and impact team placed considerable emphasis on hosting small community screenings—including in schools and universities across the country. Malakunas said that watching audiences, especially young audiences, engage with the climate challenge through the film, and feel empowered by the heroism of the activists at the center of it, has been one of the most meaningful experiences of his professional life. "Just their eyes and the expressions on their face," he said. "To me, that's the impact."[6]

But the film has also led to several other major actions. At the global level, in addition to screenings and circulating petitions, Malakunas and his film team partnered with the environmental organization Global Witness to help activate support for European Union legislation that will hold European companies accountable for the environmental abuses that their companies or subsidiaries are committing in the Philippines and elsewhere. The influential International NGO also invited Malakunas to Thailand to screen the film and address the Human Rights Commission and environmental defenders from around the Asia-Pacific. The day before we spoke for this book, in the summer of 2023, Malakunas had also just received an email

DEMONSTRATING ACTIVISM   137

Image 6.3 Description: *Delikado*: The film's participants receiving a standing ovation at the Philippine premiere of the film to a full house of 1,500 people in Manila in 2022. Copyright Delikado LLC.

Image 6.4 Description: *Delikado*: The film's participants receiving a standing ovation at the Philippine premiere of the film to a full house of 1,500 people in Manila in 2022. Copyright Delikado LLC.

138 RADICAL REALITY

from Al Gore's influential Climate Reality Project, which shared their plans to make community and strategic screenings of *Delikado* a core part of their three-year strategic plan to engage communities around the Philippines on issues of climate change and justice. The film team has also helped activists in the film with connections, including facilitating meetings between them and the British ambassador, and other government officials, for support and protection.

At the same time, Malakunas said that every step of the filmmaking process brought massive challenges. Over the last decade, he has come to expect the risks and barriers of working in an authoritarian country, so he knew that he would need to take extreme precautions to safeguard the participants of the film and those on the film team. But what Malakunas hadn't anticipated being as much of an issue was the politics of funding and distributing the film. While *Delikado* was fortunate enough to receive early financial support from foundations, including from ITVS, Doc Society (which also provided vital legal support), the Bertha Foundation, and the Sundance Institute, Malakunas said that making *Delikado* opened his eyes to how difficult it is to finance a film that critiques power. Even with the privilege of foundational grants, he would not have been able to complete the film if he didn't keep his position with AFP as a day job. The struggle for funding also carried over to the world of distribution, which brought some disturbing insights into the machinery of commercial media today, even for a veteran journalist like Malakunas. Before securing a distributor in POV/American Documentary, Malakunas said that his team had discussions with several commercial streamers, only to learn of their concerns that the activist work at the center of the film would threaten their business relationships with the authoritarian country at the center of the film.

> We were looking at engaging with streamers and I was at one industry event, one of the pitching events, and we met with one of the streamers, and she said, "Well, if you have a film on Imelda Marcos's shoes, I'd be interested. But we're not going to go near such a touchstone issue like [Indigenous land defenders]. It would endanger our Philippine market." . . . Well, our jaw dropped.[7]

Getting commercial network distribution in the Philippines was also a challenge. The country's media landscape has been demolished under its former president Rodrigo Duterte, Malakunas said, and his team found that "it's not in the business interests of anyone in the Philippines, who own the commercial venues and the media outlets, to show this story."[8] Difficulties over distribution also limited the film team's ability to safely screen the documentary in locations where some of the film's participants were expecting it to be made freely available;[9] such tensions around distribution expectations, between Malakunas and some of the film's participants, point to the importance of filmmakers supporting and establishing clear "duty of care" frameworks and explicit agreements of understanding with the communities centered in documentaries before filming even begins (a vital approach discussed in Chapter 7).

Despite the barriers, the impact and value that *Delikado* has had in elevating the stories of the activists in Philippines has exceeded anything that Malakunas imagined for his career, and the experience has exceeded what he thinks could have been possible had he continued to tell the story of climate justice only through daily journalism.

> I'm going to go into the office now and will work for the next ten hours on all the daily news that's happening around Asia Pacific. And I'm in charge of 220 people around the region and we're running, whether it's the Typhoon that's going to hit India and Pakistan tomorrow. We're following up on [Antony] Blinken's visit to Beijing on the weekend. And it's a voom! It's a whir and it keeps us so busy. And it's so important for us to be able to be that frontline of information around the world. And I really love that, and I feel very committed to that. And, yet, I can also see the incredible power of this film. I've had nothing like it in my journalism career.[10]

At nearly every juncture in history where justice and equity are expanded, we see the work of activists as they create networks and inspire others, changing political systems along the way, for better or worse.[11] The making of *Delikado* touches on documentary's unique power in providing activists with a greater platform, telling fuller stories about their cause and the risks they face, helping them to build a larger profile among high-level officials and organizations (which can, sometimes, help them to access greater security), countering narratives that seek to criminalize or disrupt their work by reframing it as inspirational and heroic, and centering activist solutions and objectives, among other roles. These themes are all centered and

140 RADICAL REALITY

further expanded upon in this chapter, which aims to spotlight the work of documentaries that demonstrate activism and activists—individual people who find themselves in extraordinary times, called or forced to stand up against injustice and fight for their families and communities—along with some of the challenges, contradictions, and opportunities of this function of documentary today. At the same time, the making of *Delikado* also speaks to part of a longer history of documentary filmmaking—an old, yet still prevailing, trend of filmmakers from more distant countries traveling to territories that have been underrepresented in the media ecosystem and endeavoring to tell the stories of communities they are not from. This history informs the relationships, approach, decisions, and experiences of all the filmmakers spotlighted in this chapter; and it reflects a context that should be recognized by any exploration of the role of documentary historically, and today.

Nearly every film in this book could be categorized as a film that demonstrates activism. And while many of the films in this chapter are recent examples of the experiences, triumphs, and challenges of filmmakers who endeavor to use the power of film to expose injustice and advance or spotlight the work of activists around the world, the tradition of activism in documentary filmmaking hearkens back for many decades. The work of documentaries in shaping activist histories, framing and advancing social justice movements and agendas, centering underrepresented communities and those from oppressive systems of colonialism, occupation and authoritarianism, and in reimagining identity and notions of global citizenship, to name a few roles, have long been the focus of studies, books, academic courses, celebration, and critique within filmmaking communities.[12] In other words, beyond its artistic and creative elements, the function of documentary film as vehicles for activism and change—through the stories it tells onscreen and the strategic engagements it inspires afterward—has long been a popular topic of conversation in media studies and activism circles.

Work that references the activist roots of documentary film often does so as either a celebration or a warning—directing attention to its long track record of work with good intentions or its colonial past and history as tools for intervention, oppression, and manipulation by groups that wish to extend their dominance.[13] While it is important to spotlight documentaries that are doing the work of social justice and activism well, it is the position of the authors that the warnings of the latter group also strongly merit greater deliberation than they have yet received. As the renowned filmmaker Raoul Peck once noted on the power of film: "Movies, as innocent as they might appear, are vehicles for ideology, for politics, for culture, for merchandise."[14] The very nature of film and storytelling means that every documentary serves to advocate for a certain way of seeing or understanding the world. The vital films of Raoul Peck, for instance, have not only helped expose the history and lingering impact of racism and colonialism in the United States and around the world, they have also drawn attention to the power of film as a tool for building—and correcting—the narratives through which one comes to understand the very society and country in which they live (a topic that is expanded on in Chapter 7, "Creating Spaces for Reconciliation and Healing.") In this way, films always demonstrate a form of activism whether the audience knows it or not.

Consequently, to celebrate the history of activism in documentary without also addressing the colonial roots through which film has also been used to harm, demean, and repress communities would be to misappropriate and deny the very roots of activism and role of documentary film in many places in the world today.[15] In a study of the work of Cameroonian filmmaker Jean-Marie Teno, film scholar Olivier J. Tchouaffe discusses the role of documentary as both a tool of the colonizer and of the formerly colonized.[16] Tchouaffe argues that it is essential to understand that "ethics in documentary stands to rupture with the naive notion of objectivity in order to confront the complex notion that documentary making is not immune from the compromises of power and, thus, can become quickly deficient in ethics."[17] To understand the work of many African filmmakers working in documentaries today, like Teno, Tchouaffe asserts that it is necessary to know the long history of injustice and colonialism that documentaries made by Western filmmakers helped perpetuate, through which Africans were "used as props for colonial propaganda" and as subjects to advance the objectives of Western powers. Tchouaffee writes of an "anti-documentary" perspective through which filmmakers of former colonies are now working to decolonize images and harmful representations of their communities—manufactured and disseminated by documentary filmmakers of the past—by:

> taking advantage of the tools and techniques of the documentary to interrogate processes in which they were documented, produced, humiliated, and alienated by the colonizers and the ethical necessity to answer back and express a more legitimate representation of blackness in terms of

142 RADICAL REALITY

history, memory, and Indigenous democratic cultural and political codes to midwife new ways of being and new ways of seeing.[18]

As the work of Tchouaffe suggests, documentaries have a long history of both oppressing and liberating communities.

This historical foregrounding—which is distinct and expressed differently depending on the country and region of the world—raises the importance of always considering "activism for whom?" in the context of documentary, interrogating how power and perspective is shared or subverted by the filmmaker, and understanding that the ethics and practices of documentary are both still actively evolving and hold lingering historic imbalances, social ills and inequities. This understanding serves as the foundation for this chapter's exploration of the intersection of documentary and activism today, and how the filmmakers of four films navigated a range of issues, including storytelling power, ideology, journalistic convention, and market pressures, in pursuit of activist and social justice goals.

In summary, while the *intent* of filmmakers is often the prevailing lens through which activism in documentary film is observed, this chapter endeavors to shift greater focus toward the specific *practices* that are being used, and to interrogate the degree to which filmmakers are changing old patterns and transferring *power* to the activists portrayed in their film and the activists' goals, preferred frames, and visions. Through these films, this chapter also examines why activism matters in a global context, and it unpacks the inside machinations and influence of documentaries that seek to do more than simply show activism at work, but which endeavor to use film as a tool for the advancement of activist work, including by centering activist stories and recasting them as leaders and heroines, lifting up activist solutions, correcting stereotyped portrayals, and contributing to and building social movements for underrepresented and historically disenfranchised communities.

Centering Activist Stories and Recasting Them as Leaders and Heroines

Within the context of activism, advocacy generally means to take a position and assert it. And that is just what filmmaker Alex Pritz realized he would need to do. The decision to center the experiences of a small group of activists at the heart of the story, rather than trying to filter them through a both-sides journalistic lens or place them in a larger global context, was one of the most transformational shifts that took place while making the film *The Territory*, said its filmmaker Pritz. The film documents the struggle of the Indigenous Uru-eu-wau-wau people in Brazil, as they work to resist encroaching deforestation from the hands of farmers and illegal settlers in the Brazilian Amazon who are extracting resources and illegally burning and clearing protected Indigenous land. The film, shortlisted for Best Documentary Feature honors at the 2023 Academy Awards, was partially shot by Uru-eu-wau-wau community members themselves and utilizes vérité footage captured over three years, providing an intimate look at a community fighting for their land and against harmful media narratives in order to share the truth of their situation with audiences.

Pritz has a background in journalism and conceded that he discovered early on in the process of filming that the traditional journalistic approach and way of working was only distancing him from the experiences and perspectives of the Indigenous community at the heart of the film. One of the most consequential moments during the filmmaking process, Pritz recalled, came when he decided to stop trying to report on the climate struggle in Brazil, and to instead collaborate with a core group of activists whose lives demonstrated the implications of the climate crisis, and to give them the power to tell the story the way they felt it needed to be told.

> I came in with the idea that I was going to make a film about this [climate change] situation and that evolved over time to making a film with people about their own situation. And I think that was a really important shift, not just in terms of what the impact of the film would be or any of that, but even on the creative side. I think the perspective shift occurs when I stopped trying to put myself in the shoes of an Uru-eu-wau-wau person who's fighting for their home, and let the Uru-eu-wau-wau people describe firsthand what that is like. I think that's the type of thing that is hard to do in other parts of the news or journalism world—to collaborate with people in that deep of a way.[19]

This approach to storytelling meant that the film wouldn't be able to represent some perspectives as equally as others. And Pritz says he wrestled with the fact that he was knowingly collaborating with a specific group of Indigenous activists, since their perspectives had long been underrecognized

144 RADICAL REALITY

and disempowered by the mainstream media in Brazil, rather than with the settler farmers or other oppositional groups in the film.

> We were trying to be fair to the situation as we saw it and that meant understanding that the Uru-eu-wau-wau had been so deeply disempowered in the media, and that these White settlers were also really disadvantaged and poor, marginalized people, but at least within the media landscape, they were the hegemonic power. So we didn't feel the same obligation to collaborate with them as coproducers of the film as we did with the Uru-eu-wau-wau.[20]

The move to collaborate with the Uru-eu-wau-wau community and activists in the film also meant hiring and paying Indigenous cinematographers, and it meant centering the community's visions and objectives for impact—including how they wanted the story in the film to unfold and what they wanted it to achieve after it was complete.

The film team received financial and advisory support from organizations including Doc Society and Luminate, which prompted them to contemplate their plans for impact early, and to hire an impact producer, Marianna Olinger, a Brazilian activist. Support from outside partners was critical, they say, in allowing the film to be possible, especially since former President Bolsonaro had gutted Brazil's state budgets for anything that supported independent film or the arts, including the Brazilian film agency Ancine. With Olinger's support, the film team connected with more than 80 partners in an effort to embed its work within the broader indigenous movement in Brazil and to ensure that activists could use the film to also bring funding and support to their work in a way that would be helpful.

After several collaborative discussions with Uru-eu-wau-wau community members, the film identified a set of impact priorities, all of which centered around the goals of amplifying Indigenous voices, protecting Indigenous territory, and advancing strategic policies. Among their concerted efforts, they collectively pushed—through high-level advocacy, screenings, and targeted meetings with business leaders, government ministers and lawmakers—for the EU anti-deforestation law, which banned the import of beef, soy, leather, and a range of products that were linked to illegal deforestation (the resolution has since been adopted with European Parliament members referencing *The Territory* film and Uru-eu-wau-wau people as influencing their vote). In addition, one of the most important objectives shared by the Uru-eu-wau-wau community was the desire to ensure that they would be involved in editing the film and shaping their own media narratives after it was completed. The film team worked with Uru-eu-wau-wau collaborators to create a multimedia and cultural facility in their territory, which involved using timber that was reclaimed from illegal loggers, shipping in new media equipment, and ultimately providing a space for the community "to tell their own story, in whatever form, moving forwards."[21] This also meant translating the film and its impact website into Tupi Kagwahiva, the language of the Uru-eu-wau-wau community, which is spoken by less than 1,000 people in the world, making it the first film to ever be accessible in the Kagwahiva language.

The film found a major distributor in Disney and National Geographic, but the team had to limit much of its community-level engagement because of the distributor's activism-weary stance, including prohibiting community impact screenings after a three-month window. Given the relatively short time frame, Pritz and the film's partners worked quickly to organize about 150 impact screenings throughout the Indigenous territories of Brazil, and they were able to foster several community-level discussions, before they had to halt the efforts after three months. And, even though it was a central goal of the filmmakers to ensure that the film was made available before Brazil's October 2022 election, given that illegal deforestation and destruction of protected Indigenous land had expanded under far-right President Jair Bolsonaro, the distributors decided to avoid any potential controversy by limiting the film to a theatrical release and not making it available for streaming in Brazil until December (after the country's election and after Bolsonaro had left office and the new president, Lula da Silva, had been inaugurated). The film team also needed to be careful with any perception that they had an activist agenda, since that was something that their distributors warned against. As a result, the film team couldn't emphasize their role in pushing for things like the EU deforestation law, for instance, or other initiatives that served the interests of the Indigenous community in the film.[22]

Centering Activist Solutions and Overcoming Stereotyped Portrayals

When she started working on the film *Thank You for the Rain*, impact producer Emily Wanja said, she never would have guessed that she would be helping to build a dam months later. But that's exactly what happened.[23]

146   RADICAL REALITY

The film *Thank You for the Rain*, released in 2017, centers around Kenyan farmer Kisilu Musya, who uses his camera to capture the harm and challenges that climate change is posing to his family and rural community. Over a five-year period, the film follows Kisilu as the urgency of changing environmental conditions compels him to take on more of a leadership role in his community and motivates him to advocate for their interest in global climate events. In southeast Kenya, Kisilu films his struggle to grow mango trees and crops like cassava on his farm, for instance, which faces drought and flooding over a period of months, due to increasingly unpredictable weather. A camera, held by codirector Julia Dahr, also follows Kisilu as he organizes community meetings to help other farmers better understand the challenges they face and explore solutions together.

Wanja said that one of the important steps the film team took was in making sure that their work was anchored to the interests of the activist, Kisilu, at the center of the film and with his local organization. They wanted to ensure the film served the solutions that local community members had already identified to the climate struggles at the heart of the film, and to ensure that the film was in service to those solutions. This included asking the community which people and organizations they thought could be helpful to their efforts, along with whom they have struggled to reach/connect with in the past. And then they worked to make sure that these key actors were present at impact events so that a space could be created for those conversations, relationship-building, and engagements to take place.[24]

Wanja said it was important for them to avoid "reinventing the wheel" by going through parallel conversations of community needs and solutions that were held apart from the already existing efforts taking place in the community.[25]

> So it was always just trying to find out: what is the community working on? What are the immediate challenges? And what's standing between them and the solution? And then trying to map out which stakeholders are on the ground and [asking] why is there still a problem? Why is our community still facing these challenges?[26]

For the *Thank You for the Rain* team, early community conversations around solution-building were critical in building out a blueprint for impact. In this way, Wanja and her team were able to identify a set of community priorities and then match funding and partner organizations to those priorities (rather than the other way around). There can be a tendency to quickly zoom out, once national or international partners enter a room, Wanja said, and so they worked to pause at every funder or distributor meeting to ask, "Who are we serving?" If the answer was anyone other than the community, then that meant that they had lost their center.

> Our [marker of] success was: have we at least been able to walk with the community from one point to the next? . . . Have we at least been able to make that step [of the filmmaking and distribution process] with the community? And is that how they see it?[27]

This also meant ensuring that community activists, especially Kisilu, were placed at the front of the table in conversations the film attracted with high-ranking organizations and officials around climate change; ensuring that they weren't simply the focus of the film or its poster, but that they were given opportunities to lead conversations with key partners. As a result, the film paid for Kisilu to travel to more than 20 countries as part of the film's screenings and engagement efforts.

> Especially for international screenings, it was important for Kisilu to be there, because we understood that local communities and activists, especially those at the front line of climate change, are mostly left out in key climate events, where major negotiations are taking place. A lot of times they've not been involved. And when they have been involved, they have been seen, but not heard; it's not been meaningful participation. We knew from the beginning, any screening in any key climate event, Kisilu has to be there.[28]

Centering the solutions of Kisilu and the community also meant supporting the local-level work that they needed to take place, including supporting the construction of earth dams and irrigation projects, using funds raised by the film. While the idea that the film team would be helping to construct a dam was surprising at first, that effort has changed lives, recalled Wanja, by supporting livestock, sustainably providing water for over 300 families, and nourishing their farms. The film team also set up a fund so that people could make direct donations to support Kisilu's climate organization and activist work; funding continues to come from the film's audiences, more than six years after it was released. The film has been screened, and is still used, in hundreds of secondary schools and community gatherings across the country. After traveling with the film to community meetings across Kenya, Wanja said that she observed how effective the medium of documentary is in tapping into the long tradition of oral learning in her country, which has long served as a popular way stories are told and knowledge is shared—a powerful attribute of film that is rarely recognized in conversations around documentary, but centrally important to their power to help people to look at things in different ways and expand understandings.

When someone thinks of a climate activist, they might not think of someone like Kisilu, a dedicated father and farmer in a rural region of Kenya, said Wanja. But it's this level of intersectionality and complexity that she believes documentaries are capable of providing to audiences, allowing them to see a fuller picture of an activist's life, which goes beyond people's preconceived notions of who they are and what they do.[29] In doing so, the film has also helped Kisilu to find other activists who share similar stories or causes around climate justice—inspiring a level of recognition and coalition-building that would have been very unlikely without the film.

Image 6.5 Description: *Thank You for the Rain*: Kisilu Musya leaves Christina Wayua Kisilu. Photos credit: Julie Lillesæter. Copyright Banyak Films & Differ Media 2017.

Image 6.6 Description: *Thank You for the Rain*: Kisilu Musya at the "red line" protest in Paris. Photos credit: Julie Lillesæter. Copyright Banyak Films & Differ Media 2017.

Using Documentaries to Contribute to and Build Movements

> I believe that film is one of the pieces of how movement work happens—in helping to shape people's imaginations about what's possible. . . . There are many people who work in the corporate sector or the entertainment sector who want to do good. They just don't know which groups or how or what to do.
>
> —Tracy Sturdivant[30]

By empowering and lifting up the stories and platforms of community leaders at the heart of the two-part documentary series *And She Could Be Next*, which follows a defiant movement led by women of color political candidates and organizers in the United States, the film team endeavored to bring power to their local movements and to make women of color leaders more visible in public discourse so that they could receive greater recognition and ultimately inspire more people to follow their lead.

Beyond the stories of Rashida Tlaib, Stacey Abrams, and the other inspiring political leaders who are featured, the film places women of color

150 RADICAL REALITY

organizers, who facilitate and sustain political engagement and civic organizing in the United States, front and center. Since these organizers are often the "unseen heroes," said producer Jyoti Sarda, the film team decided early on that featuring these local activists and organizers was one way for the film to have the greatest impact.[31] This creative decision informed all subsequent stages of their approach in their release of the film, from the speakers and organizations who engaged in screening events, to the art work they used to feature the film, to the partners, goals, and strategies of their screening and engagement efforts. This decision was also informed by an early consultation held between the filmmakers and other cultural organizations that are aligned with using storytelling for social change, including the Pop Culture Collective, a philanthropic resource and funder organization dedicated to supporting pop culture creators in their pursuit of social justice goals. As part of these early consultations, the film team learned about the work of impact veteran Tracy Sturdivant and her organization called The League, a team of strategists, organizers, storytellers, advocates, and creators who work with media, brands, and social movements on creating positive change in their communities.

Sturdivant and The League worked with the *And She Could Be Next* film team to create the film's organizing phrase, "there's an organizer in all of us," which came to embody the spirit of the film's distribution and marketing drive to use the film to inspire more women of color to join organizing efforts in the country. Sturdivant and the film team then identified three ways that the film could help advance the mission of the activists it features: (1) to inspire women of color to "step into their own power" through civic actions; (2) to shift narratives around women of color leadership; (3) and to spotlight and support women of color organizers. This meant using the film to not only spark wider civic engagement, but to also help build an intersectional movement of women of color leaders and organizers across the country.

While traditional film screenings can be important, Sturdivant said, they don't always attract a diverse audience in the United States. As a result, they focused on connecting the film's main participants with targeted media outlets, and they used digital platforms that got their story in front of wider audiences. At the core, their objective centered around aligning engagement strategies with the audiences they wanted to mobilize for change.[32] One tactic involved building cross-partnerships and corporate outreach with funders and organizations that are typically outside of the norm for documentaries. This meant pursuing several partnerships that are not typically associated with documentary, ranging from a major beauty supplies brand to a big computer technology company, which gave them campaign printers to give to organizers in several states so they could print out voter registration forms, on the promise that they didn't reveal the name of their company publicly.

Sturdivant said that working within and around political sensitivities to get things done has long been part of activist work, and it's no different with documentaries. Rather than being taken by surprise, the film team worked to turn moments of resistance and political discomfort to the advantage of the film, including when they were faced with efforts by distributors to neutralize or quiet the activist leanings of the film, for instance. When this happened, the film and impact teams worked to make their messages and content louder. As Sturdivant recalled:

> We ran into some bumpy roads because there were a handful of women in the film who were running for reelection and some of the local broadcast affiliates didn't want to air the film until after the election, or after certain periods of time, or they only wanted to run it late at night because they didn't want to have to deal with equal time with other candidates. A lot of that was driven by politics at the end of the day. And so there were some periods of time, where we're like, "Let's burn it all down" . . . But then [we asked], "How do we utilize this to our advantage?"[33]

After the public broadcasters tried to delay the release of the film, Sturdivant and the film team made noise around the distributor's political hesitation.

> [We told our audiences:] "Here's the film that Georgia Public Broadcasting doesn't want you to see." And then we created the local narratives around that. So, one of the things that we did was we got a group of micro influencers, people on social media who have followings of 10,000 people or more to be a part of helping us to promote the film and to get people to watch. And these were folks who weren't necessarily political, but who had large followings and an audience of people who they could have a conversation with about why the election was so important.[34]

The importance of long-term movement building was essential for the impact and film team, so much so that they worked to share extra resources, footage, media packages, and funding to allied organizations. This included

152 RADICAL REALITY

sharing footage that didn't make it into the film, but which the producers thought could be useful to the organizations and movement. As Jyoti Sarda put it:

> During the last bit of our campaign, we took some money—because we didn't spend all of it—and we picked some organizations that are reflected in the film, and we gave them an unencumbered stipend. And then we also took a lot of clips that we thought were really interesting and illustrative, and content that we thought could be useful to other people, and we organized them, tagged them, put them online, and then pushed them out to the organizations. We basically said, this is yours. If you want it, use it in whatever way you see fit.[35]

Leaving Norms and Taking Sides

If the practices and conventions of traditional journalism were defined largely through their capacity to protect news audiences from the biases, perspectives, and hopes of any one individual,[36] the practices and conventions of the nonfiction filmmakers in this chapter can be determined by their ability to move audiences toward identifying and grappling with the specific biases, perspectives, and hopes of the individuals at the center of the story. And, in so doing, this chapter reveals how documentaries are working to provide new ways into stories that audiences thought they already knew, to spotlight the work of activists and communities who have long been minimized or pushed to the margins of news coverage and social discourse, and to help audiences better understand the urgency and motivations of the activists they feature. While many of the filmmakers were quick to point out the continued importance of daily news reporting in alerting wider audiences to important stories and events, they also emphasized the disproportionate power that such reporting continues to have over public understandings of key social issues. The choice to create a creative, independent documentary, outside of the norms and expectations of a news institution or field of traditional journalistic practice, liberated the filmmakers of this chapter to focus their attention on creating a story that best reflected the realities, experiences, and—perhaps most importantly—the vision of the activists and communities at the center of their film. Ultimately, the filmmakers were motivated by an ambition that decades of legacy news conventions and routines have functioned to safeguard against: *the desire to take sides.*

The films featured here purposefully center the stories and experiences of activists from their own perspective, without the distancing frames of neutrality, objectivity, or other vestigial conventions of traditional journalism that have historically filtered stories for media audiences. In some cases, this meant handing the camera over to the activists at the heart of the story (in the case of *The Territory* and *Thank You for the Rain*), or at least using the intimate lens of documentary to raise the profile of the activists and the urgency of their work (in the case of *Delikado* and *And She Could Be Next*). And, for every film, it meant using the form of documentary to help bring wider understanding and support to the social justice work of the activists featured.

At the same time, to end this chapter on a discussion of journalistic norms—while helpful in understanding the distinct value and conventions of evolving filmmaking practices and ethics around telling activist stories—would risk overstating the theoretical underpinnings of this exploration. Of greater consequence to the field of documentary, media scholars and filmmakers alike, are the constraints and expectations of government, commercial, and societal powers that continue to threaten and censor documentaries that lift up activist work today. And it is precisely these instances of censorship and pushback that perhaps best express the power and promise of documentary, including its ability to disrupt oppressive systems and policies and meaningfully advance the work of movements and activists that are pushing for change.

While the environmental justice focus of the film *Thank You For the Rain* did not immediately ring alarm bills inside the halls of Kenya's censors, for instance, other films that center more controversial issues—especially around LGBTQ+ stories—continue to be met with strong resistance in Kenya, and in other countries around the world. Just three years after the film *Rafiki*, a fictional story about a lesbian couple, was banned in Kenya, the documentary *I Am Samuel* met the same fate. Filmed in a vérité style over the course of five years, *I Am Samuel* shares the story of a working-class Kenyan couple—Samuel Asilikwa and his partner Alex—who face persecution, violence, and rejection in the country's capital city of Nairobi simply for being gay. The country's law criminalizes homosexuality with up to 14 years in prison if convicted, making it just one of about 64 countries with laws that criminalize homosexuality around the world today.

The filmmaker behind *I Am Samuel*, Peter Murimi, said that a central objective of the film was to help a community of people—primarily queer people from a lower-income class—to see their experience, struggle, and triumphant love represented on screen for the first time. Murimi said that being queer in Kenya is difficult no matter who you are. "Whether there are cameras there or not, [queer people] are attacked and beaten," he said, and the opening scene of the film includes footage of one such horrific act of violence.[37] However, the experiences of being queer and rich are different from being queer and poor:

> If you're middle class and wealthy, that buys you some protection because your house is isolated, you have a bigger compound and you can be who you are within confines. But if you're poor, like Samuel and the majority of gay men in Kenya, it's more difficult because you're living in confined spaces so it's hard to keep a secret. And if people find out, the results can be fatal.[38]

Murimi said that what it means to be gay and poor in Kenya has long been missing from media and film portrayals, and so he felt it was important to help "get that narrative out—not just for Samuel and the general public's information, but more so for queer people who have never seen themselves on a screen or as part of Kenya."[39] For this reason, Murimi said that having the film accessible—for free—to Kenyans was more important than its recognition by international film festivals or audiences outside of the country. However, in September of 2021, shortly after the film was released, the Kenya Film and Classification Board (KFCB) blocked the film from being seen, exhibited, distributed, or in anyone's possession, referring to it as a "clear and deliberate attempt by the producer to promote same-sex marriage as an acceptable way of life."[40] The board called the documentary "an affront to our culture and identity" and warned that anyone who attempts to find or watch the film will be met with harsh consequences. Similarly, documentaries and films with gay protagonists or content that depicts LGBTQ+ activists and communities in a positive light have recently been banned in countries around the world, including in Australia, Singapore, Russia, Saudi Arabia, Pakistan, New Zealand, Iran, China, Romania, Malaysia, Qatar, Oman, Bahrain, Jordan, Kuwait, United Arab Emirates, India, and the United States.

And, yet, people in Kenya are still finding the film and pushing for change. And Murimi continues to give interviews and speak about the film on podcasts, radio programs, and venues across the country, hoping that the documentary will help activists continue their push for change and encourage allied communities to not be silent.

> There's a strong, organised and vibrant movement in Nairobi who are giving people safe houses and legal aid. Rather than giving up and going into hiding, they're fighting for their space and saying "we're here, we're as Kenyan as you, and we want our space." As a storyteller, I hope my film contributes to that movement.[41]

Murimi said that documentaries can help bring important experiences and topics to the mainstream, and they can help overcome stereotypes. And thus, they can help to break down stigma and preconceived notions that are limiting understanding and impeding progress.

> If you're queer in Kenya people want to put you in a box and they expect you to behave a certain way, but we have shown someone like Samuel: very religious, as African as you can get, even his politics leans towards the conservative, but also he's gay. And he's allowed to be all these things. There are so many elements in his life that people can connect to, and you hope that can bring these new connections and people can look beyond his sexual orientation. So I think the film can do that in a beautiful way, bring this connection.... The more that is done the more it brings it a little bit into the mainstream, not in the periphery. And that maybe can help bring change. [It will happen] slowly, but hopefully it will be helpful.[42]

If the underlying thrust of all the films spotlighted in this chapter could be summarized into a single idea, then it might come close to this aspiration from Murimi: documentaries are not only serving to lift up the experiences of activists today, they are also endeavoring to contribute to the movements they advance. In other words, the role of the documentary filmmaker featured here is not to make a film about a movement, it's to support a movement with a film. As such, social justice isn't merely the focus of documentaries that demonstrate activism, it is often the objective.

7

Creating Spaces for Reconciliation and Healing

"Can we just take a moment to weep?"

This question came from a community participant the morning after a screening of the film *Always in Season* in Durham, North Carolina, during one of several community screenings and discussions organized by the authors and a collective of community facilitators.[1] The discussions were aimed at better understanding how (and if) independent documentaries are trusted by local communities and how they are shaping conversations about the social issues they address.[2]

Always in Season explores the lingering impact of more than a century of lynching African Americans in the United States. The film connects this form of historic racial terrorism to racial violence today through the tragic story of Lennon Lacy, a Black teenager who was found hanging from a swing set in Bladenboro, North Carolina, on August 29, 2014. Despite several inconsistencies in how his death was investigated, local officials and media quickly ruled Lennon's death a suicide, although his mother, Claudia, and several others in the community, believe Lennon was lynched. The film features Claudia's fight for justice for her son.

Even though no one at the Durham screening event expressed knowing Lennon or his family, several people said that the hard truths and emotions that the film exposed through his story resonated with their experience. One person said that they could feel these truths "in my body" after the screening. That is why, before the conversation proceeded any further, another community participant asked if they could all pause and simply cry together.[3]

This issue is not simply under-covered, it is a painful reality that has been grossly misrepresented and silenced by government policies, national and local institutions, and news organizations, for decades. And while the

Radical Reality. Caty Borum and David Conrad-Pérez, Oxford University Press. © Oxford University Press 2025.
DOI: 10.1093/9780197604298.003.0007

CREATING SPACES FOR RECONCILIATION AND HEALING   157

meticulously researched film tells a corrective history and fuller story of the legacy of lynching, it also demonstrates the distinctive ability of documentary to open up community conversations and spaces for interrogation and healing in ways that many people expressed having never experienced before.

In the independent community study we facilitated along with the film's director,[4] seven geographically, socially, and politically diverse communities were selected across the country—in Herkimer, New York; Concord, New Hampshire; Albuquerque, New Mexico; Bristol, Tennessee; Carbondale, Illinois; Twin Falls, Idaho; and Durham, North Carolina. In each community, the film *Always in Season* was screened for a diverse audience, followed by a survey and a two-hour community focus group conversation. The results were surprising. Among the findings, participants in every community shared a strong belief that local and national media outlets were "failing us" and that uncomfortable truths were being hidden from them.[5] They expressed a range of emotions—from sadness and shame to outrage and frustration—about not knowing more about cases of racial violence and suspicious suicides across the country, and a feeling that they are missing other critical stories important to them and their community. Community audiences also frequently noted feeling physical connections and reactions to the film, as the social justice challenge of racial violence in the United States was a lived reality for them and the documentary grounded the room in that challenge. Further, anonymous surveys administered to each participant who was part of the documentary screenings revealed that all but one respondent agreed with the statement that the documentary provided "a true portrayal of a real problem." In other words, audiences overwhelmingly trusted what they saw, regardless of their race, ethnicity, gender, politics, or geography.[6]

While the documentary focused on a North Carolina tragedy, participants across the country felt that it told a story that echoed with the realities of their local community. Many participants shared recent and distant experiences that they had not spoken about before and called out realities that they felt had long been hidden or ignored. Participants spoke about lynchings that have taken place in their communities and to their loved ones, with little media or public attention, while many others spoke to less overtly violent— but still painful—ways in which racial discrimination finds them, including in their community's health clinics, school systems, and trips to Walmart. They collectively expressed: the reality in the documentary is also true here.[7]

158 RADICAL REALITY

When the filmmaker, Jacqueline Olive, started her research for the film, in 2008, she said, there was "radio silence about lynching in the mainstream," including both present-day and historical racial violence.[8] As her research transitioned to nearly a decade of filming, several racial violence killings—including Oscar Grant III in 2009 and Travyon Martin in 2012—appeared and then disappeared from mainstream conversations in the country. Meanwhile, she also noted that cursory investigations into the deaths of several other Black people found hanging received little to no major news coverage—including the deaths of Danye Jones, the 24-year-old son of Black Lives Matter activist Melissa McKinnies, who was found hanging from a tree in their backyard on October 17, 2018; Titi Gulley, a 31-year-old Black transgender woman found hanging in Portland, Oregon, on May 27, 2019; and Robert L. Fuller, a 24-year-old Black man found hanging from a tree in Palmdale, California, on June 10, 2020. "We often like to think that we're walled off from history, but there is no such wall," she reflected. "So all of those things that are unresolved in history, that are unreconciled, are showing up now."[9] In thinking further about her experience making the film, Olive recalled:

> Early on, I felt it was important that people—particularly young people who, like me, were underexposed to this history in secondary education—are able to name aspects of racial violence and the systemic racism happening in their communities that they encounter every day. The country is currently grappling with the fallout of lynching, and to be able to understand and discuss the issues thoroughly, allows for greater clarity in the work towards justice and reconciliation. . . . The climate that made lynching possible historically has evolved into the dehumanization and racial violence occurring today, and it is not an irrational leap to think that a lynching could occur now, so it is crucial that law enforcement, the criminal justice system, government agencies, journalism, secondary schools and colleges and universities, and other institutions frame the work that they are charged to do around the deaths and lives of Black people with lessons from this history.[10]

After the film was released in 2019, Olive traveled the country for more than a year, with a small impact team, facilitating community engagement screenings and dialogues designed to give audiences the opportunity to unpack their connections with lynching violence and to discuss the

CREATING SPACES FOR RECONCILIATION AND HEALING   159

lingering effects of racial terrorism on their communities today. In addition to prioritizing cross-racial dialogues that could lead to deeper mutual understanding and stronger multiracial coalition-building, Olive said that her effort was also centered around strategizing ways for communities to collectively work toward justice and reconciliation at local and national levels, and to center the voices of Black families and facilitate dialogues that allowed Black people to imagine their own paths toward healing, without having to navigate the residual power dynamics of white supremacy as they define and work toward repair for themselves.[11]

While news coverage of social justice work often focuses on big headline policy changes, social demonstrations, and political clashes, less attention has been afforded to the lingering trauma and need for healing that resides in many of the communities at the center of racial violence, climate injustice, land rights, conflict, LGBTQ+ discrimination, and the other social justice challenges highlighted in this book. And yet activists, organizers, and filmmakers have all found documentaries to be uniquely capable of helping communities to enter processes of recognizing uncomfortable truths, reconciling difficult realities, and grappling with the generational harm and consequence of injustice.

This chapter highlights documentaries that are serving as corrective histories in and of themselves, by centering realities that have been misrepresented or silenced in the countries where they are based, and that are being used to provide spaces for community-based healing and interrogation, and for the recognition of underrepresented histories and communities in the governments, institutions, societies, and media systems that have historically caused them harm. The role of documentaries in doing this work—foregrounding objectives of reconciliation, healing, and reimagination—is often difficult to quantify or capture with statistics or flashy impact reports. Consequently, this level of work may represent one of the most underfunded, understudied, and underappreciated aspects of documentary endeavors for social justice.

Documentaries and Corrective Histories

For more than three decades, the documentaries of filmmaker Stanley Nelson have served to correct the historical record and contemporary understandings of Black life in America. From his film on the Black Panther

160 RADICAL REALITY

Party (*The Black Panthers: Vanguard of the Revolution*), which reclaims the organization's history from the stereotype-driven stories that have long misrepresented their work, to his films on the influence of underrecognized civil rights activists and events in America's civil rights movement (including *Freedom Riders, Freedom Summer,* and *The Murder of Emmett Till*); to the story of the 1921 massacre of African Americans in Tulsa, Oklahoma (*Tulsa Burning*); to revealing the violence and racism at the center of the deadly 1971 prison uprising at Attica Correctional Facility in upstate New York and the role it played in the country's prisoners' rights movement (*Attica*); to a film about his family's own history (*A Place of Our Own*), to name just a few, his documentaries spotlight the moments of struggle, triumph, and catastrophe that have shaped his experience along with the greater history of African Americans in the United States.[12]

Growing up in New York City in the 1950s and 1960s, Nelson said, the mainstream films and media depictions he saw of his community did not reflect his reality, and that this was a motivating force in his decision to explore filmmaking.

> I was interested in films about African Americans, and ways that we could make films that were not about, you know, "pimps and whores," which were the films coming out of the blaxploitation movement. My father's a dentist, my mother's a librarian, that was not the world that I knew.[13]

As a result, Nelson said that he felt compelled to make films about the world that he knew, "the world that most African Americans knew."[14]

In 1998, as part of his journey into filmmaking, Nelson created the independent nonprofit documentary production company, Firelight Media, with his wife, filmmaker Marcia Smith, as a production house centered around his original mission of telling stories about Black America that are underrepresented and often misrepresented in the mainstream media. But after a screening of their documentary *The Murder of Emmett Till* at the Schomburg Center for Research in Black Culture in Harlem, New York, everything changed.[15] The film tells the story of an injustice that helped spark the civil rights movement: two Mississippians bludgeoned and killed a 14-year-old Black boy, Emmett Till, for allegedly flirting with a white woman in August 1955; they were acquitted by an all-white, all-male jury shortly after committing the crime and then boasted about it in the press.

CREATING SPACES FOR RECONCILIATION AND HEALING   161

Nelson and Smith recalled their surprise at the level of emotion and engagement the film had stirred after a screening in Harlem, as people were outraged that the film had seemingly exceeded the diligence done by the country's justice system in uncovering witnesses and information that were never considered in court. Motivated by the public response, Firelight Media galvanized a community effort to petition the US Department of Justice to reopen the murder case, based on evidence revealed in the film, which led federal prosecutors to exhuming the body of Emmett Till in 2005 and finally performing an autopsy for the first time. From this moment on, Nelson recalled coming to the realization that documentaries "could do something very different than just be something that goes up on screen."[16]

Since then, the Firelight Media team has continued to support and organize community events centered around documentaries about the African American experience, along with cultivating audiences and providing industry mentorship, social justice training, incubation labs, and other valuable support for documentary filmmakers of color.

The work that Nelson, Smith, and other documentary filmmakers, particularly those from BIPOC communities, have been doing to center and evolve impact and community engagement has been vital in inspiring new industry practices and commitments to using documentaries for community engagement in the United States, and in countries around the world. Directors from groups and associations like Firelight Media, Brown Girls Doc Mafia, Asian American Documentary Network (A-Doc), Working Films, and Chicken & Egg Accelerator Lab support filmmakers in engaging with the communities at the heart of their films. Their critical work is also part of a growing effort made by public media and other nonprofit organizations that use strategically selected documentaries to facilitate grassroots community events around important public issues. For instance, the PBS-funded *Independent Lens* series and the *POV* documentary series in the United States, which collectively distribute about 50 films each year (many of which are produced by filmmakers around the world, not only the United States), collaborate with local civic and public media organizations and partners to host more 1,000 screening events of select films each year in libraries, churches, jails, community centers, local theaters, and schools across the country.

Tell Them We Are Rising: The Story of Black Colleges and Universities, directed by Stanley Nelson and Marco Williams, is one example of a film made possible through PBS funding support. And the role of such public media support was essential, said Marcia Smith, who was also a cowriter

162   RADICAL REALITY

of the film, as it provided the film team with the funding and freedom they needed to create spaces for communities to engage with the documentary and each other.[17] In addition to PBS and the Corporation for Public Broadcasting, the film's community screening efforts received media engagement funding from several other foundational grants. But they were only able to accept such funding because PBS supported the film team's impact ambitions and desire to embed the film in college campuses (something other major distributors, especially streamers, frequently do not allow for). As a result, they forged partnerships with several civic organizations and funds, including The United Negro College Fund, the Thurgood Marshall Fund, along with the Divine Nine, the umbrella association of African American sorority and fraternity associations in the United States. The partners organized several dynamic community events tied to *Tell Them We Are Rising* on campuses across the country, even bringing-in HBCU marching bands to participate in three of the events. Smith said that such support is hard to find outside of public media:

> Our experience in the commercial sector is that they, at best, don't care about [community engagement work]. At worst they're hostile. It's not important to them. It doesn't fit their values and it doesn't align with their reward structure at all.[18]

Smith recalled a previous film directed by Nelson, *Crack: Cocaine, Corruption & Conspiracy*, on the history and consequences of the 1980s crack epidemic in the United States, which disproportionately impacted African American communities. The film was released by Netflix in 2021, but the streamer had little interest in supporting community efforts around the film, outside of a virtual screening event held by an institution based in the Upper East Side, one of the most affluent and predominantly white neighborhoods of New York City.

> [T]hey didn't care. How they defined impact was that they arranged a screening hosted by the 92nd Street Y, which had a screening series. And they called that a community event. I asked, "Well, who are you even trying to reach with this?" . . . We could have conceived something different, but we were not working in an environment that valued it at all. And so that contrast has become only starker to me over time.[19]

The films produced by Nelson and Smith, and their pursuit of corrective and transformational filmmaking, can be considered as part of an ongoing effort to decolonize documentary practices by putting the authority of storyteller and historian into the hands of people from the communities being depicted. Films like *I Am Not Your Negro*, *Hale County This Morning, This Evening*, *Liquor Store Dreams*, *The Changing Same*, *Building the American Dream*, *Game Changer*, *Change the Name*, *Black Birth*, and *A Song of Grace* are other examples of recent exemplary documentaries by BIPOC creators about BIPOC individuals, families, and communities. However, the reality is that media trends toward consolidation and the growing power of streamers and their preferences—as noted by Smith and by other filmmakers engaged throughout this book—makes these types of films increasingly difficult both to create and to see.

At the center of the movement to provide corrective histories through documentary, and to provide spaces for impacted communities to grapple with the realities of these histories, is a battle to value Black filmmakers and audiences in an industry that has been, especially in the United States, predominantly white and male. Despite efforts and progress around diversity and inclusion in the field of documentary production, there is still a major discrepancy among 'who is telling whose stories' in the US film industry. In a study of 1,232 documentaries, reflecting every publicly available film distributed between 2014 and 2020 across the most watched platforms for documentary in the United States—categorized by streaming (including Netflix and Hulu), cable (CNN Films and HBO Films), and public broadcasting service channels (Independent Lens and POV)—we found that the vast majority of stories being distributed across major entertainment outlets are directed by white, men-identifying filmmakers about white men-identifying subjects.[20] The study, organized by the authors and led in collaboration with other industry leaders, revealed that 78% of documentaries were directed with only white directors on the film team, and 66% were directed by men, with BIPOC women filmmakers representing just 7% of the 1,423 credited documentary directors across 1,232 films.[21]

This trend has a direct effect on impact. In a landmark article for *Filmmaker Magazine*, Sahar Driver and Sonya Childress—co-directors of Color Congress, which serves documentary film organizations led by people of color—note an evolution from stand-alone films to the inclusion—and ultimate professionalization—of impact-oriented work in the documentary

164   RADICAL REALITY

field, with a new interest in the ways that filmmakers of color have "defined impact, the structural barriers filmmakers of color face in the industry and its implications for impact" as exemplifying its next evolutionary step.[22] One of the biggest unresolved issues facing the field, they argue, is the relentless push by streamers to prioritize films that have the broadest appeal and reach (i.e., films that will appeal to a white audience), rather than the films that are best positioned to serve specific communities. "Filmmakers of color, who face structural barriers at every turn when attempting to advance their own storytelling on their own terms, and who see value and impact potential in engaging their own communities, are the casualties of this trend," they wrote.[23] This trend constrains the ability of filmmakers to produce the type of films that are capable of creating the necessary community-level social justice work that is highlighted in this chapter. They write:

> [E]vidence shows that when (or if) impact campaigns are permitted, the commercial streamers favor those that have "broad reach" (read again: white, male). And they favor campaigns that don't rock the boat too much. This can force impact teams to neutralize the power and potential of their strategic interventions. Instead, they advance campaigns to educate audiences about issues and policies rather than take clear positions on them. They build campaigns to "humanize the other," rather than name the people and policies that perpetuate harm. The prevailing notion is that for a campaign to be noteworthy and "strategic" it must focus on shifting the hearts, minds and actions of mainstream Americans (read: white audiences) who hold positional power (be they voters, parents, business or political leaders).[24]

Among other consequences, this trend also creates barriers to the work of healing and reconciliation discussed in this chapter, further reflecting the consequences of undervaluing this role of documentary in conversations about the potential and future of film today. Driver and Childress put it this way:

> In addition to the beautiful and powerful storytelling that filmmakers of color can produce, the process itself can be a transformative experience. The agency found in a filmmaker of color being able to tell their own story on their own terms, to excavate their own histories to inform,

CREATING SPACES FOR RECONCILIATION AND HEALING 165

heal and strengthen their own communities, can be deeply meaningful, empowering, and liberatory. Equally so for the people on screen whose stories are held with care and dignity and agency. That too should be considered central to impact.[25]

Ceding Power to Communities, Working in Antioppressive Ways, and Reclaiming Spaces for Positive Experiences

Another common objective for many of the documentaries featured in this chapter is their commitment to using the process of filmmaking as a way to shift the locus of power and relationships from dominant institutions to communities. This means that while many of these films might aim for reform related to specific goals (like addressing institutional racism and mistreatment), any effort to raise awareness or educate external audiences is largely approached as a secondary outcome, choosing instead to focus primarily on processes that center the community represented on screen as the target audience.

The documentary *In My Blood It Runs*[26] represents one exemplary way that filmmakers are centering community collaboration in how they make and distribute their films. Released in 2019, *In My Blood It Runs* shares the perspective and life of Dujuan, a 10-year-old Arrernte and Garrwa Aboriginal boy living in Australia's Northern Territory, as he tries to balance his traditional Arrernte/Garrwa upbringing with a state education. The film was directed by Maya Newell in collaboration with Dujuan and Megan Hoosan, Margaret Andersen, Carol Turner, and James, Colin, and Jimmy Mawsen.

Their model of "collaboration, not consultation" was informed by the expertise and past work of a diverse team of advisors convened by the filmmakers, and by the Amiun culturally safe practices framework for film, TV, and the arts. Ultimately, in interviews conducted by the authors, the film team said that community collaboration meant valuing First Nations perspectives and the history on which they have been misrepresented in past films and other storytelling efforts. And it meant ensuring that the attention and power of the filmmaking process was constantly pointed back to the community at the heart of the film; not to the funders or audiences that might see it. William Tilmouth, a lead advisor with the film and a widely respected Arrernte leader, frames this process well:

166 RADICAL REALITY

Aboriginal people do their everyday living in [collaboration and consultation] with each other, it's par for the course in how we do business. In a traditional life setting things didn't just happen, they happened because people got together, talked about it and worked out the best way forward together. Our daily lives were and are all about [collaboration and consultation] in conversation. This didn't happen through written text the way that the west does it but the process is still one we still do today. It's not one of 'I've got an idea and lets do it this way,' it's one that means you take your time to sit with the community and work though the community process until you arrive at a consensus.[27]

Given the stakes of the film and the damage done by past media stories and representation of Indigenous people in Australia, and elsewhere, it is important to not stop at good intent, but rather direct focus to positive impact, said the filmmakers. Rachel Naŋinaaq Edwardson, a First Nations filmmaker from Alaska and an impact producer on the film, put it this way:

As my partner says, it boils down to being aware of not only our *intent*, but our *impact* for the community, and being conscious of not creating a film, or story, or project that is about using an Aboriginal community to educate a mainstream audience.

I can't tell you, as a First Nations person, the amount of times I get requests from people saying, "We want to come and tell a story about your community, so the whole rest of the world can learn how terrible this or that impact is." [In other words,] "we want to use your community to educate everybody else." Which, of course, there's a reason for that. However, if the impact of using our pain and struggles to educate a broader audience is negative for our community, whose stories, bodies, energy, and resources are being used, then we've missed the point.

So for us, on IMBIR, it was pivotal that we were constantly checking the project impacts on Dujuan, his family and on the community—whose stories the film was telling.[28]

Community collaboration meant requesting permission to work with the community before a camera lens ever opened, discussing what type of film to make, providing spaces for feedback during editing sessions (with rough cuts being viewed and discussed with the community on an ongoing basis), and allowing for sufficient time for the community to be meaningfully involved in every step, including final editing, distribution, and impact screening stages. Community members and partners were also paid for their time through a shared profit model. While *In My Blood It Runs* is not the first or only example of profit sharing within the field of impact and collaborative work (and the film team made a point of emphasizing that they aren't the first to use this approach), it is an exemplary and rare example of this model being applied in the field of documentary film. The *In My Blood It Runs* team set up a royalty distribution structure that shared the profits of the film with the community contributors. This meant that Dujuan and his family received profit that was equal to the director, and more than any producer. The family decided to use the funds to set up a trust fund for Dujuan and his brother.

The film team acknowledged that the process of sharing the camera, the profits, and the editing process with a community is notably different from how filmmakers are often taught to make documentaries. The typical mantra that filmmakers often hear is that they should never give power to their subjects, said Naŋinaaq Edwardson, but for films that endeavor to share intimate stories of communities and people long misrepresented by the field

Image 7.1 Description: Members of the *In My Blood It Runs* film and impact team during an impact strategy planning workshop. Photo Credit: *In My Blood It Runs* film team.

168   RADICAL REALITY

of documentary and actors outside of media, this is a mantra that must be broken.

> It's all of us who went to any sort of standard film school or started in any industry. We're always told, "Never let them in the editing suite. Never talk to them about what you're doing until you are done with it and know how you want to present it to the world. Watch out they will not want you to put in the hard stuff." We took the complete opposite approach, because the desire was to ensure that we were working in anti-oppressive ways. And the only way to ensure we were working in anti-oppressive ways was to give power over to the people whose stories are being told, to raise our critical consciousness, and to recognize that an authentically anti-oppressive story is a story told with, not about.[29]

Before the film *In My Blood It Runs* was released, its filmmakers organized a three-day workshop with about 50 First Nations participants, including the families at the center of the film, along with other senior Arrernte people and advisors, and partner organization members, including from Children's Ground and Akeyulerre Healing Centre. The workshop created and held safe spaces for First Nations community members to share their perspectives on the intentions and desired outcomes of the film and any engagements that would happen around it. Early discussions at the workshop also involved recognizing the history of the First Nations people in Australia, going back before colonization, and acknowledging the harmful impact of work and collaborations that came before, including the history of First Nations stories being misrepresented in past films, media coverage, and other efforts.

By the end of the three-day meeting, the group identified four key goals for the film, all of which oriented around advancing supportive partnerships and policies to create safer spaces for First Nations people to be recognized and heard at various levels of society: (1) address racism by sharing lived experiences of First Nations people and challenging structural racism; (2) champion and build significant support for an Aboriginal and Torres Strait Islander–led education system; (3) support mainstream schools in becoming more culturally safe for Aboriginal and Torres Strait Islander students; (4) and amplify evidence-backed restorative youth justice solutions instead of punitive youth justice.

To ensure that these objectives—along with the other principles, goals, and key messages created by the First Nations community members during

CREATING SPACES FOR RECONCILIATION AND HEALING   169

the workshop—would be followed, they required their distributors, funders, and partners to sign a "memorandum of understanding," which stated that any use of the film or marketing activity associated with it must abide by these principles. Alex Kelly, a producer on the film, said that they would frequently jump on calls with organizations to help explain the reasoning and impact of different framings, and why even a couple words can make a big difference in a community feeling recognized or harmed:

> I think for some partners it seemed unusual that we would say, "As a basis of this partnership can we read your drafts of your social media posts or your press release before you send it out?" And sometimes it's only one or two words, but the conversation that we would then have on a Zoom call where we would step through why those two words undermined agency, or undermined dignity and the kinds of work that the family had identified they wanted to do, and why, and what the messages and principles were. That is a really big piece of the impact work, and it's got nothing to do with metrics, and numbers, and bums on seats. . . . We're not in every lounge room conversation. We're not reading every review with the audiences, but to the extent that we could influence the framing, the conversation, the education materials that we produced, the Q and As that we hosted, the media op-eds that were published, we tried.[30]

Central to the *In My Blood It Runs* impact team's approach was always being "conscious of what a camera can do."[31] And this meant ensuring that any community engagement around the film was "strength-based" and as much about community empowerment as it was about protection:

> We said, "Let's not just be responsive to something that's negative. Let's actually try to do work to make sure there is a positive impact." We're not just protecting [Dujuan]. We're trying to also use this as a space to give him a platform for support and development and what does that look like?[32]

At times this meant anticipating and talking about how the experience of being in a film could impact how people at Dujuan's school and in his own community (and beyond) might look at him, treat him, or relate to him in the future. In terms of timing, it also meant waiting until the community felt ready before screening the film. The impact team's efforts of ensuring that every partner agreed to the MOU was one important wellness strategy. The

170 RADICAL REALITY

team's commitment to maintaining a pace that was in step with the community was another. But one of the most important steps the film team took was working with the community to create safe-enough spaces for their participation in community events, Q&As, media interviews, and all the other impact- and engagement-related events that come with documentaries.

While unfortunate, the film team said they also had to prepare for the inevitable mainstream media practice of putting First Nations people in the position of being asked questions solely based on their identification with a First Nations community. In order to prepare the film's participants for the potential for these challenging situations, the impact team supported the family and community members in writing their own stories, articles, and speeches based around the perspective they felt was important to share. The film's lead director, Maya Newell, recalled:

> Something that I've learnt through this process is that it's not just creating the opportunities for people to have a platform or to invite people to Sydney Film Festival, but it's preparing the space so that is a positive experience. And that is actually a huge part of the work, which is really labor-intensive.[33]

To return to a point raised earlier in this chapter, Naŋinaaq Edwardson noted that "preparing the space" meant ensuring that the film and the postfilm experience wouldn't just be in service of educating people "outside" the community, but that it would also—and primarily—be in service to the community represented in the film.

> For us, it was about making sure that we're not using Black bodies to educate everybody else. Rather, we're doing something that will benefit both the internal community where the film has come from and the greater community that needs to hear these stories.[34]

Putting Participant Wellness Models at the Core of Social Justice and Documentary Work

Centered around the intimate stories of survivors and insiders, *Pray Away* is a documentary film that exposes the horrific practice and devastating consequences of LGBTQ+ conversion therapy—the practice of attempting to force a person to change their sexual orientation, gender identity, or

CREATING SPACES FOR RECONCILIATION AND HEALING   171

gender expression—through an investigation of the world's largest conversion therapy organization, Exodus International. The film is another example of a burgeoning movement toward creating better models of care for the protagonists of documentaries and in ensuring that participant wellness is centered in both the processes of making a film and the processes of putting it out into the world.

For the producers of *Pray Away*, screening efforts shouldn't start-and-stop with provocative discussion guides and "expert" panels—although that remains a dominant practice in the field of documentary. Instead, they argue, screening events should involve the inclusion of engaging care team members (not just subject experts) in any community event and provide support resources for the participants and audiences. Anya Rous, producer of *Pray Away* and advisor for its impact campaign, said that the film's director, Kristine Stolakis, and her producing partner Jess Devaney at Multitude Films, started talking about a care-informed approach in the earliest stages of the filmmaking process. Kristine underwent a thorough research process in the development of the film to ensure the film was grounded in an extensive understanding of the movement and practice of conversion therapy, informed by historical record, the experiences of survivors, and those leading at the forefront of the movement to end conversion therapy (one of the primary goals of the film).[35]

Central to these early stages was also building the right team for production, and, later on, who were engaged in their planning conversations for the impact campaign. This included forming relationships with organizations like the National Center for Lesbian Rights, the Trevor Project, PFLAG, GLAAD, and others who provided early guidance and partnership. The team also brought on Myles Markham as consulting producer. In addition to bringing his experience as a survivor of conversion therapy, he had a depth-of-issue expertise as an organizer working at the intersection of faith & LGBTQ+ inclusion for years and remained connected to a broader community of survivors and Queer Christian communities. He played a central role in helping the team think about its casting, and in contributing to the storylines in the film and its representations of the movement, and he charted the goals and strategies of its impact campaign after distribution. After Myles launched the campaign for its first events, he then passed the baton to Shae Washington, another leader in the faith & LGBTQ+ facilitation world, to helm the continuation of the multicity community engagement campaign.

Image 7.2 Description: A screening event and resource table for the film *Pray Away* in Washington, D.C. Photo courtesy of *Pray Away* film team.

During this early stage of design and preparatory work around the impact campaign, the team focused not only on better understanding where the leadership and power in the conversion movement was located but also on considering the ways that the practice and movement cause lasting emotional and spiritual harm. Rous emphasized that this dual-approach of addressing external structures that are causing harm and need to change, while not losing sight of considering the wellness and healing of the impacted participants and protagonists at the center of the film and conversation, was a critical organizing principle for them.[36]

As part of this effort, the team particularly leaned on the Trevor Project and NCLR's Born Perfect Campaign in being cognizant that "this is a high risk, vulnerable population with a lot of survivors who are dealing with PTSD symptoms from the ongoing reverberations of their experience with conversion therapy."[37] In the LGBTQ+ community generally, and especially among those who are survivors of conversion therapy, there are much higher rates of suicide or suicidal attempts and ideations about self-harm, along with people who have had direct experiences of losing loved ones or close

CREATING SPACES FOR RECONCILIATION AND HEALING   173

Image 7.3 Description: A screening event and resource table for the film *Pray Away* in Washington, D.C. Photo courtesy of *Pray Away* film team.

community members and have seen the harm of the conversion therapy movement up close.

The impact team felt strongly that a care-oriented approach meant ensuring that screenings were "hyper-localized" in order to ensure that they

Image 7.4 Description: Left to right: Earl S. Mowatt (one PULSE Foundation), Rev. Stanley Ramos (Alabanza MCC), Patty Sheehan (conversion therapy survivor, Orlando City Council), Heather Wilkie (Zebra Youth), and *Pray Away* impact producer Shae Washington. Photo courtesy of *Pray Away* film team.

reflected and built on the unique histories, partners, issues, experiences, conversations, and work already taking place in that community. Local organizations and leaders were part of planning each event, and each screening was then resourced with therapists, trauma specialists, and allies who were prepared ahead of time to provide support to audiences, help them find care and qualified support after the screenings, and, for those interested, in ways to be involved in advocacy efforts to end conversion therapy.

Rous said the film team also discussed with survivor participants the types of questions, environment, and conversation that they feel would be helpful or healing to participate in, and what would feel unhelpful or even retraumatizing:

> We had conversations . . . on what is okay to share? What are the kinds of questions that could come up in Q and As that you feel comfortable talking about? What does not feel comfortable talking about? What are the kinds

CREATING SPACES FOR RECONCILIATION AND HEALING   175

of questions that we as a film team should take on, so that this isn't your responsibility? We were conscientious about if there was a Q and A, it's okay for participants to not be there afterwards for people to come up to them and unload on them.[38]

Considering the wellness of the community at the center of the film also meant recognizing the reality that most people who would engage with their documentary would do so outside of the safe spaces they were building. This became of even greater importance when Netflix became the film's main distributor. As part of its early conversations and negotiations with Netflix, the *Pray Away* team worked to create trauma-informed messages, cultural glossaries, and audience guides that aimed to serve people who would find the film online or in their homes. And they emphasized that these materials should be made explicit by Netflix in both the film cut it uses and on its distribution page.

Concern over the framing and representation of the film also carried over to the film team's media engagement efforts. The *Pray Away* team worked to inform journalists and media organizations about the role they have historically played in perpetuating a limited understanding of the movement and the harm caused to the community in the film. For several years, media portrayals of conversion therapy have predominantly framed it as a fringe issue, without providing a fuller picture of its prevalence and the power structures that are maintaining it.

> Predominantly the way that conversion therapy is covered [by the media] is as a fringe movement which exists in the most extreme forms, like electroshock therapy. But we wanted to show the fact that, actually, it's just as harmful when it's in counseling and Bible studies and when the wallpaper of your community is continually telling you that there's something wrong and broken with you. All of those different ways contribute to people internalizing these messages and leading to high rates of self-harm. So, when the media talks about electroshock therapy, for instance, if a lot of churches say they don't do conversion therapy, because they're identifying it with that kind of practice. They're like, "No, we are just giving people choices around their lives and we're showing them there's another way."[39]

In other words, while the film team placed a heavy emphasis on media engagements around the film, the focus was never about "getting more

176   RADICAL REALITY

coverage." Instead, the organizing premise for all their partnerships and efforts pointed back to wellness and ensuring that the film would be in service to the people at the center of the film and to creating spaces for greater recognition and healing.

Building Trust and Connection Between Communities That Have Historically Been Exploited and Isolated

The experiences of filmmakers Rosemarie Lerner and Maria Ignacia Court, and the team who worked on *The Quipu Project,* an interactive form of participatory research and documentary storytelling with communities affected by forced sterilization in Peru, point to the role that documentaries are playing in helping to not only engage but to build communities. Lerner said that a driving motivation for their documentary was to help build a community among women groups who were often geographically isolated and struggling with the trauma of their experience separately, without support from other women who had survived the same things.

The Quipu Project focuses on telling stories of women—many of whom are poor, marginalized women with an Indigenous background—who were tricked or forced into sterilization by the Peruvian government in the mid-1990s. The forced sterilization affected an estimated 200,000 women and yet no punishment or justice or reparation process had taken place, and, since many of the affected women remain in remote communities of Peru, few know that it even happened. Meanwhile, national and international media alike have provided little attention to the tragic injustice.

When Lerner first learned about the sterilization campaign, she thought that it would be an important issue for the focus of a traditional feature documentary. But her thinking changed after she spoke to community members.[40] A truth that is too often underrecognized by filmmakers and other media creators, is the reality that the same storytelling tools filmmakers bring to communities have likely been brought to that community before and have caused them more harm than good. And while the intentions of the filmmaker might be better than those of the person who came before, collaboration and partnership isn't developed by intentions, said Lerner, it is born through a dedication to collaborative processes. In her early conversations with the women's organizations and community activists in Peru, Lerner

CREATING SPACES FOR RECONCILIATION AND HEALING   177

said that they could sense hesitation among the women's groups to invite any type of media worker into their community:

> We noticed that there was a lot of fear and a lot of distance. They were very careful in their relationship with the media because they had already been betrayed or used so many times, even by international production companies that were doing documentaries or photographers or artists or the local media. They felt that people always took from them and then they never saw anything in return. Not even a photo, a copy of a photo that they took. Because this was also a reality that we had to face, it was like, okay, we have to be very careful and go very slowly and also go through all the steps and the necessary people to actually reach the women, but also we want to make sure that, first of all, they know what they are gaining and that there's something concrete and clear for them to actually want to collaborate with us.[41]

After the filmmakers met directly with communities of women who had survived the sterilization campaign, heard their stories, and learned what was important to them, they realized that a feature film—even though it might interest an international audience—would not be in service to these women.

> And that's when I approached Maria and told her: "Look, I think this story would be great for an interactive documentary, because I think it's much bigger and the story is much bigger than what can be told through a traditional two-hour film." ... And that's when we started to collaborate, started thinking, "Okay, how can we use [new media tools] that allow for people to participate and have agency in how to tell their own stories."[42]

Ultimately, Lerner and her team decided that an interactive online and mobile website was the best platform for their project, since it would allow for stories to be anonymous while still facilitating a wider community of sharing and engagement. It would allow for community-building and create an initiative that would be ongoing, with more stories added over time. It would allow women to share their stories via mobile phones, listen to other stories, and engage with a wider community of people who were affected by the sterilization campaign or who want to send them support. It would, in other words, provide a safe space for the women to document and share their

178 RADICAL REALITY

stories themselves, using a platform (mobile phones) that many of them had daily access to, on an ongoing basis.

Given the history of mistrust in the community, the filmmakers emphasized the importance of "informed consent," ensuring that every community member who participated in the project knew of its potential benefit and harm, its purpose, and that their participation was entirely voluntary. One of the reasons the sterilization campaign violated and harmed hundreds of thousands of women was because the government did not inform them—in their own language—about what they were doing. Lerner put it this way:

> The sterilization [campaign] happened because there were no considerations around informed consent.... For example, we were speaking with women who didn't have Spanish as a first language. And during the sterilization campaign, many times no one ever bothered to translate to the original language . . . and explain to [the women] what they were going to sign. Also, a lot of times, they were asking women who were illiterate to sign documents that they didn't even understand. Other times they were asking the husbands for permission for the procedure that was going to be done to the women's bodies. For us, informed consent was crucial.[43]

Given the sensitive and traumatic nature of the sterilization campaign, and how infrequently many of the women had spoken or revisited the issue before the documentary project arrived, the filmmakers said that ensuring their work was co-owned by the local women's groups was critical in helping to earn the trust of the women and allow them to feel safe enough and supported enough to participate:

> Most of the places where the testimonies were shared were during events with multiple women, and usually it was one woman sharing their testimony, getting emotional and two or three other women hugging her or holding her when they were sharing. And for us, it was really, really important to do this with care; to be really careful.[44]

Helping to ensure the project had local leadership and co-ownership, one of the women (Esperanza) was paid and empowered as a lead organizer for the effort. Esperanza helped the filmmakers identify women to interview, and she encouraged women to participate in the work. Because Esperanza also had ambitions to serve in a more leadership and activist role against

CREATING SPACES FOR RECONCILIATION AND HEALING   179

sterilizations, she was one of the few women who didn't ask for anonymity. Esperanza also helped the women and organizers of the documentary to see how the initiative would help them improve their ability to communicate with each other—and to officials and prosecutors—about the lasting pain and consequences of their experience. In this way, Lerner said that Esperanza played a central role in transforming the project from an experimental documentary and into a social justice action and capacity-building opportunity for local communities to support one another in processes of justice and healing.[45]

> For them, it was not only cathartic, but Esperanza [said] "this is a tool for us to learn how to communicate better with other people, for other people to listen to us and to speak back to us."[46]

At its core, the work of *The Quipu Project* demonstrates how documentaries are working to lift the stories of communities in a way that honors their experience through a process where they feel co-ownership and recognition throughout. It also illustrates how creating a space for such radical realities to be shared and grappled with is more important for some filmmakers working today than the film itself, even more important than creating a film at all.

Toward New Ways of Identifying, Supporting, and Assessing Impact in Documentary Film

The previous chapters of this book have demonstrated myriad ways that documentaries are advancing social justice work around the world, including in raising awareness of critical social issues and inequities, interrogating government power, documenting atrocities, witnessing conflict and resistance, fighting for free expression, demanding human rights, correcting damaging historical narratives, mobilizing communities, and demonstrating activism. Given the urgency of the issues and struggles at the core of many of the documentaries spotlighted here, it can be easy to give disproportionate focus to the films that were able to generate concrete policy changes, mobilize broad movements, raise the most funds, and influence high-level governance and global discussions, while missing the ways in which documentaries are also functioning to help communities to pause: to stop what they are doing, and the way they have been doing things, and to collectively look back, recognize, and grapple with the realities that some have tried to deny, reframe, or to simply put in the rearview mirror. But it is through this type of work that many filmmakers say the process of healing, reimagination, and transformation becomes possible—through which communities, not filmmakers, are positioned to decide what should come next in the story, the change that should happen, how it should happen, and why it should happen. The films highlighted in this chapter reflect some examples of how documentaries are uniquely capable of facilitating this type of vital engagement.

8

Building a Future for Global Independent Documentary Storytelling to Survive and Thrive

In November 2023, Doc Society, the UK-based global documentary organization, summoned a far-reaching closed-door group of comrades to chilly London for its most urgent convening yet. For nearly two decades, Doc Society—founded as erstwhile BRITDOC by documentary activists Jess Search, Beadie Finzi, and Maxyne Franklin—has helped to incubate a growing network of documentary professionals and impact producers around the world. Alongside an expansive cadre of international collaborators, Doc Society and its allies have funded and developed films, created resources to support social impact efforts, brokered relationships between civil society and storytellers, and hosted legendary gatherings to build cultural power among what some affectionately call "the ecosystem" of documentary people.

This time, an unusual and expanded mix of constituents, often siloed with their own kind, gathered at Doc Society's inaugural Democracy Story Lab: documentary filmmakers, civil society organizations, philanthropists, academics, and journalists. Participants came from Estonia, Germany, Hungary, Europe, Russia, Kenya, Mexico, Lebanon, Brazil, India, the United Kingdom, Taiwan, the United States, and other corners of the world. The starting place: authoritarianism tendencies are thriving in fertile ground, global capitalism is a challenge to free and independent media, and democracy weakens and wanes in all corners. The guiding question: Given the erosion of trust in democracy, what is the role that narrative strategy can play in rebuilding and reimagining the social contract? It was not a "nice to do," but a critical call to arms, said Doc Society cofounder and codirector Beadie Finzi:

> What Doc Society wanted to do was to bring together in one room people who do not speak with each other, who have these conversations in silos,

Radical Reality. Caty Borum and David Conrad-Pérez, Oxford University Press. © Oxford University Press 2025.
DOI: 10.1093/9780197604298.003.0008

but yes, the extraordinary, resilient, tenacious, entrepreneurial people working in independent film all over the world, our brothers and sisters, but also our cousins in journalism and development media.... We need to ally with all those other brilliant, brilliant colleagues working in public interest media from journalism to folks working in development. We need to figure out how we are going to collaborate to meet this onslaught.[1]

Building and strengthening global networks of like-minded documentary storytellers, journalists, philanthropists, thinkers, and freedom activists is a must-do—a requirement to resist unprecedented modern-day political, technological, and economic systems of power. "That is what this moment, what this time, this post-truth moment calls for," said Finzi. "What is the strategic contribution we can all make in this fight—the fight of our lives?"[2] Independent documentary storytelling, always perched on precarious ground, is endangered around the world—particularly when it comes to human rights topics. How that trajectory can shift is a perennial, messy proposition without perfect answers. It starts with articulating why it matters, where we are, and ultimately, what is needed to evolve in an uncertain future.

Image 8.1 Description: Shanida Scotland, Doc Society Codirector, Head of Film, speaking at Doc Society's inaugural Democracy Story Lab in London in November 2023. Photo courtesy of Doc Society and Shanida Scotland.

Creative, cinematic independent documentaries have always served a unique function in our storytelling culture and democratic discourse, sitting somewhere between entertainment and journalism. Documentary makers take their cues not from news desk assignments or entertainment marketing agendas, but from stories bubbling from the ground up—within communities and movements. Then as now, documentary's editorial independence is unique among media industries, and this authorial freedom is deeply revered among filmmakers.[3] This matters to us as participants in the public sphere, particularly when we consider the democratic value of seeing stories shaped by voices often neglected elsewhere in the media landscape—women, people of color, members of the disability community, LGBTQ+, undocumented immigrants. With artistic freedom and a motivation for social progress, contemporary documentary storytelling is nimble and deep, forecasting local stories and serving as harbingers of looming realities—often months and years before dominant media narratives take hold. They shine a light on real people, shaped by artistic impulses that can capture our emotional selves and remind us of the limits of reducing every reality to an ideological binary.

But independent documentaries are, and always have been, more than mere entertainment. With free media and freedom of expression in clear duress as commercial media dominates global markets and authoritarianism simmers, independent documentaries are the proverbial canaries in the coal mine. And it's past time, said Finzi, that we framed the discussion and the stakes appropriately; building urgent mechanisms for their survival requires this resetting:

> We need to take the system of independent film seriously. Independent filmmakers are the grit in the oyster. They always have been. They sit in places where there is absolute market failure, where there is absolute repression and suppression of voices. And, these storytellers, alongside a few of their scattered cousins in journalism, who are predominantly kind of underground or as precarious as they are, are the only ones left speaking truth to power. Let us be really fucking clear. Documentary is not a lifestyle choice. Organizations like Doc Society and all of the sisters and brothers working in this field, we're defending people who are speaking truth to power, who are representing communities who have no voice, no visibility, day after day, under extraordinary conditions.[4]

184 RADICAL REALITY

The throughline of the reality: Decades into fantastical neoliberal hopes, the market alone is clearly unable to uphold public interest values and protections.[5] Free and independent media, including documentary storytelling, cannot survive in an economic climate driven entirely—or dominantly—by the norms and ethos of global capitalism. And, yet, even among the most presumably progressive organizations and individuals, who advocate for social progress on a range of issues, the gap of attention, urgency, and meaningful reform in areas of deteriorating public discourse and media seems to be widening around the world. "Somehow, liberal, progressive funders and governments don't value the public sphere," said Finzi. "It has been entirely corrupted, co-opted, fully controlled," not only by authoritarian tendencies even in open democracies but also by corporate interests. Rampant, broadly unregulated global capitalism does not serve democracy,[6] and consequently, consolidated commercial media systems work harmoniously with constraints to full expression, even when politically "inconvenient." Even at the most basic level, the fundamental business model of global commercial streaming media does not align with independent documentaries that advance human rights and agitate political themes. Scholar Victor Pickard's parallel argument about journalism's decline rings precisely true here: "If society treats news as only a commodity, then it is rational to maximize profits by any means possible.... Commercial constraints have long created barriers for particular voices and views in the press."[7]

Checks on staggering networked tiers of power are shockingly elusive: In the age of global capitalism and media systems run increasingly by Big Tech, scant meaningful regulation exists.[8] Generative AI is fully unleashed, creating conditions that are destructive to democracies and free societies around the world, even as it offers creative potential for good in other aspects. Alongside unchecked capitalism is a global economic and political system not driven and shaped entirely by the rules and norms of capital, but by tech company "feudalism" and turf wars.[9] The same technology companies shape and drive the broader cultural narratives around a range of issues, from social to political. Human rights are not the dominant interest.

Where does it all lead? It's impossible to say for sure. Independent documentary storytellers are a tenacious lot. And yet, they are in trouble, and the stakes of losing them are high if we value freedom of expression, information, and human rights. As a public good and a form of public interest media, what does it mean to preserve, protect, and resource independent documentary storytelling around the world as we head deeper into the uncharted territory of information collapse? What are the imperative elements and truths? What can the journey of this book—and the many conversations with civil society leaders, documentary activists and filmmakers around the world—tell us?

Five overarching themes emerge from nearly every film story and interview within these pages. While no single framework can reasonably be seen as absolutely conclusive or complete for a forward trajectory, we offer these core fundamentals as a hopeful road map for the future. To survive and thrive, independent documentary stories and storytellers need expanded investment and support to build and uphold these essentials: strong global and regional professional networks, editorial independence, healthy synergistic journalism systems, distribution for human rights themes, and robust infrastructure for financial and security resources. They are inseparably intertwined with one another, each reinforcing and belonging to the next— and all in need of serious exploration, dedication, focus, norm-building, and training.

Global and Regional Networks

Allied and organized global and regional professional networks are crucial for stories that speak truth to power and the artists who make them. The vast majority of independent documentary filmmakers are not employed by journalism or entertainment companies, a reality that sometimes permits greater editorial freedom but that also poses incredible challenges for getting important work out into the world. Documentary filmmakers work within loose, norm-based communities of practice, and those who exist as members of local and global networks benefit directly by sharing craft tools, resources, and support when they need it the most.[10]

It's already happening to a degree, but network-building and strengthening requires real expanded financial investment and intentional work to bring in allies across professional lines beyond documentary. The Global Impact Producers Assembly (GIPA) connects and works regularly with documentary movement builders and impact producers across the globe. Film festivals like the International Documentary Festival Amsterdam (IDFA) act as sites to forge and deepen relationships. During the pandemic, Doc Society joined forces with regional organizations from across the globe to create a loose cooperative, DISCO (Decentralized Independent Story and Cultural Organizers) to intentionally address shared problems and evolve their

186   RADICAL REALITY

shared future. Together, the groups—which include Ambulante, DocsMX, DocSP, In-Docs, Docubox, and AFLAMUNA, alongside Doc Society—serve thousands of independent nonfiction filmmakers across 40 countries in Central and South America, the United States, Europe, Africa, MENA regions, and South and Southeast Asia. Finzi explained:

> We rebuild for everybody. In the midst of this corporate political climate, polycrisis comes an opportunity to collectively imagine a decentralized, decolonized system for global funding and global distribution of independent media. . . . We've been thinking about remedies for the systemic challenges, but from the perspective of global majority.[11]

These networks are not luxuries, but imperatives. Supportive amplifying networks—including collaborations and impact partnerships with civil society organizations and grassroots groups—often play *the* crucial role in ensuring that politically sensitive independent documentaries are funded, produced, or distributed.

The film and social impact team for *The Territory*, for instance, relied heavily on network power and knowledge to shape the film and its ethical approach to telling Indigenous stories. To engage meaningful screening discussions in conjunction with the theatrical release of the film in Brazil, the focus of the documentary, it was up to the team's impact producers, including Marianna Olinger, who facilitated close to 90 regional partners to work harmoniously with existing Brazilian indigenous movements. But global networks and partnerships were also particularly vital, said director Alex Pritz, because Brazil's crucial national funder network was gutted under Present Bolsonaro. He recalled: "Our whole team was basically first-time filmmakers. Being able to understand everything from the precedent set by other films and how other people navigate some of these tricky ethical issues around collaboration and paying people to the nitty-gritty of contract negotiation was crucial."[12] A global network of documentary activists, funders, and organizations enabled a series of grassroots screenings and public engagement outside the country—not the formal distributor.

For Nanfu Wang, the widely respected, Peabody Award–winning documentary filmmaker known for exposing and agitating sensitive human rights topics (through films like *Hooligan Sparrow* and *One Child Nation*), global networks are especially important since some funders in China can't touch her documentaries for political reasons. In this case, the flip side of the network argument highlights the vulnerabilities of local ones, which balance decisions around what films and work to support with a desire to not upset government authorities and risk their ability to operate in China. Wang said: "The help that has been great for me is institutions in the US . . . all of these nonprofits that, if they didn't exist, or if they were so neutral . . . then my films wouldn't have existed."[13] Vera Krichevskaya, the director of *F@ck This Job*, which explores the last bastion of independent journalism in Russia, said that international donors and documentary networks were invaluable; her film was a critical hit among audiences around the world even as she was forced to flee the country. And the film team behind *El Tema*, a six-part docuseries, released in 2022, that explores different aspects of the climate crisis in Mexico, said that global funding and support networks were critical to both producing their film and organizing impact efforts around it. They employed several creative approaches to fundraising—including a campaign that involved tarps, blankets, chalk signs, and cans to ask people on the streets to donate money so they could "bribe the Ministry of Environment" into doing more to help the communities who were impacted by the climate crisis and featured in the film. The bribery-based fundraising effort was a bit "absurd," admitted Pablo Montaño, lead impact producer behind the docuseries, and only one part of a strategy that also included a robust educational campaign, but it helped them to raise unprecedented attention from influential national media outlets that had been largely ignoring the key issues highlighted by the docuseries, leading to tangible changes that included supportive policy and legislative changes.[14] It also helped them to build a larger support network of people and organizations around the film and climate crisis. A critical ingredient to the success of such efforts, they said, was having the support of an international funder and network, including Doc Society's Climate Story Fund, which allowed them to feature important—even if controversial—climate change realities that are impacting communities across their country, and to be able to take risks in local coalition-building efforts and in raising attention around their work.

At the same time, "international support" does not—and indeed must not—only mean sources of support, guidance, and funding from organizations operating out of the United Kingdom and other Western countries. What documentary support networks will look like, and should look like, is dependent on many contexts.

In East Africa, for instance, filmmakers say that the sustainability of networks and funders rooted in their region is vital for building local power,

188   RADICAL REALITY

capacity, and leadership in the documentary community; providing guidance and protection from attempts of government interference; fostering relationships with local audiences and communities; and offering alternative models of support from the tired Western-led media and development models of the past. There has been a long history of Western institutions and governments launching experimental funding models and media efforts in countries and communities in Africa, using the seemingly well-intentioned language of democratic development and innovation to drive short-sighted efforts that often stem more from a drive to advance Western agendas than to meet locally driven needs and interest. And in the documentary and non-fiction storytelling space, there remains a widely held understanding that many Western funders are looking for a "certain kind of story" and a "certain kind of impact" in the region. As Chloe Genga, a documentary impact-producer working in Kenya, describes it, "There's often a certain kind of impact that [NGOs] want, especially when it comes to African stories, there are certain things that they consider important issues and there are those that they don't consider important."[15] Among other consequences, years of externally driven media campaigns have even conditioned many distributors and broadcasters in Kenya, and elsewhere in the region, to expect financial payments from filmmakers and journalists in order to air their films and projects, since NGOs have been setting-up such expectations for decades, which in itself has created a barrier of entry for filmmakers who can't afford to pay.[16] Given this history, alongside a legacy of colonialism, the need for a more dynamic understanding of—and a more robustly supported—regional institutional network around documentary film is vital.

For filmmaker Sam Soko, this point is critical. Soko's films have been essential in critiquing power, defending freedom of expression, humanizing the work of activists, and exploring important sociopolitical issues in Kenya. His 2020 film *Softie* follows the work of activist Boniface "Softie" Mwangi, as he struggles against injustices and divisive politics in Kenya. In *Free Money*, released in 2022, the first documentary to be acquired by Netflix Africa, he explores the repercussions of a feel-good mission gone awry, in profiling an ongoing initiative of the US nonprofit organization GiveDirectly, which donates free money as universal basic income to a rural village in Kenya. In the film, Soko raises important questions and attention around the often overlooked consequences of foreign aid programs, the role of NGOs in poverty alleviation, and the legacy of Western powers using towns in Africa for grand experimentation. Further, Soko is also behind the organization

Lightbox Africa, a Kenyan production company dedicated to supporting films and filmmakers, especially in areas of fundraising and social impact work. Akuol de Mabior, the filmmaker behind the South Sudan–based film *No Simple Way Home* (discussed in Chapter 3), said that Soko and Lightbox Africa provided centrally important guidance in how to navigate many aspects of filmmaking in the region, including in fundraising. "In Kenya, like in many other African countries, information is gold," said Soko. "Historically, those who came before rarely shared their experiences and lessons. If they did it was at a great price that many can't afford."[17] This is a trend that Soko said he is trying to break with his work and organization—by sharing his lessons, challenges, and experiences with others—and through building supportive local networks that can share both funding and useful experiences and information for capacity building. This local support is critical, said Akuol de Mabior and other filmmakers interviewed for this book: it not only ensures that they are supported by people who understand the unique contexts they are working in, but also helps them to develop local audiences and secure support from organizations that can bring longer-term commitments and sustainability to their work.

Further, any conversation about documentary impact or filmmaking, especially in East Africa, would be incomplete without recognizing the legacy and work of Docubox and its founder, Judy Kibinge, a filmmaker whose work has been credited as helping to launch the current era of contemporary documentary and filmmaking in Kenya.[18] Launched in December 2012, Docubox is one of the first East African documentary film funds and organizations, and several filmmakers point to its importance in the development of the filmmaking and documentary ecosystem in the region. Docubox not only has provided support to the films of Soko but also has been foundational to the careers of several filmmakers whose works have been spotlighted in this book (including Emily Wanja, Toni Kamau, and Peter Murimi). Following a study of the rise of documentary film in East Africa, it would not be an overstatement to say that most roads lead back to Docubox, as the birthplace or champion for many of the documentary community groups, networks, and funding support groups operating throughout the region today.

"It was arguably the first fund of its kind on the continent and grew to be not only a fund, but a home for independent documentary filmmakers," said Kibinge.[19] Docubox originated with a mission that initially went beyond the typical work of a production house, and this was intentional; Kibinge says she wanted the organization to serve as a community building space,

190   RADICAL REALITY

networking force, and physical meeting place for filmmakers, as well. Over the years, Docubox has supported award-winning films, including *I Am Samuel, The Letter, Thank You for the Rain, New Moon*, and *Softie*, among many others.

Toni Kamau, one of the most revered rising producers working today and the founder of the independent production house We Are Not The Machine, points to Docubox as serving a critically important role in her career and journey into filmmaking. Kamau has produced some of the most successful documentaries of the last few years—including *I Am Samuel, Softie*, and *The Battle for Laikipia*—and she was a 2024 recipient of the prestigious Amazon MGM Studies Nonfiction Producer of the year honors, which is awarded annually at the Sundance Film Festival in recognition of the world's best producers.[20] Helping to provide her with connections, support and a pathway to growth in the field of filmmaking, Kamau credits Docubox with no less than "introducing her to the world of indie documentary production" in 2013, while she was producing *I Am Samuel*.[21] In an interview, she recalled how Kibinge and the Docubox team "were very intentional about introducing us to mentors, taking us to festivals, and creating a safe space and community [for us] to grow as independent filmmakers."[22] A further indication of its influence in shaping the ecosystem of documentary film in the region, Docubox also served as the incubator for organizations like DocA (Documentary Africa), which bring grants and other support to filmmakers working across the continent. In an interview about the state of the documentary ecosystem in Kenya, Kamau recently called for more organizations and wealthy players to get behind Docubox's endowment fund "so that they can continue to support ambitious and creative storytellers who are interested in creating narrative shifts around how we as Africans are perceived."[23]

To be specific, providing a source of funding and support to East African filmmakers, something that did not exist in a significant way until the founding of Docubox, has not only led to the development of some of the most successful and important documentaries from the last decade, it has helped to foster the very ecosystem of documentary filmmaking in East Africa that has gained the world's attention in recent years through honors at the Oscars, Sundance, Cannes, and all of the industry's most prestigious events. "You can honor and bring back and agitate with documentary," said Kibinge during a convening around the role of documentaries in telling important stories of Africa's "Erased Heritage."[24] Kibinge says that she created the organization in response to the general lack of funding available to creative documentary filmmakers in the region. And while Docubox received much of its seed funding and financial support from international funders and organizations, it was also designed to offer an important buffer between the interests—both real and perceived—of global agendas and local, creative content. In doing so, Docubox provides vital support to filmmakers who endeavor to tell stories that are relevant and important to them and their communities, regardless of their relevance to typical international and NGO-funding interest buckets.[25] In an interview shortly after creating Docubox, Kibinge noted:

> Being a filmmaker in Kenya is very difficult and I will say this for most of Africa. In the beginning I found myself taking on more NGO docs. It paid the rent, but it wasn't why I took the enormous risk for, what turned out to be, a successful career in filmmaking. It became evident how many people like me have amazing ideas up their sleeves but no means of achieving them. Kenya doesn't have great film schools. People like Spike Lee who make shorts on no budgets can do so thanks to the enormous bonds they made in school. So in this market it becomes very difficult to get films made, which is why I set up Docubox.[26]

Since then, Kibinge and Docubox, alongside production houses like We Are Not The Machine and LightBox Africa, have worked to foster community-building spaces and activities among filmmakers in the region, and they have supported films that have lifted-up several important social issues in the region for wider engagement. In addition to offering financial support, part of the urgent work they are interested in doing is supporting the identification and preservation of existing archival video footage of the region's history, much of which has been destroyed or is still to be found around the country, reflecting the multidimensional role that filmmakers and regional networks are playing not only in strengthening the field of filmmaking but also in protecting works of cultural history, spaces for public dialogue, and social progress.

Yet, filmmakers say more investment in regional networks is needed. While documentaries are quickly gaining popularity across East Africa, fundraising remains a difficult pursuit, and active government interference and censorship pressures around films that critique power or center around important social justice challenges and issues are also impediments. The very recent arrival of major streamers is bringing many of the same challenges of control

192 RADICAL REALITY

and influence as shared in other countries around the world. Filmmakers in the region say that streamers are trying to get films earlier in their development so that they can have greater influence over their stories, and they are slow to show an interest in films that could endanger their markets. "It definitely is a challenge, because especially for independent filmmakers, [the streamers and big distributors] have these huge machines, they have the marketing power, they have all these different things, and you are just this single filmmaker who's been able to put in different grants together and make an amazing film so it can get some light," said impact producer Chloe Genga. "It's like going against a giant."[27] In the face of such challenges, Genga says that filmmaker networks are providing critically needed support, resources, and community.

While its selection as the first documentary acquired by Netflix Africa was a point for celebration for the film team of *Free Money*, for instance, it also brought challenges. Most of the people in the Kenyan village of Kogutu, the town at the center of the film, didn't have access to Netflix Africa and so they couldn't see it. As a result, the film team had to organize their own screening events in the community, something that they were only able to pursue because they knew the importance of negotiating for community screening rights ahead of time. At the same time, given the documentary's focus on a US-based nonprofit, and the consequences of foreign intervention that often go unseen, the film team had a hope that international audiences in the United States and Europe could also access the film; but Netflix allowed streaming access to their African market alone, rather than Netflix Global.

Like other parts of the world, filmmakers in East Africa are increasingly rising to cover critically important issues in the region, often with little personal and financial security. More needs to be done to support their work, especially given the interest and demand filmmakers have seen for such films from audiences across their countries.

Navigating the funding landscape for filmmaking is no small feat. Although organizations like Docubox, Documentary Africa (DocA), and the Kenya Film Commission provide some financial relief, their support often barely scratches the surface of the actual costs involved. This leaves many creators resorting to grant applications, accruing debt, and seeking external financiers who resonate with our storytelling ambitions—a challenging and risky endeavor. We argue that the path to long-term sustainability hinges on shifting the perspective of local investors including the

BUILDING A FUTURE   193

government. Unfortunately, the prevailing view in the continent is that artists are hobbyists rather than viable entrepreneurs. This mindset needs to evolve, especially given the tremendous global potential of the industry.[28]

The bottom line: Independent documentary storytellers rely on support, not only from one another but also from an ever-growing and powerful network of philanthropies, attorneys, civil society organizations, and journalists who understand the stakes and believe in the work. Without supportive global and regional networks, it's unreasonable to imagine how filmmakers working alone—without protections, resources, and support from formal employers—would consistently be able to make it through the many challenges of fundraising, production, risk and security protocol, post-production, distribution, and marketing that allow their work to happen. And parallel social impact efforts rely heavily on collaborative partnerships and screenings with a wide range of civil society groups and communities. It takes a village—and often relying on the global or regional ones are the only way for a filmmaking team to circumvent the political or economic roadblocks within their own countries.

Editorial Independence

For documentaries that speak truth to power—wherever that power may reside, from corporate to political—filmmakers *must* maintain dominant creative and editorial independence. It is at the very heart of the work and an endangered value in the realm of big international streaming entertainment. The number of large-scale distributing networks and studios that will acquire fully produced independent films has dwindled to only a handful, despite a boom moment a few years before the COVID-19 pandemic; this structural reality poses a direct impediment to editorial independence in the hands of the filmmaker.[29] The political economy of the global commercial documentary industry has moved swiftly to a dominant commissioning model—ideas bought and produced with media companies' input and creative control in varying degrees, à la scripted entertainment. This system may work for filmmakers who craft stories about music, true crime, sports, and celebrity, but not for those working in contemporary human rights and public affairs, other than a few outliers that slip through. The basic business model is anathema to independent documentary: Commercial media organizations need to maintain operations in valuable markets by appeasing the political realities and power in place. They do not exist to serve the public interest.

The Cave, the 2019 documentary focused on Syria's ongoing conflict, is a case in point. The film featured a dangerous reality that wasn't widely known or reported at the time—Russia's involvement with chemical weapons strikes in Syria—and the film team needed to convince its distributors about the importance of keeping this controversial reality in the film. Today, members of the film team wonder if their film would even be acquired in today's risk-averse media environment and how their film would have been different as a commissioned work; it couldn't have been shaped "in house" inside an entertainment media company in the same way, they said. In parallel terms, Alex Pritz, director of *The Territory* (Brazil), reflected: "I don't think this film would have been made" if its distributor had been involved from the very beginning of the creative process.[30] This concern was shared by filmmakers of nearly every documentary featured in this book.

In practice, editorial independence is hard to maintain. Like some other themes in this final chapter, it's a double-edged sword: On the one hand, a fierce commitment to editorial and creative independence is vital, filmmakers say, for making a documentary with untainted integrity. But the same impulse can make the job even harder. *Writing with Fire* directors Sushmit Ghosh and Rintu Thomas were deeply committed to telling their story without interference, which made for a slow road, as Thomas explains:

> Our experience as filmmakers is in a country [India] where there are extremely frugal systems to support development production or even distribution of docs. We had really taught ourselves how to make our own films, we were always producers on our films to make sure that we had editorial independence. And then you have to build your own audiences because you just have to find a way to show these films because theatrically and on television are the only two ways. All of these are undernourished systems in India.[31]

Ultimately, what are the stakes when investigative independent documentaries are editorially compromised or censored in some way—not produced or distributed without financial, political, or special-interest interference? We risk missing entire stories and points of view, says Robert Bahar, codirector of *The Silence of Others*:

What I think is happening in the documentary world right now is, first, a filtration of what films are even getting made. And second, it's the self-censorship—that if I have the great opportunity to work with a platform, am I self-censoring myself in the form that the film should take? Or in how much I want to push the line politically? That's especially the question of what films are getting made right now.[32]

When it comes to nonfiction films that can challenge the status quo, critique corporate power, or take on politically sensitive topics, editorial independence is the necessary mode of production—central to the discourse. And it's an increasingly uphill battle. Editorial independence is a vital tradition to protect and preserve within the future of independent documentary storytelling as a public good. It's a hard skill, not a soft one, and building decision-making norms and policies for funders, foundations, investors, and distributors is a requirement for the integrity of the stories that will emerge.

Journalism Synergies

High-quality journalism plays a dynamic synergistic part in ensuring that the stories of independent, human-rights-focused documentaries reach broad publics for awareness, engagement, and potential reform. Without news media coverage, muckraking documentaries are limited in their ability to make an impact. While the independent documentary tradition fights for its survival in an ever-evolving maze of shifting economics, technology, and markets, so too, does high-quality journalism. There is a shared fate here that could benefit from a greater degree of professional collaboration and mutual support between journalists and independent documentary filmmakers; they are sectors and individuals in peril for similar economic and political reasons, and yet, their power can be multiplied with greater network-building, resource-sharing, and amplifying of one another's work.

Almost without exception, the wildly disparate documentaries profiled in this book benefited directly from parallel high-quality journalism on their topics—from helping to spark filmmakers' interest in a deeper story to driving public understanding and engagement in completed documentaries released into the public sphere. For instance, *Welcome to Chechnya*, the 2020 film about LGBTQ+ persecution in Russia, was inspired by a *New Yorker* article by Masha Gessen. Similarly, *The Silence of Others* was loosely sparked by

196 RADICAL REALITY

emerging Spanish news coverage about atrocities and stolen children during the Franco dictatorship; that same journalistic news media network was vital, said the filmmakers, in reaching a wide public in Spain to engage in the finished film and broader conversations about reconciliation and healing. The director of *Delikado*, a journalist by training and profession, felt that his years of reporting about land defenders in the Philippines didn't get the attention it deserved, so he turned to the independent documentary format for a deeper dive and bigger audience. But without the journalism, the story would not have emerged, he said. Amplifying news media coverage of documentary films is a key tool for social impact producers working across both physical grassroots engagement and social media platforms.

On the other hand, journalistic excellence, accuracy, and cultural expertise is not a given. When it is harmful, dehumanizing, and extractive, particularly for historically marginalized and neglected communities—as cited by several filmmakers interviewed for this book—patterns of journalistic coverage can spark documentary filmmakers to create films that can act as vehicles for healing, reconciliation, and corrective narratives. The filmmakers behind *Always in Season* (United States), *The Quipu Project* (Peru), and *No Simple Way Home* (South Sudan) all cite harmful journalistic practices and coverage as motivating factors for their own storytelling. To re-emphasize a learning offered in Chapter 7, Rosemarie Lerner, director of *The Quipu Project*, spoke directly about Indigenous women protagonists' apprehension to work with a film team because of past experiences with media organizations: "There was a lot of fear and a lot of distance. They were very careful in their relationship with the media because they had already been betrayed or used so many times, even by international production companies that were doing documentaries or photographers or artists or the local media. They felt that [media] people always took from them and then they never saw anything in return." With more consistent trusted pathways between them, independent documentary storytellers and journalists can together critique, correct, and agitate harmful narratives that perpetuate oppression.

New and robust efforts to bolster public interest journalism and media are encouraging as they build new networked models for resourcing, training, and protecting independent media—both news and documentaries, locally and globally. In the United States, for instance, organizations like the Institute for Nonprofit News (INN) are setting up resource-sharing models for independent journalists to benefit from legal and editorial support; as INN's Emily Roseman explains, "building a network of public service, high-quality news organizations that can collaborate editorially to expand their editorial reach and power, but also collaborate to build and earn revenue."[33] Similarly, an unprecedented group of more than 20 influential foundations pooled $500 million to fund local news in pockets of the United States decimated by market inequities in commercial journalism, an initiative called Press Forward.[34] On a global level, the International Fund for Public Interest Media, the first multilateral organization to attempt such a high-level solution set, is deeply embedded in the structural problems—economic, organizational, political—that face quality public interest journalism and media around the world, particularly in regions that have been consistently neglected in all manner of debate and investment in information systems. "The goal of the fund," says its CEO Nishant Lalwani,

> is to radically increase the amount of support for public interest media, and to use that money to develop systemic solutions for the economic resilience of media in the long run so that independent media can survive, which is not a given in many places, unfortunately. So that independent media can survive, in service of inclusive democratic societies, accessible to everyone in society.[35]

To do the work, Lalwani says, the organization aims to build and work within "a truly global coalition." It's the right assessment and approach. As free and independent news media outlets decline at shocking rates around the world, the call is increasingly urgent for this kind of allyship and collaboration between independent documentary and public interest journalism. Blurred boundaries will always exist between cinematic nonfiction storytelling and investigative reporting, but rather than endlessly theorizing about the distinctions, time and collective energy can be spent carefully documenting and building infrastructure that honors both—despite their divergent qualities, distribution mechanisms, and norms of craft.[36]

Distribution

Distribution is an infuriating, complicated challenge in the contemporary documentary world—some call it an outright crisis. Global commercial media distributors are not regularly licensing fully produced independent documentaries, particularly those that speak truth to power, regardless of their critical acclaim at prestigious festivals and awards circuits. The obvious consequence: it's harder and harder for audiences to watch documentaries that shed light on injustice in some way. Social critique of power is often silenced by business models that prioritize capital accumulation alone.

It's a systemic pattern, not anecdotal. According to one dataset, produced by the advocacy coalition Distribution Advocates, in collaboration with the authors of this book, more than 80% of the independently produced documentaries shown at major international documentary festivals in 2022—sales ground zero for nonfiction storytelling—did not receive licensing deals from distributors.[37] As journalist Anthony Kaufman neatly summarized,

> The abundance of new streaming platforms gobbling up as much as diverse content as possible has given way to corporate consolidation and retrenchment, with companies such as Netflix, Amazon, and CNN now turning away from the acquisitions of independently made documentaries and focusing more on internally produced "mainstream" nonfiction content.[38]

In past work, one of the authors of this book has made the distinction between "authorial" documentaries—that is, when the filmmaker maintains editorial freedom and discretion and then licenses the finished film to a distributor—and "executive-produced" documentaries, those commissioned by distributors (streaming platforms, TV networks) with some varying degree of shared editorial decision-making.[39] Those distinctions are important for describing the troubled state of documentary distribution and ultimately, freedom of expression, particularly acute for stories about social justice or politics in regions that aren't friendly to the critique. Placed together in the appropriate structural context—that is, commercial entertainment business models that adhere to political dynamics of valuable markets like India, for instance, regardless of how their governments are policing freedom of speech and expression—these are troubling realities. As filmmaker Julia Bacha noted, "Increasingly, the ways in which our media landscape has shifted over time have in many ways created the conditions for creeping authoritarianism."[40] Editorial independence is a key idea here once more, but this is a deeper critique and call for redress and structural rebuilding and imagining. Brandon Kramer, the director behind *The First Step*, says that distributors— large and small—have developed an "extraordinary allergy" to stories that deal with sensitive, difficult, or controversial topics in a nuanced way:

It's been really disheartening for me because I understand the sensitivities, but what I don't understand is that these contentious issues, they're really, really consequential. They're life and death for a lot of people. And our ability to navigate these polarizing topics [is] really critical. So, if the main gatekeepers for presenting stories that help shape our culture are saying that there is not a space to have debates around topics or people that are contentious or where it's sensitive or heated. To me, it's like, then what do we do?[41]

What started as a quiet creeping concern has become an urgent, industry-wide question. How do we intervene in a documentary field increasingly dominated by a global entertainment marketplace and political forces that are uninterested in releasing and marketing films that critique political and corporate power, or human rights topics that move across them? There are no perfect predictive models, but movements to radically reimagine the future are underway. In its global network of collaborators, for instance, the DISCO network advocates for entirely new streaming services dedicated to public interest material:

> the development of a free global streaming service to carry independent film and public interest media into every continent. In the short-term, we're recommending the community takeover of an existing, failing platform to start to experiment, to pilot what's possible with new models of ownership, with new models of collaboration, with journalism organizations, with all the other public interest media collaboratives, to start to pilot what might be possible.[42]

It's also vital to resource, expand, and support existing public media systems around the world, still the dominant home for independently produced documentaries that reveal lived realities often missing from the mainstream entertainment fare. "We need to protect what is still working," says Finzi. Compared to commercial networks, public media outlets are much more likely to license independent films and distribute stories about human rights topics—and those made by diverse storytellers.[43] Public media shouldn't be forgotten amid entrepreneurial thinking about building from scratch. How to properly fund this infrastructure—taxes, regulation, philanthropy, other fee structures—is its own set of questions and answers, some of which the International Fund for Public Interest Media aims to tackle. IMPIM can't

200 RADICAL REALITY

stand alone as the only such model, nor the only entity that emerges to engage in this level of world-building. And yet, any conversation about bolstering or bringing forward public media models must also recognize and center the reality that public broadcasting, especially in the United States, has a mixed history. It has perhaps been easier to celebrate it through the frames of intention and theory, rather than practice. In theory, public media stands as a bulwark of storytelling for the wider public interest, for instance, but in practice it has long housed many of the same institutional inequities that its stories have functioned to undo in society, including a model of distribution that persistently targeted high-income, white audiences. There have been significant changes in public broadcasting leadership and strategies in recent years, leading to notable progress in supporting more diverse creators and efforts to engage more inclusive audiences, but this legacy is real.

At the same time, in many ways, the chaos of the contemporary documentary marketplace brings back some documentary basics from which to build. From their first days to the present, independent documentaries have often existed in what we have described before as a "dual distribution model"— that is, one layer of distribution is the marketplace (TV, streaming, theaters) but the other is the wide network of grassroots and community places where people can come together to view and discuss in schools, workplaces, election offices, houses of faith, libraries.[44] As documentary director Julia Bacha says, "A lot of our distribution relies on civil society groups and universities and campuses and think tanks and women's groups and peace groups. For our films, we never really know if it's going to get any commercial distribution. We're always prepared for not getting any of it, and we're going to have to do it all ourselves."[45]

Social impact engagement with documentary storytelling, a long practice in the field, relies heavily on screening films in grassroots places—that is, sharing the work with communities most impacted, most readily able to engage meaningfully in the work and the stories shared on screen. For example, even without a commercial distributor for several years after a successful film festival circuit run, the directors of *The First Step* (United States) facilitated a robust grassroots engagement tour to bring their film to prisons and other communities for people and families involved in the criminal justice system—that is, the people most affected by the film—to engage. For *Uýra, The Rising Forest* (Brazil), the film team leveraged drag and other performances to connect with community audiences. Filmmakers of *The Quipu Project* (Peru) used mobile stories to reach and engage with rural Indigenous women, the heart of their story. There are now hundreds, if not thousands, of contemporary examples of successful, meaningful grassroots engagement programs with documentary stories.

And yet, this has emerged as a distinct tension between commercial distributors and filmmakers working in a grassroots tradition. In a growing number of whispered-about cases, media companies have blocked filmmakers from screening their films in grassroots environments, fearing that this appears to be "political" engagement in some way. If grassroots engagement is able to survive and thrive into the future, assuming this practice is properly funded and resourced, filmmakers—and the funders who support them—will need to effectively advocate for this activity before an evolving set of business practices is codified for the foreseeable future.[46] This is easier said than done, of course, and the onus can't be placed on individual filmmakers working alone, but as part of collective network power. Without distribution—reliable, affordable, resourced, accessible for wide audiences—there's little chance independent documentaries can agitate injustice, uphold democracy, or resist harmful abuses of power.

Essential Infrastructure: Financial and Security Resources

Despite promising networks of documentary filmmakers and impact producers around the world, the essential structural infrastructure required to make independent nonfiction storytelling—particularly for topics that are political or human-rights-focused—is weak. Filmmakers, like independent journalists, require financial support to make documentaries, along with reliable, accessible risk and security resources to ensure their work can see the light of day. Even the most lauded and celebrated filmmakers profiled in this book are not immune from the absolute madness of trying to access funding and protection resources—legal, physical, technological—for their work. They piece it all together from one film to the next. Financial and other risk is exponentially greater for the films that expose and resist harmful power, and for women and creators of color, already marginalized in the broader media ecology. For instance, Karl Malakunas, director of the award-winning investigative environmental film, *Delikado*, doubts he will ever make another film because funding it was so difficult; and having a full-time job was the only way he managed to create this one. Nanfu Wang, recipient of a prestigious MacArthur "genius fellowship" in the United States, says it's becoming nearly impossible to make a documentary about controversial political and human rights topics; the funding intricacies are a maze and distribution is increasingly not available to these kinds of films. The ripple effect is consistent and insidious. Returning to a concern raised by Wang in Chapter 5:

> There are less channels and less distributors who are brave enough to touch on issues that are politically sensitive. . . . And I worry that it means the public will see less and less films around issues that are challenging, that are questioning, that are radical, that are controversial. . . . I think people who are making films around human rights, politically sensitive films are facing challenges from multiple levels and directions. For example, people who are making a film in China that is reflecting the repression, they are not only risking their personal safety within China from the Chinese authority, they also face the challenges of getting it supported and funded outside of China. It forces a lot of people to give up on those stories.[47]

Danielle Turkov Wilson, founder of the Think-Film Impact Production company based in the United Kingdom, who has worked with films like *The Cave, The Territory, Nalvany,* and others, is blunt about the precariousness of the system: "I feel pain when I hear an artist say, 'I've set up an NGO, and at the same time, have been working on this film for five years, and I've been raising funds and running a charity.' And I wonder, when's your next film coming? Never."[48]

It's impossible to separate the delicate instability of financial and risk resources available for independent nonfiction makers. For documentary storytellers who create material that showcases little-seen lived experiences or reform-minded content, the "entire fragility of the ecosystem," as human rights attorney and scholar Peter Noorlander puts it, is the greatest intertwined threat to the continuation of this tradition of artistic, journalistic independent storytelling. Every manner and form of risk—psychological, economic, political, physical, mental health—comes into play when documentary filmmakers operate without security, without any kind of promise or guarantee that they can make a living or sell their films to distributors in the marketplace, without consistent access to funding or shared protections and training; as Noorlander, who also serves as a board member for Doc Society, said in an interview:

> All of it [specific political, technological, economic challenges] comes together. . . . The underlying feeling of insecurity, I think is actually one of the

BUILDING A FUTURE   203

hardest of the biggest pressures. And that results in greater vulnerability because somebody who's under pressure to make ends meet, they just want to complete the project.[49]

Legal threats imperil film distribution deals, economic realities of the commercialized global media system make human rights stories less viable, political actors can use regulatory actions and direct intimidation tactics to shut down critics, and lack of funding from country to country (and even international funds) makes independent media-making an increasingly frustrating and dangerous career choice. All of it incubates a silent, systemic kind of censorship, well beyond (but often including) direct hazards from political leaders, governments, and the commercial marketplace that dominates the space.

On the financial side, what might be done to develop reliable, accessible funding for independent documentary filmmakers around the world, including and particularly the ones working in environments with fleeting media freedom? Solutions, if we can boldly use this word, are crucial in two arenas: innovations in mixed revenue and funding models, and attempting to fix market structure and failure by pushing to regulate technology platforms in a range of areas, including paying content producers for material that populates them. Ideas are on the table, ripe for continued leadership and investment. The DISCO network has identified this pursuit as central, including the development of a global fund for the most politically perilous topics, albeit governed by regional voices:

> We call for the establishment of a decentralized, decolonized global fund worth 500 million to underpin the practice of independent filmmaking around the world for the next decade to increase plurality and defend freedom of expression, funds which should be controlled by regional cultural organizations.[50]

Actionable experimentation is also suggested from parallel journalistic recommendations: taxes and subsidies from commercial systems and governments to greater support for public media systems, regulatory decisions.[51] Nishant Lalwani and his colleagues at the International Fund for Public Interest Media—perhaps the most promising and unprecedented effort, given its vast financial scope and networked approach—are working daily to develop models for financial support across media development

204 RADICAL REALITY

organizations and philanthropies. It's a complicated and detailed effort that requires regulatory and political savvy to build models to work within and around repressive laws that increasingly prevent independent journalists and media makers from accessing funds within and outside their own countries. Innovation is also impossible without experimentation, so there must be some degree of tolerance to fund models and approaches that may work, or not work, over time.

Financial insecurity corresponds also to risk and safety resources, a huge and complicated area of focus for independent documentary storytelling to survive and thrive. The work is not safe in many ways, well beyond funding: legal threats and lack of access to E&O ("errors and omissions") insurance for the most politically sensitive films can effectively end a documentary's opportunity for distribution, generative AI and allegations about "deep fakes" pose reputational risks for filmmakers, and surveillance technology can place documentary makers in physical danger from repressive governments and other actors. The complicated layers of insecurity also contribute to substantial mental health risks for storytellers who endeavor to document the most painful realities, from state conflict to human rights atrocities. Here, too, developing fully accessible and shared resources and consulting experts—from technology security specialists to attorneys—is a desperate need, with humans able to offer real-time help and support, as in a well-resourced newsroom with its lawyers on staff. Beyond existing resources like the Doc Society's *Safe and Secure* resource guide for independent filmmakers, a deeper level of investment to train designated producers (or other professionals, including attorneys) to act as a film's daily "safety and security" expert might be a worthwhile idea.

As with every idea discussed in this chapter, the underlying challenges are immense—how to develop and fund the working ideas at scale, with deep cultural respect for, and understanding of, regional nuances. But they, like the films profiled within the pages of this book, are not impossible.
Beadie Finzi has the final word:

> We do not have to accept the status quo. Actually, in this time of collapse and plasticity, there is an opportunity to entirely reimagine a new system, its distribution and production funding. And we need to be progressing both of those things at the same time. But together, it's not impossible. At all. Not at all. We are multitude.[52]

And thus, we return—as our path forward—to the place where this book begins, with the tenacity and ingenuity of independent documentary filmmakers. They have never had it easy but always found a way, both through their storytelling and their collective action as networks. It might be helpful, in such a conclusion, to point out the throughline of this book as a mechanism to reframe and jolt urgency into the debate: documentary people operate as a community of practice, often outside the rules, policies, norms, and protections of formal employers, and it is precisely this reality that makes meaningful, fruitful institutional critique and repair difficult. Historically, as the field has evolved, it is a challenge to point to any one legacy organization to target for repair and correction, or to do so in a way that leads to meaningful change. This work lives in the hands of individuals working on their own—also left to agitate massive power structures alone. These are unrealistic odds if we hope to imagine a new future into being.

Documentary work today is dominated by major institutional gatekeepers—led by global media companies—that operate with unprecedented power to shape what gets seen, how it gets seen, and who tells the stories. Collective action and power are desperately needed for real criticism and correction. Technology platform dominance and global media consolidation threaten to stifle the meaningful progress that documentary people have forged together as a community of practice— see, for instance, the concerted work to resource and network BIPOC filmmakers—through the hard and conscientious work of individuals and organizations coming together. If a healthy independent public interest media system is to be built, it's clear that collective power is the only way to build systems that honor a full plurality of voices, where entertainment and information can coexist. No one organization can do it all. Innovation, collective action, and experimentation are vital to empower the storytellers who will show us the necessary radical reality in the global fight for social justice—now and in the future.

APPENDIX A

Interviews

Miriam Ayoo (*No Simple Way Home*)
Julia Bacha (*Boycott*)
Robert Bahar (*The Silence of Others*)
Alison Byrne Fields (*Welcome to Chechnya*)
Almudena Carracedo (*The Silence of Others*)
Maurice Clifton (*The First Step*)
Lisa Cortés (*All In: The Fight for Democracy*)
Juliana Curi (*Uýra, The Rising Forest*)
Akuol de Mabior (*No Simple Way Home*)
Rachel Naɲinaaq Edwardson (*In My Blood It Runs*)
Hollie Fifer (*The Opposition*)
Beadie Finzi (Doc Society)
Chloe Genga (*Softie, Free Money*, LBx Africa)
Sushmit Ghosh (*Writing with Fire*)
Yana Gorokhovskaia (Freedom House)
Lindsay Guetschow (*All In: The Fight for Democracy* and *He Named Me Malala*)
Alice Henty (*Welcome to Chechnya*)
Hanka Kastelicová (HBO Europe)
Alex Kelly (*In My Blood It Runs*)
Brandon Kramer (*The First Step*)
Lance Kramer (*The First Step*)
Nishant Lalwani (International Fund for Public Interest Media)
Rosemarie Lerner (*Quipu Project*)
Karl Malakunas (*Delikado*)
Cara Mertes (International Resource for Impact and Storytelling)
Sarah Mosses (Together Films, *For Sama*)
Maya Newell (*In My Blood It Runs*)
Peter Noorlander (The Global Rights Hub)
Jacqueline Olive (*Always in Season*)
Alex Pritz (*The Territory*)
Emily Roseman (The Institute for Nonprofit News)
Anya Rous (*Pray Away*)
Jyoti Sarda (*And She Could Be Next*)
Vinay Shukla (*An Insignificant Man*)
Marcia Smith (Firelight Media)
Megha Sood (Doc Society)
Rintu Thomas (*Writing with Fire*)
Kate Townsend (Netflix UK)
Danielle Turkov Wilson (*Peace for Nina and The Cave*)
Nanfu Wang (*Hooligan Sparrow* and *One Child Nation*)
Emily Wanja (*Thank You for the Rain*)

APPENDIX B

Filmography

Chapter 1: Fighting The Good Fight Around the World

An Insignificant Man

Chapter 2: Confronting Government Power

All In: The Fight for Democracy
The Silence of Others

Chapter 3: Witnessing Conflict and Resilience

The Cave
For Sama
No Simple Way Home
A House Made of Splinters
Peace for Nina

Chapter 4: Upholding Freedom of Expression

A Thousand Cuts
Writing with Fire
The First Step

Chapter 5: Demanding Human Rights

Hooligan Sparrow
One Child Nation
Welcome to Chechnya
He Named Me Malala
Uýra, The Rising Forest

Chapter 6: Demonstrating Activism

Delikado
The Territory
Thank You for the Rain

210 APPENDIX B

And She Could Be Next
I Am Samuel

Chapter 7: Creating Spaces for Reconciliation and Healing

Always in Season
The Murder of Emmett Till
Tell Them We Are Rising: The Story of Black Colleges and Universities
In My Blood It Runs
Pray Away
The Quipu Project

Chapter 8: Building a Future for Global Independent Documentary Storytelling to Survive and Thrive

Softie
Free Money

Notes

Chapter 1

1. Brittany Joyce, "The Political Documentary That Was Banned by the Indian Government," *Vice News*, December 19, 2017, https://www.vice.com/en_us/article/8xvnd4/the-political-docu mentary-that-was-banned-by-the-indian-government.
2. Liz Shackleton, "*An Insignificant Man* Wins Battle with Indian Censors," *Screendaily*, August 22, 2017, https://www.screendaily.com/news/an-insignificant-man-wins-battle-with-indian-cens ors/5121549.article
3. Liz Shackleton, "*An Insignificant Man* Wins Battle with Indian Censors," *Screendaily*, August 22, 2017, https://www.screendaily.com/news/an-insignificant-man-wins-battle-with-indian-cens ors/5121549.article.
4. "*An Insignificant Man*, Movie Based on Arvind Kejriwal's Life, Gets SC Nod," *The Economic Times India*, November 16, 2017, https://economictimes.indiatimes.com/magazines/panache/ an-insignificant-man-movie-based-on-arvind-kejriwals-life-gets-sc-nod/articleshow/61672 827.cms?utm_source = contentofinterest&utm_medium = text&utm_campaign = cppsthttps:// economictimes.indiatimes.com/magazines/panache/an-insignificant-man-movie-based-on- arvind-kejriwals-life-gets-sc-nod/articleshow/61672827.cms.
5. Vinay Shukla, Zoom interview with author, May 4, 2023.
6. The Economist Intelligence Unit, *Democracy Index 2019: A Year of Democratic Backsliding and Popular Protest* (London, UK: The Economist Intelligence Unit, 2019), 10, https://www.eiu. com/n/campaigns/democracy-index-2019/.
7. The Economist Intelligence Unit, *Democracy Index 2019: A Year of Democratic Backsliding and Popular Protest* (London, UK: The Economist Intelligence Unit, 2019), 16, https://www.eiu. com/n/campaigns/democracy-index-2019/.
8. John Corner, "Performing the Real: Documentary Diversions," *Television & New Media* 3, no. 3 (August 2002): 255–269, https://doi.org/10.1177/152747640200300302.
9. Caty Borum Chattoo, *Story Movements: How Documentaries Empower People and Inspire Social Change* (New York, NY: Oxford University Press, 2020).
10. Erik Barnouw, *Documentary: A History of the Non-Fiction Film*, 2nd rev. ed. (New York: Oxford University Press, 1993); Bill Nichols, *Representing Reality* (Bloomington: Indiana University Press, 2010).
11. Michael Chanan, *Politics of Documentary* (London: Palgrave Macmillan, 2008), 23.
12. Thomas Waugh, *Show Us Life: Toward a History and Aesthetics of the Committed Documentary* (Lanham, MD: Scarecrow Press, 1984); Jonathan Kahana, *Intelligence Work: The Politics of American Documentary* (New York: Columbia University Press, 2008); Betsy A. McLane, *A New History of Documentary Film*, 2nd ed. (New York: Bloomsbury Academic, 2012); Patricia R. Zimmerman and Helen De Michiel, *Open Space New Media Documentary: A Toolkit or Theory and Practice* (New York: Routledge, 2018); Dave Saunders, *Direct Cinema: Observational Documentary and the Politics of the Sixties* (London: Wallflower Press, 2007); Angela J. Aguayo, *Documentary Resistance: Social Change and Participatory Media*. Oxford University Press, 2019.
13. Steve Presence, Mike Wayne, and Jack Newsinger, *Contemporary Radical Film Culture: Networks, Organisations, and Activists* (New York: Routledge, 2020).
14. William Stott, *Documentary Expression in 1930s America* (Chicago: University of Chicago Press, 1973), 9.
15. Brian Winston, *Claiming the Real II: Documentary; Grierson and Beyond* (London: Palgrave Macmillan, 2008), 20.
16. Patricia Aufderheide, *Documentary: A Very Short Introduction* (New York: Oxford University Press, 2007), 2–3.
17. Michael Renov, ed., *Theorizing Documentary* (New York: Routledge, 1993), 21.

212 NOTES

18. Caty Borum Chattoo, *Story Movements: How Documentaries Empower People and Inspire Social Change* (New York, NY: Oxford University Press, 2020), 13.
19. Caty Borum Chattoo, *Story Movements: How Documentaries Empower People and Inspire Social Change* (New York, NY: Oxford University Press, 2020), 5.
20. Caty Borum Chattoo, *Story Movements: How Documentaries Empower People and Inspire Social Change* (New York, NY: Oxford University Press, 2020), 13.
21. Caty Borum Chattoo, *Story Movements: How Documentaries Empower People and Inspire Social Change* (New York, NY: Oxford University Press, 2020), 15.
22. Caty Borum Chattoo, *Story Movements: How Documentaries Empower People and Inspire Social Change* (New York, NY: Oxford University Press, 2020), 17–18.
23. Caty Borum, David Conrad-Pérez, and Bryan Bello, "Creative Independent Investigative Documentary Storytellers in the Streaming Age: Toward a Community of Practice Framework," *Journalism Practice* 18, no. 7 (2022): 1867–1885. https://doi.org/10.1080/17512 786.2022.2126993.
24. Caty Borum Chattoo, *Story Movements: How Documentaries Empower People and Inspire Social Change* (New York, NY: Oxford University Press, 2020), 18–19.
25. Heather L. LaMarre and Kristen D. Landreville, "When Is Fiction as Good as Fact? Comparing the Influence of Documentary and Historical Reenactment Films on Engagement, Affect, Issue Interest, and Learning," *Mass Communication and Society* 12, no. 4 (2009): 537–555, https://doi.org/10.1080/15205430903237915.
26. Caty Borum Chattoo and Lauren Feldman, "Storytelling for Social Change: Leveraging Documentary and Comedy for Public Engagement in Global Poverty," *Journal of Communication* 67, no. 5 (2017): 678–701, https://doi:10.1111/jcom.12318.
27. Caty Borum Chattoo and Lauren Feldman, "Storytelling for Social Change: Leveraging Documentary and Comedy for Public Engagement in Global Poverty," *Journal of Communication* 67, no. 5 (2017): 678–701, https://doi:10.1111/jcom.12318.
28. Victor Pickard, *Democracy Without Journalism? Confronting the Misinformation Society* (New York, NY: Oxford University Press, 2020), 63–64.
29. Victor Pickard, *Democracy Without Journalism? Confronting the Misinformation Society* (New York, NY: Oxford University Press, 2020), 64.
30. International Fund for Public Interest Media, *Enabling Media Markets to Work for Democracy: An International Fund for Public Interest Media (Summary)* (n.p.: International Fund for Public Interest Media), 3, accessed October 1, 2023, https://ifpim.org/resources/feas ibility-study/.
31. International Fund for Public Interest Media, *Enabling Media Markets to Work for Democracy: An International Fund for Public Interest Media (Summary)* (n.p.: International Fund for Public Interest Media), 4, accessed October 1, 2023https://ifpim.org/resources/feas ibility-study/.
32. Caty Borum Chattoo, *Story Movements: How Documentaries Empower People and Inspire Social Change* (New York, NY: Oxford University Press, 2020), 62–75.
33. Manuel Castells, *Networks of Outrage and Hope: Social Movements in the Internet Age* (Cambridge, UK; Malden, MA: Polity, 2012).
34. Cara Mertes, Zoom interview with author, May 16, 2023.
35. Caty Borum Chattoo, *Story Movements: How Documentaries Empower People and Inspire Social Change* (New York, NY: Oxford University Press, 2020), 71.
36. Cara Mertes, email correspondence with author, January 30, 2024; Caty Borum Chattoo, *Story Movements: How Documentaries Empower People and Inspire Social Change* (New York, NY: Oxford University Press, 2020), 87–95.
37. Caty Borum Chattoo, *Story Movements: How Documentaries Empower People and Inspire Social Change* (New York, NY: Oxford University Press, 2020).
38. David Conrad-Pérez, et al., "Breaking Cultures of Silence: Learnings from a Participatory Community-Centred Approach to Leveraging and Researching Documentaries for Social Change," *Journal of Alternative and Community Media* 7, no. 1 (April 2022): 3–22, https://doi. org/10.1386/jacm_00102_1.
39. "The First-Ever Global Directory of Impact Producers," The StoryBoard Collective, January 23, 2023, https://www.storyboard-collective.org/new/first-global-directory-of-impact-producers.
40. International Documentary Association, 2018 Attendees of the Building Networks Across Borders Convening, furnished to the author by IDA, 2018.
41. Cara Mertes, Zoom interview with author, May 16, 2023.

NOTES 213

42. Caty Borum, David Conrad-Pérez, and Bryan Bello, "Creative Independent Investigative Documentary Storytellers in the Streaming Age: Toward a Community of Practice Framework," *Journalism Practice* 18, no. 7 (2022): 1867–1885, https://doi.org/10.1080/17512 786.2022.2126993.

43. Sarah Stonbely, "Cross-Field Collaboration: How and Why Journalists and Civil Society Organizations Around the World Are Working Together," Center for Cooperative Media, March 28, 2022, https://medium.com/centerforcooperativemedia/cross-field-collaboration-how-and-why-journalists-and-civil-society-organizations-around-the-world-f7828d5ccd.

44. Cara Mertes, email correspondence with author, January 30, 2024.

45. Freedom House, *Freedom in the World Report 2023* (Washington, DC: Freedom House, March 2023), https://freedomhouse.org/sites/default/files/2023-03/FIW_World_2023_Digtal PDF.pdf.

46. "Brazil: Bolsonaro Threatens Democratic Rule: Harasses Supreme Court, Signals He May Cancel Elections, Violates Free Speech," Human Rights Watch, September 15, 2021, https://www.hrw.org/news/2021/09/15/brazil-bolsonaro-threatens-democratic-rule.

47. "A Journalist Was Harassed Online Every Three Seconds During Brazil's Election Campaign," Reporters Without Borders, April 28, 2023, https://rsf.org/en/journalist-was-harassed-online-every-three-seconds-during-brazil-s-election-campaign.

48. Raphael Tsavkko Garcia, "Bolsonaro's Social Media War with the Press Keeps Bleeding into the Real World, *Slate*, July 6, 2020, https://slate.com/technology/2020/07/brazil-president-bolson aro-attacks-press-journalists.html.

49. Marvin Kalb, *Enemy of the People: Trump's War on the Press, the New McCarthyism, and the Threat to American Democracy* (Washington, DC: Brookings Institution Press, 2018).

50. Caty Borum, David Conrad-Pérez, and Bryan Bello, "Creative Independent Investigative Documentary Storytellers in the Streaming Age: Toward a Community of Practice Framework," *Journalism Practice* 18, no. 7 (2022): 1867–1885, https://doi.org/10.1080/17512 786.2022.2126993.

51. Documentary field leaders and makers at the Copenhagen International Documentary Film Festival, confidential conversations with author, 2023.

52. Lauren Harris, "The Journalism Crisis Across the World," *Columbia Journalism Review*, March 31, 2021, https://www.cjr.org/business_of_news/the-journalism-crisis-across-the-world.php.

53. Anthony Kaufman, "At Sundance 2023, Corporate Docs Nab the Spotlight, but Bold Independent Nonfiction Shines," International Documentary Association, January 31, 2023, https://www.documentary.org/online-feature/sundance-2023-corporate-docs-nab-spotlight-bold-independent-nonfiction-shines.

54. Kate Townsend, Zoom interview with author, May 18, 2023.

55. Caty Borum Chattoo, *Story Movements: How Documentaries Empower People and Inspire Social Change* (New York, NY: Oxford University Press, 2020), 50.

56. Caty Borum Chattoo, *Story Movements: How Documentaries Empower People and Inspire Social Change* (New York, NY: Oxford University Press, 2020).

57. Matthew Carey, "Lisa Nishimura's Netflix Exit Shocks Documentary World: 'She Has Massively Helped Grow This Industry,'" *Deadline*, March 31, 2023, https://deadline.com/2023/03/lisa-nishimura-netflix-exit-shocks-documentary-world-news-1235315200/.

58. Kate Townsend, Zoom interview with author, May 18, 2023.

59. Arwa Mahdawi, "As *Making a Murderer* Returns, Is the Obsession with True Crime Turning Nasty?," *The Guardian*, October 16, 2018, https://www.theguardian.com/tv-and-radio/2018/oct/16/making-a-murderer-is-our-obsession-with-true-crime-turning-nasty-serial#:~:text = Making%20a%20Murderer%20quickly%20became,helped%20put%20Avery%20behind%20 bars.

60. Kate Townsend, Zoom interview with author, May 18, 2023.

61. Cara Mertes, Zoom interview with author, May 16, 2023.

62. Matthew Carey, "Lisa Nishimura's Netflix Exit Shocks Documentary World: 'She Has Massively Helped Grow This Industry,'" *Deadline*, March 31, 2023, https://deadline.com/2023/03/lisa-nishimura-netflix-exit-shocks-documentary-world-news-1235315200/.

63. Brian Welk, "Scaling Back CNN Films Means 'Troubling' Times for Documentaries," *IndieWire*, November 2, 2022, https://www.indiewire.com/features/general/cnn-films-cuts-documentar ies-analysis-1234777933/.

64. Kate Townsend, Zoom interview with author, May 18, 2023.

65. Hanka Kastelicova, Zoom interview with author, May 18, 2023.

214 NOTES

66. Brian Steinberg, "ABC News Executive Team Cut Following Disney Layoffs," *Variety*, March 30, 2023, https://variety.com/2023/tv/news/abc-news-layoffs-executives-disney-restructure-123 5568713/.

67. Cara Mertes, Zoom interview with author, May 16, 2023.

68. This multiyear initiative is funded by a grant from the Perspective Fund, a nonpartisan US-based foundation.

69. "Documentary Power Research Institute," Center for Media & Social Impact, accessed October 1, 2023, https://cmsimpact.org/program/documentary-power-research-institute/.

70. Caty Borum Chattoo, *Story Movements: How Documentaries Empower People and Inspire Social Change* (New York, NY: Oxford University Press, 2020), 17.

71. For more insight on who is, and is not, represented in contemporary documentary work, we encourage readers to see our earlier research on this topic: Caty Borum, Paula Weissman, and David Conrad-Pérez, "The Lens Reflected: What Stories and Storytellers Get the Greenlight in Documentary's Streaming Age?," Center for Media & Social Impact, American University School of Communication, Washington, DC, 2022, https://cmsimpact.org/program/document ary-representation/

72. Caty Borum Chattoo, *Story Movements: How Documentaries Empower People and Inspire Social Change* (New York, NY: Oxford University Press, 2020), 27–53.

73. Amnesty International, *Laws Designed to Silence: The Global Crackdown on Civil Society Organizations* (London, UK: Amnesty International, 2019), https://www.amnesty.org/downl oad/Documents/ACT3096472019ENGLISH.PDF.

Chapter 2

1. Maria Ressa and Nishant Lalwani, "Tyranny's Propagandists Are Winning," Project Syndicate, March 30, 2023, https://www.project-syndicate.org/commentary/saving-democracy-by-sup porting-public-interest-news-media-by-maria-ressa-and-nishant-lalwani-2023-03.

2. Robert Kuttner, *Can Democracy Survive Global Capitalism?* (New York: W. W. Norton, 2018), xiii.

3. V-Dem, *Democracy Report 2023: Defiance in the Face of Autocratization* (Gothenburg, Sweden: V-Dem Institute, 2023), 7, https://www.v-dem.net/publications/democracy-reports/.

4. V-Dem, *Democracy Report 2023: Defiance in the Face of Autocratization* (Gothenburg, Sweden: V-Dem Institute, 2023), 7, https://www.v-dem.net/publications/democracy-reports/.

5. The Economist, "A New Low for Global Democracy," *The Economist*, February 9, 2022, https://www.economist.com/graphic-detail/2022/02/09/a-new-low-for-global-democracy.

6. Freedom House, *Freedom in the World Report 2023* (Washington, DC: Freedom House, March 2023), https://freedomhouse.org/sites/default/files/2023-03/FIW_World_2023_Digtal PDF.pdf.

7. Ozan O. Varol, "Stealth Authoritarianism," *Iowa Law Review* 100, no. 4 (2015): 1677, https://ilr.law.uiowa.edu/print/volume-100-issue-4/stealth-authoritarianism.

8. Christian Davenport, "State Repression and Political Order," *Annual Review of Political Science* 10 (2007): 1–23, https://doi.org/10.1146/annurev.polisci.10.101405.143216.

9. Robert Kuttner, *Can Democracy Survive Global Capitalism?* (New York: W. W. Norton, 2018), xiii.

10. Robert Kuttner, *Can Democracy Survive Global Capitalism?* (New York: W. W. Norton, 2018), xix.

11. Michael Kazin, *The Populist Persuasion: An American History*, rev. ed. (Ithaca, NY: Cornell University Press, 2017), 1.

12. Michael Kazin, *The Populist Persuasion: An American History*, rev. ed. (Ithaca, NY: Cornell University Press, 2017), xiii-4.

13. John B. Judis, *The Populist Explosion: How the Great Recession Transformed American and European Politics* (New York: Columbia Global Reports, 2016), 15.

14. John B. Judis, *The Populist Explosion: How the Great Recession Transformed American and European Politics* (New York: Columbia Global Reports, 2016), 16–17.

15. Ece Temelkuran, *How to Lose a Country: The 7 Steps from Democracy to Dictatorship* (London: 4th Estate, 2020), 10.

NOTES 215

16. The Economist Intelligence Unit, *Democracy Index 2022: Frontline Democracy and the Battle for Ukraine* (London, UK: The Economist Intelligence Unit, 2023), https://www.eiu.com/n/campai gns/democracy-index-2022/; Robert R. Barr, *The Resurgence of Populism in Latin America* (Boulder, CO: Lynne Rienner, 2017); Heike Paul, Ursula Prutsch, and Jürgen Gebhardt, eds., *The Comeback of Populism: Transatlantic Perspectives* (Heidelberg: Universitätverlag Winter, 2019); John B. Judis, *The Populist Explosion: How the Great Recession Transformed American and European Politics* (New York: Columbia Global Reports, 2016); and Ece Temelkuran, *How to Lose a Country: The 7 Steps from Democracy to Dictatorship* (London: 4th Estate, 2020).

17. Carlos de la Torre, "What Can We Learn from Latin America to Understand Trump's Populism?," in *The Comeback of Populism: Transatlantic Perspectives*, ed. Heike Paul, Ursula Prutsch, and Jürgen Gebhardt (Heidelberg: Universitätverlag Winter, 2019), 254.

18. Jenifer Whitten-Woodring, "Watchdog or Lapdog? Media Freedom, Regime Type, and Government Respect for Human Rights," *International Studies Quarterly* 53, no. 3 (September 2009): 597, https://doi.org/10.1111/j.1468-2478.2009.00548.x.

19. Anon, "What the Media and Hollywood Got Wrong About Selma," *NBC News*, 2015, March 8, 2015, https://www.nbcnews.com/news/nbcblk/media-studies-selma-n319436.

20. Aniko Bodroghkozy, *Equal Time: Television and the Civil Rights Movement* (Champaign: University of Illinois Press, 2012), 115–116.

21. Aniko Bodroghkozy, *Equal Time: Television and the Civil Rights Movement* (Champaign: University of Illinois Press, 2012), 115–116.

22. "The Civil Rights Division Marks the 57th Anniversary of the Voting Rights Act," Civil Rights Division, courtesy of Assistant Attorney General Kristen Clarke, US Department of Justice, August 5, 2022, https://www.justice.gov/opa/blog/civil-rights-division-marks-57th-annivers ary-voting-rights-act.

23. "Section 2 of the Voting Rights Act," Civil Rights Division, US Department of Justice, last updated April 5, 2023, https://www.justice.gov/crt/section-2-voting-rights-act#:~:text=Sect ion%202%20of%20the%20Voting%20Rights%20Act%20of%201965%20prohibits,)(2)%20 of%20the%20Act.

24. "The Civil Rights Division Marks the 57th Anniversary of the Voting Rights Act," Civil Rights Division, courtesy of Assistant Attorney General Kristen Clarke, US Department of Justice, August 5, 2022, https://www.justice.gov/opa/blog/civil-rights-division-marks-57th-annivers ary-voting-rights-act.

25. "The Civil Rights Division Marks the 57th Anniversary of the Voting Rights Act," Civil Rights Division, courtesy of Assistant Attorney General Kristen Clarke, US Department of Justice, August 5, 2022, https://www.justice.gov/opa/blog/civil-rights-division-marks-57th-annivers ary-voting-rights-act.

26. "*Shelby County v. Holder*," Court Case Tracker, Brennan Center for Justice, last updated June 25, 2023, https://www.brennancenter.org/our-work/court-cases/shelby-county-v-holder.

27. "Effects of *Shelby County v. Holder* on the Voting Rights Act," Brennan Center for Justice, June 21, 2023, https://www.brennancenter.org/our-work/research-reports/effects-shelby-county-v- holder-voting-rights-act.

28. Kareem Crayton and Kendall Karson, "*Shelby County v. Holder* Turns 10, and Voting Rights Continue to Suffer from It," Brennan Center for Justice, June 20, 2023, https://www.brennancen ter.org/our-work/research-reports/shelby-county-v-holder-turns-10-and-voting-rights-conti nue-suffer-it; and "Vote Suppression," Brennan Center for Justice, accessed December 5, 2023, https://www.brennancenter.org/issues/ensure-every-american-can-vote/vote-suppression.

29. *All In: The Fight for Democracy*, directed by Liz Garbus and Lisa Cortés (2020; Culver City, CA: Amazon Studios), digital streaming, https://www.amazon.com/All-Fight-Democracy-Sta cey-Abrams/dp/B08FRQQKD5.

30. "*All In: The Fight for Democracy*—Meet the Women Behind New Voter Suppression Documentary, Mobilization Campaign Featuring Stacey Abrams," Southern Poverty Law Center, August 29, 2020, https://www.splcenter.org/news/2020/08/29/all-fight-democracy- meet-women-behind-new-voter-suppression-documentary-mobilization.

31. "Inspiring Compilation from *All In: The Fight for Democracy* | Prime Video," Prime Video, November 1, 2020, video, 10:11, https://www.youtube.com/watch?v=tCy9F5BIk24.

32. "Inspiring Compilation from *All In: The Fight for Democracy* | Prime Video," Prime Video, November 1, 2020, video, 10:11, https://www.youtube.com/watch?v=tCy9F5BIk24.

33. Glenn Kessler, "Did Racially Motivated Voter Suppression Thwart Stacey Abrams?," *Washington Post*, October 30, 2019, https://www.washingtonpost.com/politics/2019/10/30/did-racially- motivated-voter-suppression-thwart-stacey-abrams/.

216 NOTES

34. Ella Lee, "Fact Check: Post Online About Georgia Gov. Brian Kemp's 2018 Win Is Partly False," *USA Today*, November 18, 2020, https://www.usatoday.com/story/news/factcheck/2020/11/18/fact-check-partly-false-claim-gov-brian-kemp-and-2018-election/6327447002/; and Angela Caputo, Geoff Hing, and Johnny Kauffman, "They Didn't Vote . . . Now They Can't," American Public Media, October 19, 2018, https://www.apmreports.org/story/2018/10/19/georgia-voter-purge.

35. *All In: The Fight for Democracy*, directed by Liz Garbus and Lisa Cortés (2020; Culver City, CA: Amazon Studios), digital streaming, https://www.amazon.com/All-Fight-Democracy-Stacey-Abrams/dp/B08FRQQKD5.

36. Lisa Cortés, Zoom interview with author, September 29, 2023.

37. Lindsay Guetschow, Zoom interview with author, July 11, 2022.

38. Amazon Staff, "Amazon Studios Announces 50 State Initiative #AllInForVoting to Get Out the Vote," Policy News & Views, Amazon, August 25, 2020, https://www.aboutamazon.com/news/policy-news-views/amazon-studios-announces-50-state-initiative-allinforvoting-to-get-out-the-vote; and Mia Galuppo, "Stacey Abrams Voter Rights Doc *All In* Sets Release Date on Amazon," *Hollywood Reporter*, July 26, 2020, https://www.hollywoodreporter.com/news/general-news/stacey-abrams-voter-rights-doc-all-sets-release-date-amazon-1304472/.

39. Mia Galuppo, "Stacey Abrams Voter Rights Doc *All In* Sets Release Date on Amazon," *Hollywood Reporter*, July 26, 2020, https://www.hollywoodreporter.com/news/general-news/stacey-abrams-voter-rights-doc-all-sets-release-date-amazon-1304472/.

40. *All In: The Fight for Democracy* Impact Campaign Evaluation (n.d.), Internal document supplied to the authors by Lindsay Guetschow, impact strategist; and Lindsay Guetschow, Zoom interview with author, July 11, 2022.

41. *All In: The Fight for Democracy* Impact Campaign Evaluation (n.d.), Internal document supplied to the authors by Lindsay Guetschow, impact strategist.

42. Lisa Cortés, Zoom interview with author, September 29, 2023.

43. Dulce Chacón, *La Voz Dormida/The Sleeping Voice*, Penguin Random House, accessed December 5, 2023, https://www.penguinrandomhouse.com/books/579208/la-voz-dormida--the-sleeping-voice-by-dulce-chacon/.

44. Elizabeth Nash, "*The Sleeping Voice*, by Dulce Chacón, trans Nick Caistor," *The Independent*, January 13, 2006, https://www.independent.co.uk/arts-entertainment/books/reviews/the-sleeping-voice-by-dulce-chac-oacute-n-trans-nick-caistor-6111911.html.

45. Elizabeth Nash, "*The Sleeping Voice*, by Dulce Chacón, trans Nick Caistor," *The Independent*, January 13, 2006, https://www.independent.co.uk/arts-entertainment/books/reviews/the-sleeping-voice-by-dulce-chac-oacute-n-trans-nick-caistor-6111911.html.

46. Fionnuala Halligan, "The Sleeping Voice," *Screen Daily*, September 21, 2011, https://www.screendaily.com/the-sleeping-voice/5032361.article.

47. Madeleine Davis, "Is Spain Recovering Its Memory? Breaking the 'Pacto del Olvido,'" *Human Rights Quarterly* 27, no. 3 (August 2005): 858–880, https://www.jstor.org/stable/20069813; and Richard Gunther, José Ramón Montero, and José Ignacio Wert, "The Media and Politics in Spain: From Dictatorship to Democracy," in *Democracy and the Media: A Comparative Perspective*, ed. Richard Gunther and Anthony Mughan (Cambridge, UK: Cambridge University Press, 2000).

48. Richard Gunther, José Ramón Montero, and José Ignacio Wert, "The Media and Politics in Spain: From Dictatorship to Democracy," in *Democracy and the Media: A Comparative Perspective*, ed. Richard Gunther and Anthony Mughan (Cambridge, UK: Cambridge University Press, 2000), 4.

49. Madeleine Davis, "Is Spain Recovering Its Memory? Breaking the 'Pacto del Olvido,'" *Human Rights Quarterly* 27, no. 3 (August 2005): 860, https://www.jstor.org/stable/20069813.

50. Madeleine Davis, "Is Spain Recovering Its Memory? Breaking the 'Pacto del Olvido,'" *Human Rights Quarterly* 27, no. 3 (August 2005): 860, https://www.jstor.org/stable/20069813.

51. Omar G. Encarnación, *Democracy Without Justice in Spain: The Politics of Forgetting* (Philadelphia: University of Pennsylvania Press, 2014).

52. Enrique Moradiellos, *Franco: Anatomy of a Dictator* (London: I.B. Tauris, 2018), 1–2.

53. Richard Gunther, José Ramón Montero, and José Ignacio Wert, "The Media and Politics in Spain: From Dictatorship to Democracy," in *Democracy and the Media: A Comparative Perspective*, ed. Richard Gunther and Anthony Mughan (Cambridge: Cambridge University Press, 2000), 4.

54. Omar G. Encarnación, *Democracy Without Justice in Spain: The Politics of Forgetting* (Philadelphia: University of Pennsylvania Press, 2014).

NOTES 217

55. Guy Hedgecoe, "What Digging Up Franco Has to Do with Democracy," *New Republic*, September 17, 2018, https://newrepublic.com/article/151257/digging-franco-democracy.
56. Enrique Moradiellos, *Franco: Anatomy of a Dictator* (London: I.B. Tauris, 2018), 11.
57. Omar G. Encarnación, Forgetting, in Order to Move On," *New York Times*, January 22, 2014, https://www.nytimes.com/roomfordebate/2014/01/06/turning-away-from-painful-chapters/forgetting-in-order-to-move-on#:~:text=The%20pact%20to%20forget%20meant,democracy%20against%20Franco's%20fascist%20coup.
58. Omar G. Encarnación, *Democracy Without Justice in Spain: The Politics of Forgetting* (Philadelphia: University of Pennsylvania Press, 2014), 1; and Omar G. Encarnación, "Forgetting, in Order to Move On," *New York Times*, January 22, 2014, https://www.nytimes.com/roomfordebate/2014/01/06/turning-away-from-painful-chapters/forgetting-in-order-to-move-on#:~:text=The%20pact%20to%20forget%20meant,democracy%20against%20Franco's%20fascist%20coup.
59. Omar G. Encarnación, *Democracy Without Justice in Spain: The Politics of Forgetting* (Philadelphia: University of Pennsylvania Press, 2014), 7
60. Almudena Carracedo, Zoom interview with author, September 29, 2023.
61. Robert Bahar, Zoom interview with author, September 29, 2023.
62. Alejandro Lerena Garcia, "Overview of the Argentine Lawsuit Against the Crimes of the Franco Regime: Outcomes and Challenges," *Journal of Political Sciences & Public Affairs* 9, no. 12 (2021): 2, https://www.longdom.org/open-access-pdfs/overview-of-the-argentine-lawsuit-against-the-crimes-of-the-franco-regime-outcomes-and-challenges.pdf.
63. "*The Silence of Others*," The Silence of Others Website, accessed December 5, 2023, https://thesilenceofothers.com/.
64. Almudena Carracedo, Robert Bahar, and Charlotte Groult, "*The Silence of Others*: A Conversation with the Filmmakers," *Violence: An International Journal* 1, no. 1 (2020): 214, https://doi.org/10.1177/2633002420913751.
65. *The Silence of Others*, Impact Presentation (internal PowerPoint), shared by the filmmakers, October 2023, slide 16.
66. *The Silence of Others*, Impact Presentation (internal PowerPoint), shared by the filmmakers, October 2023, slide 35.
67. Almudena Carracedo, Robert Bahar, and Charlotte Groult, "*The Silence of Others*: A Conversation with the Filmmakers," *Violence: An International Journal* 1, no. 1 (2020): 215, https://doi.org/10.1177/2633002420913751.
68. Almudena Carracedo, Zoom interview with author, September 29, 2023.
69. "About," The Silence of Others Website, accessed December 5, 2023, https://thesilenceofothers.com/about.
70. *The Silence of Others*, Impact Presentation (internal PowerPoint), shared by the filmmakers, October 2023, slide 69.
71. Almudena Carracedo, Robert Bahar, and Charlotte Groult, "*The Silence of Others*: A Conversation with the Filmmakers," *Violence: An International Journal* 1, no. 1 (2020): 205–218, https://doi.org/10.1177/2633002420913751.
72. Robert Bahar, Zoom interview with author, September 29, 2023.
73. Almudena Carracedo, Robert Bahar, and Charlotte Groult, "*The Silence of Others*: A Conversation with the Filmmakers," *Violence: An International Journal* 1, no. 1 (2020): 215, https://doi.org/10.1177/2633002420913751.
74. *The Silence of Others*, Impact Presentation (internal PowerPoint), shared by the filmmakers, October 2023, slides 28–34.
75. Almudena Carracedo, Robert Bahar, and Charlotte Groult, "*The Silence of Others*: A Conversation with the Filmmakers," *Violence: An International Journal* 1, no. 1 (2020): 216, https://doi.org/10.1177/2633002420913751.
76. *The Silence of Others*, directed by Almudena Carracedo and Robert Bahar (2018; Semilla Verde Productions and Lucernam Films in association with El Deseo).
77. Guy Lodge, "Film Review: *The Silence of Others*," *Variety*, April 24, 2019, https://variety.com/2019/film/reviews/the-silence-of-others-review-1203196525/.
78. Robert Bahar, Zoom interview with author, September 29, 2023.
79. Almudena Carracedo, Zoom interview with author, September 29, 2023.
80. Julia Bacha, Zoom interview with author, September 29, 2023.
81. Julia Bacha, Zoom interview with author, September 29, 2023.

218 NOTES

82. Steven Levitsky and Daniel Ziblatt, *How Democracies Die* (Harlow, England: Penguin Books, 2019), 5.
83. Ece Temelkuran, *How to Lose a Country: The 7 Steps from Democracy to Dictatorship* (London: 4th Estate, 2020), "Contents" page.
84. Daehee Bak, Surachanee Sriyai, and Stephen A. Meserve, "The Internet and State Repression: A Cross-National Analysis of the Limits of Digital Constraint," *Journal of Human Rights* 17, no. 5 (2018): 642–659, https://doi.org/10.1080/14754835.2018.1456914.
85. Lisa Cortés, Zoom interview with author, September 29, 2023.

Chapter 3

1. Feras Fayyad, "Syrian Director Feras Fayyad on His New Documentary *The Cave*," interview by Kim Masters, *The Business*, KCRW, October 21, 2019, audio, 28:34, https://www.kcrw.com/cult ure/shows/the-business/syrian-director-feras-fayyad-on-his-new-documentary-the-cave.
2. "About Us," Organization for the Prohibition of Chemical Weapons, accessed November 11, 2023, https://www.opcw.org/about-us.
3. "Conference of the States Parties Adopts Decision to Suspend Certain Rights and Privileges of the Syrian Arab Republic Under the CWC," OPCW News, Organization for the Prohibition of Chemical Weapons, April 22, 2021, https://www.opcw.org/media-centre/news/2021/04/con ference-states-parties-adopts-decision-suspend-certain-rights-and.
4. "2023 World Press Freedom Index—Journalism Threatened by Fake Content Industry," Reporters Without Borders, accessed November 11, 2023, https://rsf.org/en/2023-world-press-freedom-index-journalism-threatened-by-fake-content-industry.
5. Vera Slavtcheva-Petkova et al., "Conceptualizing Journalists' Safety Around the Globe," *Digital Journalism* 11, no. 7 (2023): 1211–1229, https://doi.org/10.1080/21670811.2022.2162429.
6. Lokman Tsui and Francis Lee, "How Journalists Understand the Threats and Opportunities of New Technologies: A Study of Security Mind-Sets and Its Implications for Press Freedom," *Journalism* 22, no. 6 (2019), https://doi.org/10.1177/1464884919849418.
7. Robert Mahoney, "Going It Alone: More Freelancers Means Less Support, Greater Danger," *Committee to Protect Journalists*, April 27, 2015, https://cpj.org/2015/04/attacks-on-the-press-more-freelancers-less-support-greater-danger/.
8. Caty Borum, David Conrad-Pérez, and Bryan Bello, "Creative Independent Investigative Documentary Storytellers in the Streaming Age: Toward a Community of Practice Framework," *Journalism Practice* 18, no. 7 (2022): 1867–1885, https://doi.org/10.1080/17512 786.2022.2126993.
9. Barbie Zelizer, *About to Die: How News Images Move the Public* (Oxford: Oxford University Press, 2010).
10. David Conrad, "Misguided Benevolence: How 'Moments of Need' Came to Motivate American Journalism" (PhD diss., University of Pennsylvania, 2018).
11. David Conrad, "Misguided Benevolence: How 'Moments of Need' Came to Motivate American Journalism" (PhD diss., University of Pennsylvania, 2018).
12. Barbie Zelizer, *About to Die: How News Images Move the Public* (Oxford: Oxford University Press, 2010), 187.
13. Barbie Zelizer, *About to Die: How News Images Move the Public* (Oxford: Oxford University Press, 2010), 188.
14. Barbie Zelizer, *About to Die: How News Images Move the Public* (Oxford: Oxford University Press, 2010), 326.
15. Sandra Ristovska, "Video and Witnessing at the International Criminal Tribunal for the Former Yugoslavia," in *The Routledge Companion to Media and Human Rights*, ed. Howard Tumber and Silvio Waisbord (London: Routledge, 2017).
16. Sandra Ristovska, "Video and Witnessing at the International Criminal Tribunal for the Former Yugoslavia," in *The Routledge Companion to Media and Human Rights*, ed. Howard Tumber and Silvio Waisbord (London: Routledge, 2017), 363.
17. Caty Borum Chattoo, *Story Movements: How Documentaries Empower People and Inspire Social Change* (New York: Oxford University Press, 2020).

NOTES 219

18. Sandra Ristovska, *Seeing Human Rights: Video Activism as a Proxy Profession* (Cambridge, MA: MIT Press, 2021).
19. Barbie Zelizer, *About to Die: How News Images Move the Public* (Oxford: Oxford University Press, 2010).
20. Caty Borum Chattoo, *Story Movements: How Documentaries Empower People and Inspire Social Change* (New York: Oxford University Press, 2020).
21. Sarah Mosses, interview with author and Aras Coskuntuncel, April 18, 2022.
22. Sarah Mosses, interview with author and Aras Coskuntuncel, April 18, 2022.
23. Amy Kaufman, "Feras Fayyad Almost Couldn't Visit the U.S. Because He's Syrian. Now He's Going to the Oscars," *Los Angeles Times*, February 7, 2020, https://www.latimes.com/entertainment-arts/movies/story/2020-02-07/oscars-syria-feras-fayyad-the-cave.
24. Shorty Social Good Awards, "*The Cave*: Winner in Human Rights," https://shortyawards.com/5th-socialgood/tbd.
25. Danielle Turkov, interview with author, July 26, 2023.
26. Danielle Turkov, interview with author, July 26, 2023.
27. Brooke Kroeger, *Undercover Reporting: The Truth About Deception* (Evanston, IL: Northwestern University Press, 2012).
28. Caty Borum Chattoo, *Story Movements: How Documentaries Empower People and Inspire Social Change* (New York: Oxford University Press, 2020).
29. Brian Winston, *Claiming the Real: Documentary; Grierson and Beyond* (London: Palgrave Macmillan, 2008).
30. Stella Bruzzi, *New Documentary: A Critical Introduction* (London: Routledge, 2000), 6.
31. Simon Allison, "Was South Sudan a Mistake?" *Guardian Africa Network*, January 8, 2014, https://www.theguardian.com/world/2014/jan/08/south-sudan-war-mistake#:~:text=The%20father%20of%20South%20Sudanese,if%20everything%20else%20had%20failed.
32. John Garang, Speech at Iowa State University, 2002, https://www.youtube.com/watch?v=tW6doQxxwzo.
33. Akuol de Mabior, interview with author, August 8, 2023.
34. Akuol de Mabior, interview with author, August 8, 2023.
35. Akuol de Mabior, interview with author, August 8, 2023.
36. Akuol de Mabior, interview with author, August 8, 2023.
37. Akuol de Mabior, interview with author, August 8, 2023.
38. Akuol de Mabior, interview with author, August 8, 2023.
39. Danielle Turkov, interview with author, August 8, 2023.
40. Bill Nichols, *Representing Reality: Issues and Concepts in Documentary* (Bloomington: Indiana University Press, 1991); Fiona Otway, "The Unreliable Narrator in Documentary," *Journal of Film and Video* 67, nos. 3–4 (Fall/Winter 2015): 3–23, https://doi.org/10.5406/jfilmvideo.67.3-4.0003.
41. John Ellis, "How Documentaries Mark Themselves Out from Fiction: A Genre-Based Approach," *Studies in Documentary Film* 15, no. 2 (2021): 140–150, https://doi.org/10.1080/17503280.2021.1923144.
42. "2023 World Press Freedom Index—Journalism Threatened by Fake Content Industry," Reporters Without Borders, accessed November 11, 2023, https://rsf.org/en/2023-world-press-freedom-index-journalism-threatened-fake-content-industry.
43. Sandra Ristovska, *Seeing Human Rights: Video Activism as a Proxy Profession* (Cambridge, MA: MIT Press, 2021).
44. Sandra Ristovska, *Seeing Human Rights: Video Activism as a Proxy Profession* (Cambridge, MA: MIT Press, 2021), 200.

Chapter 4

1. "Carl von Ossietzky—Facts," The Nobel Prize, accessed November 12, 2023, https://www.nobelprize.org/prizes/peace/1935/ossietzky/facts/.
2. "Maria Ressa—Nobel Prize Lecture," The Nobel Prize, accessed November 12, 2023, https://www.nobelprize.org/prizes/peace/2021/ressa/lecture/.

220 NOTES

3. "Maria Ressa—Nobel Prize Lecture," The Nobel Prize, accessed November 12, 2023, https://www.nobelprize.org/prizes/peace/2021/ressa/lecture/.

4. "Maria Ressa—Nobel Prize Lecture," The Nobel Prize, accessed November 12, 2023, https://www.nobelprize.org/prizes/peace/2021/ressa/lecture/.

5. "Philippines' 'War on Drugs,'" Human Rights Watch, accessed November 12, 2023, https://www.hrw.org/tag/philippines-war-drugs.

6. "Duterte's History of Clashes with Philippine Media," News Desk, *Agence France-Presse*, June 15, 2020, https://www.france24.com/en/20200615-duterte-s-history-of-clashes-with-philipp ine-media; and James Griffiths, "Duterte's War on the Press in the Philippines Could Provide a Model for Hong Kong and Beyond," *CNN*, June 15, 2020, https://edition.cnn.com/2020/06/15/asia/philippines-ressa-hong-kong-national-security-intl-hnk/index.html.

7. James Griffiths, "Duterte's War on the Press in the Philippines Could Provide a Model for Hong Kong and Beyond," *CNN*, June 15, 2020, https://edition.cnn.com/2020/06/15/asia/philippines-ressa-hong-kong-national-security-intl-hnk/index.html.

8. Scott Neuman, "Philippine Journalist Maria Ressa Found Guilty of Violating Cyber Libel Law," NPR, June 15, 2020. https://www.npr.org/2020/06/15/876943655/philippine-journalist-maria-ressa-found-guilty-of-violating-cyberlibel-law

9. "Maria Ressa—Nobel Prize Lecture," The Nobel Prize, accessed November 12, 2023, https://www.nobelprize.org/prizes/peace/2021/ressa/lecture/.

10. Ramona S. Diaz, "Ramona S. Diaz on Making *A Thousand Cuts*, a Docu-film on the Unfolding Story of Maria Ressa," interview by Jannelle So, *SoJanenelleTV*, January 17, 2021, YouTube video, 25:47, https://www.youtube.com/watch?v=5XzpA6JgeQM.

11. *A Thousand Cuts*, film, accessed November 12, 2023, https://www.athousandcuts.film/; "*A Thousand Cuts* Wins News Emmy for Outstanding Social Issue Documentary," Rappler, September 30, 2022, https://www.rappler.com/entertainment/movies/a-thousand-cuts-wins-news-emmy-outstanding-social-issue-documentary-2022/; and "*A Thousand Cuts*, Award Profile," Peabody Awards, accessed November 12, 2023, https://peabodyawards.com/award-profile/a-thousand-cuts/.

12. *A Thousand Cuts*, directed by Ramona S. Diaz (2020; Los Angeles: Concordia Studios, 2021), https://www.youtube.com/watch?v=JQpjfWV_p6E.

13. Ramona S. Diaz, "Ramona S. Diaz on Making *A Thousand Cuts*, a Docu-film on the Unfolding Story of Maria Ressa," interview by Jannelle So, *SoJanenelleTV*, January 17, 2021, YouTube video, 25:47, https://www.youtube.com/watch?v=5XzpA6JgeQM.

14. Maria Ressa and Ramona Diaz, "*A Thousand Cuts*, Roundtable Conversation ft. Maria Ressa and Ramona Diaz," interview by Christiane Amanpour, *Amanpour and Company*, January 8, 2020, YouTube video, 15:12, https://www.youtube.com/watch?v=ReAc4m237qY.

15. "Philippines: Next Steps for ICC Probe of Duterte-Era Killings: Q&A on International Criminal Court Decision to Resume Investigation," Human Rights Watch, February 13, 2023, https://www.hrw.org/news/2023/02/13/philippines-next-steps-icc-probe-duterte-era-killings.

16. Richard R. John, "Freedom of Expression in the Digital Age: A Historian's Perspective," *Church, Communication and Culture* 4, no. 1 (2019): 25–38, https://doi.org/10.1080/23753 234.2019.1565918; and Howard Tumber and Silvio Waisbord, eds., *The Routledge Companion to Media and Human Rights* (London: Routledge, 2017), 5–6.

17. UNESCO, *World Trends in Freedom of Expression and Media Development: Global Report 2017/2018* (Paris: UNESCO, 2018), https://www.unesco.org/en/world-media-trends/previ ous-reports; and Sarah Repucci, *Freedom and the Media 2019: Media Freedom: A Downward Spiral* (Washington, DC: Freedom House, 2019), https://freedomhouse.org/report/freedom-and-media/2019/media-freedom-downward-spiral.

18. Maria Ressa and Ramona Diaz, "*A Thousand Cuts* Roundtable Conversation ft. Maria Ressa and Ramona Diaz," interview by Christiane Amanpour, *Amanpour and Company*, January 8, 2020, YouTube video, 15:12, https://www.youtube.com/watch?v=ReAc4m237qY.

19. Howard Tumber and Silvio Waisbord, eds., *The Routledge Companion to Media and Human Rights* (London: Routledge, 2017), 5.

20. Richard R. John, "Freedom of Expression in the Digital Age: A Historian's Perspective," *Church, Communication and Culture* 4, no. 1 (2019): 25, https://doi.org/10.1080/23753 234.2019.1565918.

21. Richard R. John, "Freedom of Expression in the Digital Age: A Historian's Perspective," *Church, Communication and Culture* 4, no. 1 (2019): 25, https://doi.org/10.1080/23753 234.2019.1565918.

NOTES 221

22. Richard R. John, "Freedom of Expression in the Digital Age: A Historian's Perspective," *Church, Communication and Culture* 4, no. 1 (2019): 25–38, https://doi.org/10.1080/23753 234.2019.1565918; and Howard Tumber and Silvio Waisbord, eds., *The Routledge Companion to Media and Human Rights* (London: Routledge, 2017), 5–6.

23. Jenifer Whitten-Woodring, "Watchdog or Lapdog? Media Freedom, Regime Type, and Government Respect for Human Rights," *International Studies Quarterly* 53, no. 3 (September 2009): 598, http://www.jstor.org/stable/27735113.

24. Jenifer Whitten-Woodring, "Watchdog or Lapdog? Media Freedom, Regime Type, and Government Respect for Human Rights," *International Studies Quarterly* 53, no. 3 (September 2009): 595, http://www.jstor.org/stable/27735113.

25. "The Issue," International Fund for Public Interest Media, accessed November 21, 2023, https://ifpim.org/the-issue/.

26. Lauren Harris, "The Journalism Crisis Across the World," *Columbia Journalism Review*, March 31, 2021, https://www.cjr.org/business_of_news/the-journalism-crisis-across-the-world.php.

27. "2023 World Press Freedom Index—Journalism Threatened by Fake Content Industry," Reporters Without Borders, accessed November 11, 2023, https://rsf.org/en/2023-world-press-freedom-index-journalism-threatened-fake-content-industry.

28. Freedom House, *Freedom in the World Report 2023* (Washington, DC: Freedom House, March 2023), https://freedomhouse.org/sites/default/files/2023-03/FIW_World_2023_Digtal PDF.pdf.

29. Yana Gorokhovskaia, Interview with author, May 16, 2023.

30. "Home," International Fund for Public Interest Media, accessed November 22, 2023, https://ifpim.org/.

31. "The Issue," International Fund for Public Interest Media, accessed November 21, 2023, https://ifpim.org/the-issue/.

32. Nishant Lalwani, Zoom interview with author, May 18, 2023.

33. International Fund for Public Interest Media, *Enabling Media Markets to Work for Democracy: An International Fund for Public Interest Media (Summary)* (n.p.: International Fund for Public Interest Media), 3, accessed October 1, 2023, https://ifpim.org/resources/feas ibility-study/.

34. International Fund for Public Interest Media, *Enabling Media Markets to Work for Democracy: An International Fund for Public Interest Media (Summary)* (n.p.: International Fund for Public Interest Media), 3, accessed October 1, 2023, https://ifpim.org/resources/feas ibility-study/.

35. Yana Gorokhovskaia, interview with author, May 16, 2023.

36. "The Issue," International Fund for Public Interest Media, accessed November 22, 2023, https://ifpim.org/the-issue/.

37. Nishant Lalwani, Zoom interview with author, May 18, 2023.

38. "New Indian FCRA Amendments Impact Foreign Grants to Indian NGOs," News, Council on Foundations, last updated November 12, 2020, https://cof.org/news/new-indian-fcra-ame ndments-impact-foreign-grants-indian-ngos.

39. Nishant Lalwani, Zoom interview with author, May 18, 2023.

40. Yana Gorokhovskaia, interview with author, May 16, 2023.

41. Karin Wahl-Jorgensen et al., "The Future of Journalism: Risks, Threats, and Opportunities," *Digital Journalism* 4, no. 7 (2016): 809–815, https://doi.org/10.1080/21670811.2016.1199469.

42. Freedom House, *Freedom in the World Report 2023* (Washington, DC: Freedom House, March 2023), https://freedomhouse.org/sites/default/files/2023-03/FIW_World_2023_Digtal PDF.pdf.

43. Steven Feldstein, *The Global Expansion of AI Surveillance* (Washington, DC: Carnegie Endowment for International Peace, September 17, 2019), 1, https://carnegieendowment.org/ 2019/09/17/global-expansion-of-ai-surveillance-pub-79847.

44. Caty Borum, David Conrad-Pérez, and Bryan Bello, "Creative Independent Investigative Documentary Storytellers in the Streaming Age: Toward a Community of Practice Framework," *Journalism Practice* 18, no. 7 (2022): 1867–1885, https://doi.org/10.1080/17512 786.2022.2126993.

45. Yana Gorokhovskaia, Interview with author, May 16, 2023.

46. Caty Borum, Paula Weissman, and David Conrad-Pérez, "The Lens Reflected: What Stories and Storytellers Get the Greenlight in Documentary's Streaming Age?," Center for Media &

Social Impact, American University School of Communication, Washington, DC, November 2022, https://cmsimpact.org/report/the-lens-reflected/.

47. Kate Townsend, Zoom interview with author, May 18, 2023.

48. Nishant Lalwani, Zoom interview with the author, May 18, 2023.

49. Karin Wahl-Jorgensen et al., "The Future of Journalism: Risks, Threats, and Opportunities," *Digital Journalism* 4, no. 7 (2016): 809–815, https://doi.org/10.1080/21670811.2016.1199469.

50. "Reasons Why Uttar Pradesh Is a Quintessential Indian Travel Experience," TimesTravel, *Times of India*, last updated February 27, 2022, https://timesofindia.indiatimes.com/travel/destinati ons/reasons-why-uttar-pradesh-is-a-quintessential-indian-travel-experience/photostory/89858609.cms.

51. *Encyclopedia Britannica*, s.v. "Uttar Pradesh," written by Raj B. Mathur, last updated November 21, 2023, https://www.britannica.com/place/Uttar-Pradesh; and Neha Sahgal et al., "Religion in India: Tolerance and Segregation: Attitudes About Caste," Pew Research Center, June 29, 2021, https://www.pewresearch.org/religion/2021/06/29/attitudes-about-caste/.

52. Yunping Tong, "India's Sex Ratio at Birth Begins to Normalize: What Role Does Caste Play?," Pew Research Center, August 23, 2022, https://www.pewresearch.org/religion/2022/08/23/what-role-does-caste-play/.

53. Ritika Bhatia, "Every Month Is Dalit History Month," *Khabar Lahariya*, April 28, 2021, https://khabarlahariya.org/every-month-is-dalit-history-month/.

54. Neha Sahgal et al., "Religion in India: Tolerance and Segregation: Attitudes About Caste," Pew Research Center, June 29, 2021, https://www.pewresearch.org/religion/2021/06/29/attitudes-about-caste/; Human Rights Watch, *Broken People: Caste Violence Against India's "Untouchables"* (New York: Human Rights Watch, March 1999); and Hillary Mayell, "India's 'Untouchables' Face Violence, Discrimination," *National Geographic*, June 2, 2003, https://www.nationalgeographic.com/pages/article/indias-untouchables-face-violence-discrim ination#:~:text=Because%20they%20are%20considered%20impure,and%20clearing%20a way%20dead%20animals.

55. Qura tul ain Hafeez, "Increase in Crimes Against Dalits and Other Scheduled Castes in India," Modern Diplomacy, February 12, 2023, https://moderndiplomacy.eu/2023/02/12/increase-in-crimes-against-dalits-and-other-scheduled-castes-in-india/.

56. Soutik Biswas, "Hathras Case: Dalit Women Are Among the Most Oppressed in the World," *BBC*, October 5, 2020, https://www.bbc.com/news/world-asia-india-54418513.

57. Devi Dayal Gautam, "Violence and Dalit Women in Rural Uttar Pradesh," *The Indian Journal of Political Science* 75, no. 4 (2014): 705, https://www.jstor.org/stable/26575549.

58. Murali Krishnan, "India: Will Sexual Violence Against Dalits Ever End?," *Deutsche Welle*, September 19, 2022, https://www.dw.com/en/india-will-sexual-violence-against-dalits-ever-end/a-63167654.

59. Vidhi Doshi, "India's All-Female Paper Goes Digital to Make Gender Taboos Old News," *The Guardian*, August 10, 2016, https://www.theguardian.com/global-development/2016/aug/10/india-all-female-newspaper-khabar-lahariya-gender-taboos-old-news?CMP=share_btn_tw.

60. Vidhi Doshi, "India's All-Female Paper Goes Digital to Make Gender Taboos Old News," *The Guardian*, August 10, 2016, https://www.theguardian.com/global-development/2016/aug/10/india-all-female-newspaper-khabar-lahariya-gender-taboos-old-news?CMP=share_btn_tw.

61. Snigdha Poonam, "Kidnap, Rape and 'Honour' Killings: On the Road with a Female Reporter in Rural India," *The Guardian*, March 30, 2015, https://www.theguardian.com/lifeandstyle/2015/mar/30/female-reporter-rural-india-khabar-lahariya-feminist-newspaper.

62. "India," Reporters Without Borders, accessed November 23, 2023, https://rsf.org/en/coun try/india#:~:text=The%20violence%20against%20journalists%2C%20the,the%20embodim ent%20of%20the%20Hindu.

63. Parth M. N., "In India, Warnings that Independent News Media are Teetering on a Precipice," *Los Angeles Times*, December 5, 2022, https://www.latimes.com/world-nation/story/2022-12-05/india-broadcast-media-on-a-precipice-observers-say.

64. Shalu Yadav, "With Raids, Arrests and Hostile Takeovers, India Press Freedom Continues to Decline," *NPR*, April 3, 2023, https://www.npr.org/2023/04/03/1167041720/india-press-free dom-journalists-modi-bbc-documentary.

65. "Protect Our Human Rights Work in India," Amnesty International, accessed November 23, 2023, https://www.amnesty.org/en/petition/protect-our-human-rights-work-in-india/; and Shalu Yadav, "With Raids, Arrests and Hostile Takeovers, India Press Freedom Continues to

Decline," *NPR*, April 3, 2023, https://www.npr.org/2023/04/03/1167041720/india-press-free dom-journalists-modi-bbc-documentary.

66. Shalu Yadav, "With Raids, Arrests and Hostile Takeovers, India Press Freedom Continues to Decline," *NPR*, April 3, 2023, https://www.npr.org/2023/04/03/1167041720/india-press-free dom-journalists-modi-bbc-documentary.

67. Rintu Thomas, Zoom interview with author, July 18, 2023.

68. Sushmit Ghosh, Zoom interview with author, July 18, 2023.

69. Naman Ramachandran, "Sundance Documentary *Writing with Fire* Smashes Indian Patriarchy, Exposes Caste System," *Variety*, January 27, 2021, https://variety.com/2021/film/news/sunda nce-documentary-writing-with-fire-indian-caste-system-1234893174/; and "Rintu Thomas and Sushmit Ghosh: Courage Under Fire Award," IDA Awards 37, International Documentary Association, accessed November 26, 2023, https://www.documentary.org/awards2021/honor ees/rintu-thomas-sushmit-ghosh.

70. "Rintu Thomas and Sushmit Ghosh: Courage Under Fire Award," IDA Awards 37, International Documentary Association, accessed November 26, 2023, https://www.documentary.org/awa rds2021/honorees/rintu-thomas-sushmit-ghosh.

71. "In the Press," Khabar Lahariya, accessed November 26, 2023, https://khabarlahariya.org/kha bar-lahariya-in-the-media/.

72. Rintu Thomas, Zoom interview with author, July 18, 2023.

73. "Oscar-Nominated *Writing with Fire* Wins Peabody Award in Documentary Category," HT Entertainment Desk, *Hindustan Times*, May 10, 2023, https://www.hindustantimes.com/entert ainment/others/oscarnominated-writing-with-fire-wins-peabody-award-in-documentary-category-101683709219811.html.

74. Naman Ramachandran, "Sundance Documentary *Writing with Fire* Smashes Indian Patriarchy, Exposes Caste System," *Variety*, January 27, 2021, https://variety.com/2021/film/news/sunda nce-documentary-writing-with-fire-indian-caste-system-1234893174/.

75. Sushmit Ghosh, Zoom interview with author, July 18, 2023.

76. Sushmit Ghosh, Zoom interview with author, July 18, 2023.

77. Naman Ramachandran, "India Publishes 'Digital Media Ethics Code' for Social Media and Streaming Platforms," *Variety*, February 25, 2021, https://variety.com/2021/streaming/news/ india-digital-media-ethics-code-social-media-streaming-platforms-1234914981/.

78. Naman Ramachandran, "India Publishes 'Digital Media Ethics Code' for Social Media and Streaming Platforms," *Variety*, February 25, 2021, https://variety.com/2021/streaming/news/ india-digital-media-ethics-code-social-media-streaming-platforms-1234914981/.

79. Naman Ramachandran, "India Publishes 'Digital Media Ethics Code' for Social Media and Streaming Platforms," *Variety*, February 25, 2021, https://variety.com/2021/streaming/news/ india-digital-media-ethics-code-social-media-streaming-platforms-1234914981/.

80. Naman Ramachandran, "India Publishes 'Digital Media Ethics Code' for Social Media and Streaming Platforms," *Variety*, February 25, 2021, https://variety.com/2021/streaming/news/ india-digital-media-ethics-code-social-media-streaming-platforms-1234914981/.

81. Naman Ramachandran, "Netflix, Amazon and Disney Adopt Self-Regulation Tool Kit as Indian Streamers Await Government Guidelines," *Variety*, February 12, 2021, https://variety.com/ 2021/streaming/news/india-streaming-self-regulation-tool-kit-adopted-by-netflix-amazon-hotstar-1234906851/.

82. Naman Ramachandran, "Netflix, Amazon and Disney Adopt Self-Regulation Tool Kit as Indian Streamers Await Government Guidelines," *Variety*, February 12, 2021, https://variety. com/2021/streaming/news/india-streaming-self-regulation-tool-kit-adopted-by-netflix-ama zon-hotstar-1234906851/; and "'Tandav' Row: SC Stays Arrest of Amazon Prime India Head Aparna Purohit," Scroll Staff, Scroll.in, March 5, 2021, https://scroll.in/latest/988434/tandav-row-sc-stays-arrest-of-amazon-prime-india-head-aparna-purohit.

83. Sushmit Ghosh, Zoom interview with author, July 18, 2023.

84. Rintu Thomas, Zoom interview with author, July 18, 2023.

85. Sushmit Ghosh, Zoom interview with author, July 18, 2023.

86. Caty Borum Chattoo, *Story Movements: How Documentaries Empower People and Inspire Social Change* (New York, NY: Oxford University Press, 2020), 111.

87. Good Pitch India 2018, *Writing with Fire* impact document, provided to the authors by Rintu Thomas and Sushmit Ghosh.

88. Rintu Thomas, Zoom interview with author, July 18, 2023.

224 NOTES

89. Sushmit Ghosh, Zoom interview with author, July 18, 2023.
90. "*Writing with Fire*," PBS Independent Lens, *PBS*, aired March 28, 2022, accessed November 26, 2023, https://www.pbs.org/video/writing-with-fire-khvke1/.
91. Geoffrey Macnab, "IDFA Best of Fests Interview: Meera Devi, Main Protagonist of *Writing with Fire*," Business Doc Europe, November 23, 2021, https://businessdoceurope.com/idfa-best-of-fests-interview-meera-devi-main-protagonist-of-writing-with-fire/.
92. Sushmit Ghosh, Zoom interview with author, July 18, 2023.
93. Michelle Ye Hee Lee, "Does the United States Really Have 5 Percent of the World's Population and One Quarter of the World's Prisoners?," *Washington Post*, April 30, 2015, https://www.washingtonpost.com/news/fact-checker/wp/2015/04/30/does-the-united-states-really-have-five-percent-of-worlds-population-and-one-quarter-of-the-worlds-prisoners/.
94. Ashley Nellis, *The Color of Justice: Racial and Ethnic Disparity in State Prisons* (Washington, DC: The Sentencing Project, 2021), https://www.sentencingproject.org/reports/the-color-of-justice-racial-and-ethnic-disparity-in-state-prisons-the-sentencing-project/.
95. Lance Kramer, interview with author, February 2, 2023.
96. Brandon Kramer, interview with author, February 2, 2023.
97. Mark Jurkowitz and Amy Mitchell, "A Sore Subject: Almost Half of Americans Have Stopped Talking Politics with Someone," Pew Research Center, February 5, 2020, https://www.pewresearch.org/journalism/2020/02/05/a-sore-subject-almost-half-of-americans-have-stopped-talking-politics-with-someone/.
98. Ted Van Green, "Republicans and Democrats Alike Say It's Stressful to Talk Politics with People Who Disagree," Pew Research Center, November 23, 2021, https://www.pewresearch.org/short-reads/2021/11/23/republicans-and-democrats-alike-say-its-stressful-to-talk-polit-ics-with-people-who-disagree/.
99. "The New York Times/Siena College Research Institute February 9-22 2022 1,507 United States Residents Age 18+ MOE +/- 3.1%," New York Times/Siena College Research Institute, https://int.nyt.com/data/documenttools/free-speech-poll-nyt-and-siena-college/ef971d5e78e1d2f9/full.pdf.
100. "The New York Times/Siena College Research Institute February 9-22 2022 1,507 United States Residents Age 18+ MOE +/- 3.1%," New York Times/Siena College Research Institute, https://int.nyt.com/data/documenttools/free-speech-poll-nyt-and-siena-college/ef971d5e78e1d2f9/full.pdf.
101. The Editorial Board, "America Has a Free Speech Problem," *New York Times*, March 18, 2022, https://www.nytimes.com/2022/03/18/opinion/cancel-culture-free-speech-poll.html.
102. CMSI, "The First Step: Stories of a Documentary in Community Building, Social Change, and Pushing for Progress After the Credits Roll," Center for Media and Social Impact, Forthcoming.
103. CMSI, "The First Step: Stories of a Documentary in Community Building, Social Change, and Pushing for Progress After the Credits Roll," Center for Media and Social Impact, Forthcoming.
104. CMSI, "The First Step: Stories of a Documentary in Community Building, Social Change, and Pushing for Progress After the Credits Roll," Center for Media and Social Impact, Forthcoming.
105. CMSI, "The First Step: Stories of a Documentary in Community Building, Social Change, and Pushing for Progress After the Credits Roll," Center for Media and Social Impact, Forthcoming.
106. CMSI, "The First Step: Stories of a Documentary in Community Building, Social Change, and Pushing for Progress After the Credits Roll," Center for Media and Social Impact, Forthcoming.
107. CMSI, "The First Step: Stories of a Documentary in Community Building, Social Change, and Pushing for Progress After the Credits Roll," Center for Media and Social Impact, Forthcoming.
108. Lance Kramer, interview with author, February 2, 2023.
109. Lance Kramer, interview with author, February 2, 2023.
110. Lance Kramer, interview with author, February 2, 2023.
111. Yana Gorokhovskaia, interview with author, May 16, 2023.

Chapter 5

1. Nanfu Wang, "How the Truth Disappears: Chinese Censorship and My Film *One Child Nation*," *Daily Beast*, January 3, 2020, https://www.thedailybeast.com/how-the-chinese-government-is-censoring-my-oscar-shortlisted-film-about-chinas-brutal-one-child-policy.
2. Nanfu Wang, "How the Truth Disappears: Chinese Censorship and My Film *One Child Nation*," *Daily Beast*, January 3, 2020, https://www.thedailybeast.com/how-the-chinese-government-is-censoring-my-oscar-shortlisted-film-about-chinas-brutal-one-child-policy.
3. Nanfu Wang, "How the Truth Disappears: Chinese Censorship and My Film *One Child Nation*," *Daily Beast*, January 3, 2020, https://www.thedailybeast.com/how-the-chinese-government-is-censoring-my-oscar-shortlisted-film-about-chinas-brutal-one-child-policy.
4. Nanfu Wang, interview with author, June 12, 2023.
5. Nanfu Wang, interview with author, June 12, 2023.
6. Matthew Carlson and Seth C. Lewis, eds., *Boundaries of Journalism: Professionalism, Practices and Participation* (London: Routledge, 2015), https://doi.org/10.4324/9781315727684.
7. Richard Brody, "*One Child Nation*, Reviewed: A Powerful Investigation of a Chinese Policy's Personal Toll," *New Yorker*, August 9, 2019, https://www.newyorker.com/culture/the-front-row/one-child-nation-reviewed-a-powerful-investigation-of-a-chinese-policys-personal-toll.
8. Nanfu Wang, interview with author, June 12, 2023.
9. Nanfu Wang, quoted in Han Zhang, "In *One Child Nation*, Nanfu Wang Confronts China's History, and Her Own," *New Yorker*, August 27, 2019, https://www.newyorker.com/culture/persons-of-interest/in-one-child-nation-nanfu-wang-confronts-chinas-history-and-her-own.
10. Hannah Arendt, *The Origins of Totalitarianism* (New York: Harcourt, Brace, and Co., 1951; Wilmington: Houghton Mifflin Harcourt Trade & Reference Publishers, 1973), 296.
11. Howard Tumber and Silvio Waisbord, eds., *The Routledge Companion to Media and Human Rights* (London: Routledge, 2017), 3.
12. Howard Tumber and Silvio Waisbord, eds., *The Routledge Companion to Media and Human Rights* (London: Routledge, 2017).
13. Kate Nash, "Film That Brings Human Rights to Life," *Public Culture* 30, no. 3 (2018): 393–412.
14. Kate Nash, "Film That Brings Human Rights to Life," *Public Culture* 30, no. 3 (2018): 393–412.
15. Richard Rorty, "Human Rights, Rationality, and Sentimentality," in *On Human Rights: The Oxford Amnesty Lectures 1993*, ed. Stephen Shute and Susan Hurley (New York: Basic Books, 1994).
16. Lilie Chouliaraki, *The Ironic Spectator: Solidarity in the Age of Post-Humanitarianism* (Cambridge, UK: Polity Press, 2012).
17. Kate Nash, "Film That Brings Human Rights to Life," *Public Culture* 30, no. 3 (2018): 393–412.
18. See Roland Bleiker and Amy Kay, "Representing HIV/AIDS in Africa: Pluralist Photography and Local Empowerment," *International Studies Quarterly* 51, no. 1 (March 2007): 139–163, https://doi.org/10.1111/j.1468-2478.2007.00443.x; Lilie Chouliaraki, *The Spectatorship of Suffering* (London: SAGE Publishers, 2006); Lilie Chouliaraki, "The Mediation of Suffering and the Vision of a Cosmopolitan Public," *Television New Media* 9, no. 5 (2008): 371–391, https://doi.org/10.1177/1527476408315496; Lilie Chouliaraki, "'Improper Distance': Towards a Critical Account of Solidarity as Irony," *International Journal of Cultural Studies* 14, no. 4 (2011): 363–381, https://doi.org/10.1177/1367877911403247; Lilie Chouliaraki, *The Ironic Spectator: Solidarity in the Age of Post-Humanitarianism* (Cambridge, UK: Polity Press, 2012); Simon Cottle and David Nolan, "Global Humanitarianism and the Changing Aid-Media Field: 'Everyone Was Dying for Footage,'" *Journalism Studies* 8, no. 6 (2007): 862–878, https://doi.org/10.1080/14616700701556104; Birgitta Höijer, "The Discourse of Global Compassion: The Audience and Media Reporting of Human Suffering," *Media, Culture, & Society* 26, no. 4 (2004), https://doi.org/10.1177/0163443704044215; Mervi Pantti, Karin Wahl-Jorgensen, and Simon Cottle, *Disasters and the Media* (New York: Peter Lang Publishing, 2012); Barbie Zelizer, *About to Die: How News Images Move the Public* (Oxford: Oxford University Press, 2010).
19. Luc Boltanski, *Distant Suffering: Morality, Media, and Politics* (Cambridge: Cambridge University Press, 1999).
20. Susan Moeller, *Compassion Fatigue: How the Media Sell Disease, Famine, War and Death* (New York: Routledge, 1999).

226 NOTES

21. Wazhmah Osman, *Television and the Afghan Culture Wars* (University of Illinois Press, 2020).
22. Slavoj Žižek, *On Belief* (London: Routledge, 2001).
23. Lilie Chouliaraki, "'Improper Distance': Towards a Critical Account of Solidarity as Irony," *International Journal of Cultural Studies* 14, no. 4 (2011): 363–381, https://doi.org/10.1177/1367877911403247; and Lilie Chouliaraki, *The Ironic Spectator: Solidarity in the Age of Post-Humanitarianism* (Cambridge, UK: Polity Press, 2012).
24. David Conrad, "Misguided Benevolence: How 'Moments of Need' Came to Motivate American Journalism" (PhD diss., University of Pennsylvania, 2018).
25. Kate Nash, "Film That Brings Human Rights to Life," *Public Culture* 30, no. 3 (2018): 394.
26. Kate Nash, "Film That Brings Human Rights to Life," *Public Culture* 30, no. 3 (2018): 393–412; Wendy Hesford, *Spectacular Rhetorics: Human Rights Visions, Recognitions, Feminisms* (Durham, NC: Duke University Press, 2011).
27. Kate Nash, "Film That Brings Human Rights to Life," *Public Culture* 30, no. 3 (2018): 393–412.
28. Kate Nash, "Film That Brings Human Rights to Life," *Public Culture* 30, no. 3 (2018): 391.
29. Kate Nash, "Film That Brings Human Rights to Life," *Public Culture* 30, no. 3 (2018): 391.
30. Lilie Chouliaraki, *The Ironic Spectator: Solidarity in the Age of Post-Humanitarianism* (Cambridge, UK: Polity Press, 2012).
31. Lilie Chouliaraki, *The Ironic Spectator: Solidarity in the Age of Post-Humanitarianism* (Cambridge, UK: Polity Press, 2012): 205.
32. Lilie Chouliaraki, *The Ironic Spectator: Solidarity in the Age of Post-Humanitarianism* (Cambridge, UK: Polity Press, 2012): 205.
33. "10 Things We Learned When Greta Thunberg Met David Attenborough," Today, BBC Radio 4, https://www.bbc.co.uk/programmes/articles/270DpZjTRtdscc0qbQbmDH7/10-things-we-learned-when-greta-thunberg-met-david-attenborough#:~:text=Greta%20Thunberg%20says%20watching%20nature,to%20do%20something%20about%20it.%E2%80%9D.
34. Amnesty International, *Amnesty International Annual Report 2019* (London: Amnesty Internation, 2019), https://www.amnesty.org/en/documents/amr01/1353/2020/en/#:~:text=Review%20of%202019,-February%2027%2C%202020&text=Inequality%2C%20corruption%2C%20violence%2C%20environmental,violations%20for%20millions%20of%20people.
35. Amnesty International, *Amnesty International Report 2022/23: The State of the World's Human Rights* (London: Amnesty International, 2023), https://www.amnesty.org/en/documents/pol10/5670/2023/en/.
36. "*Welcome to Chechnya*: Higher Education Resource," developed by Blueshift Education, 8, accessed November 26, 2023, https://www.musicboxfilms.com/wp-content/uploads/2020/11/CHECHNYA_Guide_print.pdf.
37. Alice Henty, interview with author, June 13, 2023.
38. Masha Gessen, "The Gay Men Who Fled Chechnya's Purge," *New Yorker*, June 26, 2017, https://www.newyorker.com/magazine/2017/07/03/the-gay-men-who-fled-chechnyas-purge.
39. Alice Henty, interview with author, June 13, 2023.
40. "*Welcome to Chechnya*: Higher Education Resource," developed by Blueshift Education, 6, accessed November 26, 2023, https://www.musicboxfilms.com/wp-content/uploads/2020/11/CHECHNYA_Guide_print.pdf.
41. Susan Sontag, *Regarding the Pain of Others* (New York: Farrar, Straus, and Giroux, 2003), 114–115.
42. "*Welcome to Chechnya*: Higher Education Resource," developed by Blueshift Education, 20, accessed November 26, 2023, https://www.musicboxfilms.com/wp-content/uploads/2020/11/CHECHNYA_Guide_print.pdf.
43. Alison Byrne Fields, interview with author, August 1, 2023.
44. Alison Byrne Fields, interview with author, August 1, 2023.
45. Alice Henty, interview with author, June 13, 2023.
46. Alice Henty, interview with author, June 13, 2023.
47. "*Welcome to Chechnya*: Higher Education Resource," developed by Blueshift Education, 18, accessed November 26, 2023, https://www.musicboxfilms.com/wp-content/uploads/2020/11/CHECHNYA_Guide_print.pdf.
48. "*Welcome to Chechnya*: Higher Education Resource," developed by Blueshift Education, 18, accessed November 26, 2023, https://www.musicboxfilms.com/wp-content/uploads/2020/11/CHECHNYA_Guide_print.pdf.
49. "*Welcome to Chechnya*: Higher Education Resource," developed by Blueshift Education, 19, accessed November 26, 2023, https://www.musicboxfilms.com/wp-content/uploads/2020/11/CHECHNYA_Guide_print.pdf.

NOTES 227

50. *"Welcome to Chechnya*: Higher Education Resource," developed by Blueshift Education, 18, accessed November 26, 2023, https://www.musicboxfilms.com/wp-content/uploads/2020/11/CHECHNYA_Guide_print.pdf.
51. *"Welcome to Chechnya*: Higher Education Resource," developed by Blueshift Education, 24, accessed November 26, 2023, https://www.musicboxfilms.com/wp-content/uploads/2020/11/CHECHNYA_Guide_print.pdf.
52. Alison Byrne Fields, Interview with author, August 1, 2023.
53. Alison Byrne Fields, Interview with author, August 1, 2023.
54. *"Welcome to Chechnya*: Impact Campaign Case Study," developed by Aggregate, 22, accessed November 26, 2023, https://impactguide.org/static/library/WELCOMETOCHECHNYACaseStudy.pdf.
55. Malala Yousafzai, "16th Birthday Speech at the United Nations," Newsroom, Malala Fund, July 12, 2013, https://malala.org/newsroom/malala-un-speech.
56. Lindsay Guetschow, interview with author, May 17, 2022.
57. Lindsay Guetschow, interview with author, May 17, 2022.
58. Lindsay Guetschow, interview with author, May 17, 2022.
59. Lindsay Guetschow, interview with author, May 17, 2022.
60. Juliana Curi, interview with author, August 16, 2023.
61. Juliana Curi, interview with author, August 16, 2023.
62. Juliana Curi, interview with author, August 16, 2023.
63. Juliana Curi, interview with author, August 16, 2023.
64. Jericho Tadeo, "Exclusive: Director Juliana Curi Talks Frameline World Premiere of *UÝRA: The Rising Forest*," Movieweb, June 23, 2022, https://movieweb.com/uyra-the-rising-forest-juliana-curi-interview/.
65. Rhea Rollmann, "Uýra of *UÝRA: The Rising Forest* on Nature's Trans[formational] Power," popMatters, July 11, 2022, https://www.popmatters.com/uyra-interview-uyra-rising-forest.
66. Juliana Curi, interview with author, August 16, 2023.
67. Juliana Curi, interview with author, August 16, 2023.
68. Juliana Curi, interview with author, August 16, 2023.
69. Alice Henty, interview with author, June 13, 2023.
70. Alice Henty, interview with author, June 13, 2023.
71. James Carey, "Where Journalism Education Went Wrong" (speech, Middle Tennessee State University, Murfreesboro, TN, 1996), accessed November 26, 2023, https://lindadaniele.wordpress.com/2010/08/11/carey-where-journalism-education-went-wrong/.
72. Alice Henty, interview with author, June 13, 2023.
73. Alice Henty, interview with author, June 13, 2023.
74. Nanfu Wang, interview with author, June 12, 2023.
75. Nanfu Wang, interview with author, June 12, 2023.

Chapter 6

1. Karl Malakunas, interview with author, June 13, 2023.
2. Karl Malakunas, interview with author, June 13, 2023.
3. Karl Malakunas, interview with author, June 13, 2023.
4. *James Carey: A Critical Reader*, ed. Eve Stryker Munson (University of Minnesota Press, 1997).
5. Karl Malakunas, interview with author, June 13, 2023.
6. Karl Malakunas, interview with author, June 13, 2023.
7. Karl Malakunas, interview with author, June 13, 2023.
8. Karl Malakunas, interview with author, June 13, 2023.
9. Rosalind Donald, et al., "'Film Is Like a Fire': Analyzing the Cultural Influence of Three Environmental Justice Documentaries," Center for Media & Social Impact, forthcoming.
10. Karl Malakunas, interview with author, June 13, 2023
11. Caty Borum Chattoo, *Story Movements: How Documentaries Empower People and Inspire Social Change* (New York, NY: Oxford University Press, 2020).
12. J. A. Stover III, "Framing Social Movements Through Documentary Films," *Contexts* 12, no. 4 (2013): 56–58, https://doi.org/10.1177/1536504213511218;Sherry Ortner, *Screening*

228 NOTES

Social Justice: Brave New Films and Documentary Activism (Durham, NC: Duke University Press, 2023); Josepha Ivanka Wessels, "Cosmopolitanism, Activism and Arab Documentary Film," *Middle East Journal of Culture and Communication* 13, no. 2 (2020): 210–231, https://:doi.org/10.1163/18739865-01302003.

13. Caty Borum Chattoo, *Story Movements: How Documentaries Empower People and Inspire Social Change* (New York, NY: Oxford University Press, 2020); Caty Borum et al., "The Lens Reflected: What Stories and Storytellers Get the Green Light in Documentary's Streaming Age?" Center for Media and Social Impact, https://cmsimpact.org/wp-content/uploads/2016/08/CMSI_LensReflected_final.12.1.pdf.

14. Eliana Miller, "Acclaimed filmmaker Raoul Peck discusses identity, history," *Bowdoin Orient.* October 27, 2017. https://bowdoinorient.com/2017/10/27/acclaimed-filmmaker-raoul-peck-discusses-identity-history/#:~:text=%E2%80%9CMovies%2C%20as%20innocent%20as%20they,wanted%20to%20make%20Hollywood%20films.%E2%80%9D.

15. Edwin Martinez, "Navigating the River: The Hidden Colonialism of Documentary," International Documentary Association, July 19, 2016, https://www.documentary.org/feature/navigating-river-hidden-colonialism-documentary;Olivier Tchouaffe, "Colonial Visual Archives and the Anti-Documentary Perspective in Africa," *Journal of Information Ethics* 19, no. 2 (2010): 82–99, https//:doi.org/10.3172/JIE.19.2.82.

16. Olivier Tchouaffe, "Colonial Visual Archives and the Anti-Documentary Perspective in Africa," *Journal of Information Ethics* 19, no. 2 (2010): 82–99, https//:doi.org/10.3172/JIE.19.2.82.

17. Olivier Tchouaffe, "Colonial Visual Archives and the Anti-Documentary Perspective in Africa," *Journal of Information Ethics* 19, no. 2 (2010): 82–99, 83, https//:doi.org/10.3172/JIE.19.2.82.

18. Olivier Tchouaffe, "Colonial Visual Archives and the Anti-Documentary Perspective in Africa," *Journal of Information Ethics* 19, no. 2 (2010): 82–99, 84, https//:doi.org/10.3172/JIE.19.2.82.

19. Alex Pritz, interview with author, June 13, 2023.

20. Alex Pritz, interview with author, June 13, 2023.

21. Alex Pritz, interview with author, June 13, 2023.

22. Alex Pritz, interview with author, June 13, 2023.

23. Emily Wanja, interview with author, April 22, 2022.

24. Emily Wanja, interview with author, April 22, 2022.

25. Emily Wanja, interview with author, April 22, 2022.

26. Emily Wanja, interview with author, April 22, 2022.

27. Emily Wanja, interview with author, April 22, 2022.

28. Emily Wanja, interview with author, April 22, 2022.

29. Emily Wanja, interview with author, April 22, 2022.

30. Tracy Sturdivant, interview with author, May 3, 2022.

31. Jyoti Sarda, interview with author, February 2, 2023.

32. CMSI, "Making Social Change with Documentaries: What Works, Why and How?: And She Could Be Next Case Study," Center for Media & Social Impact, August 2023, https://cmsimpact.org/wp-content/uploads/2016/08/DPRI_ASCBN_web-1.pdf.

33. Tracy Sturdivant, interview with author, May 3, 2022.

34. Tracy Sturdivant, interview with author, May 3, 2022.

35. Jyoti Sarda, interview with author, February 2, 2023.

36. H. J. Gans, *Deciding What's News: A Study of CBS Evening News, NBC Nightly News, Newsweek, and Time* (Evanston, IL: Northwestern University Press, 1979); G. Tuchman, *Making News* (New York: The Free Press, 1978).

37. Peter Murimi, quoted in Gary Ryan, "*I Am Samuel* and the Fight for Gay Rights in Kenya: "It's Not Safe for Them Here," NME, June 4, 2021, https://www.nme.com/features/i-am-samuel-peter-murimi-interview-2957727.

38. Peter Murimi, quoted in Gary Ryan, "*I Am Samuel* and the Fight for Gay Rights in Kenya: "It's Not Safe for Them Here," NME, June 4, 2021, https://www.nme.com/features/i-am-samuel-peter-murimi-interview-2957727.

39. Peter Murimi, quoted in Soila Kenya, "How a Queer Kenyan Film Is Outpacing Homophobic Colonial Censorship Law," openDEMOCRACY, March 19 2022. https://www.opendemocracy.net/en/5050/i-am-samuel-lgbtiq-kenya-film-outpacing-homophobic-colonial-censorship-law/.

40. Peter Murimi, quoted in Soila Kenya, "How a Queer Kenyan Film Is Outpacing Homophobic Colonial Censorship Law," openDEMOCRACY, March 19 2022. https://www.opendemocracy.net/en/5050/i-am-samuel-lgbtiq-kenya-film-outpacing-homophobic-colonial-censorship-law/.

NOTES 229

41. Peter Murimi, quoted in Gary Ryan, "*I Am Samuel* and the Fight for Gay Rights in Kenya: "It's Not Safe for Them Here," NME, June 4, 2021, https://www.nme.com/features/i-am-samuel-peter-murimi-interview-2957727.
42. Peter Murimi, quoted in Andrew Young, "In Conversation with Peter Murimi and Toni Kamau for *I Am Samuel*," Film Inquiry, November 5, 2020, https://www.filminquiry.com/peter-mur imi-interview/.

Chapter 7

1. "Radical Optimist Collective," accessed December 2, 2023, https://theradicaloptimist.com/.
2. David Conrad, Caty Borum Chattoo, and Patricia Aufderheide, *Breaking the Silence: How Documentaries Can Shape the Conversation on Racial Violence in America and Create New Communities* (Washington, DC: Center for Media and Social Impact, October 2020), https://cmsimpact.org/report/breaking-silence-documentaries-can-shape-conversation-racial-viole nce-america-create-new-communities/.
3. David Conrad, Caty Borum Chattoo, and Patricia Aufderheide, *Breaking the Silence: How Documentaries Can Shape the Conversation on Racial Violence in America and Create New Communities* (Washington, DC: Center for Media and Social Impact, October 2020), https://cmsimpact.org/report/breaking-silence-documentaries-can-shape-conversation-racial-viole nce-america-create-new-communities/.
4. David Conrad-Pérez, et al., "Breaking Cultures of Silence: Learnings from a Participatory Community-Centred Approach to Leveraging and Researching Documentaries for Social Change," *Journal of Alternative and Community Media* 7, no. 1 (April 2022): 3–22, https://doi.org/10.1386/jacm_00102_1.
5. David Conrad-Pérez, et al., "Breaking Cultures of Silence: Learnings from a Participatory Community-Centred Approach to Leveraging and Researching Documentaries for Social Change," *Journal of Alternative and Community Media* 7, no. 1 (April 2022): 3–22, https://doi.org/10.1386/jacm_00102_1.
6. David Conrad-Pérez, et al., "Breaking Cultures of Silence: Learnings from a Participatory Community-Centred Approach to Leveraging and Researching Documentaries for Social Change," *Journal of Alternative and Community Media* 7, no. 1 (April 2022): 3–22, https://doi.org/10.1386/jacm_00102_1.
7. David Conrad, Caty Borum Chattoo, and Patricia Aufderheide, *Breaking the Silence: How Documentaries Can Shape the Conversation on Racial Violence in America and Create New Communities* (Washington, DC: Center for Media and Social Impact, October 2020), https://cmsimpact.org/report/breaking-silence-documentaries-can-shape-conversation-racial-viole nce-america-create-new-communities/.
8. Jacqueline Olive, in David Conrad, Caty Borum Chattoo, and Patricia Aufderheide, *Breaking the Silence: How Documentaries Can Shape the Conversation on Racial Violence in America and Create New Communities* (Washington, DC: Center for Media and Social Impact, October 2020), 5, https://cmsimpact.org/report/breaking-silence-documentaries-can-shape-conversat ion-racial-violence-america-create-new-communities/.
9. Jacqueline Olive, in Barbara Olachea, "'Always in Season' Filmmaker Jacqueline Olive on Promoting Justice and Reconciliation Through Documentary Film," Good Docs Blog, March 28, 2020, https://gooddocs.net/blogs/behind-the-camera/jacqueline-olive-interview.
10. Jacqueline Olive, in David Conrad, Caty Borum Chattoo, and Patricia Aufderheide, *Breaking the Silence: How Documentaries Can Shape the Conversation on Racial Violence in America and Create New Communities* (Washington, DC: Center for Media and Social Impact, October 2020), 5–6, https://cmsimpact.org/report/breaking-silence-documentaries-can-shape-conve rsation-racial-violence-america-create-new-communities/.
11. Jacqueline Olive, in David Conrad-Pérez, et al., "Breaking Cultures of Silence: Learnings from a Participatory Community-Centred Approach to Leveraging and Researching Documentaries for Social Change," *Journal of Alternative and Community Media* 7, no. 1 (April 2022): 3–22, https://doi.org/10.1386/jacm_00102_1.

230 NOTES

12. Jamil Smith, "Stanley Nelson's 3 Decades of Telling Black Stories," *Vox*, March 23, 2022, https://www.vox.com/2022/3/23/22989435/stanley-nelsons-3-decades-of-telling-black-stories.

13. Stanley Nelson, in Hua Hsu, "Stanley Nelson's Lifetime of Documenting Black Experience," *New Yorker*, March 20, 2022, https://www.newyorker.com/culture/the-new-yorker-interview/stanley-nelsons-lifetime-of-documenting-black-experience#:~:text=I%20was%20interested%20in%20films,the%20world%20that%20I%20knew.

14. Stanley Nelson, in Hua Hsu, "Stanley Nelson's Lifetime of Documenting Black Experience," *New Yorker*, March 20, 2022, https://www.newyorker.com/culture/the-new-yorker-interview/stanley-nelsons-lifetime-of-documenting-black-experience#:~:text=I%20was%20interested%20in%20films,the%20world%20that%20I%20knew.

15. Caty Borum Chattoo, *Story Movements: How Documentaries Empower People and Inspire Social Change* (New York, NY: Oxford University Press, 2020), 53–55.

16. Caty Borum Chattoo, *Story Movements: How Documentaries Empower People and Inspire Social Change* (New York, NY: Oxford University Press, 2020), 55.

17. David Conrad-Pérez, et al., "Beyond the Impact Report: What's Really Needed to Produce and Sustain Social Impact in Documentary Film?," Center for Media & Social Impact, https://cmsimpact.org/general/going-beyond-the-impact-report/.

18. David Conrad-Pérez, et al., "Beyond the Impact Report: What's Really Needed to Produce and Sustain Social Impact in Documentary Film?," Center for Media & Social Impact, https://cmsimpact.org/general/going-beyond-the-impact-report/.

19. David Conrad-Pérez, et al., "Beyond the Impact Report: What's Really Needed to Produce and Sustain Social Impact in Documentary Film?," Center for Media & Social Impact, https://cmsimpact.org/general/going-beyond-the-impact-report/.

20. Caty Borum, Paula Weissman, and David Conrad-Pérez, "The Lens Reflected: What Stories and Storytellers Get the Greenlight in Documentary's Streaming Age?," Center for Media & Social Impact, American University School of Communication, Washington, DC, 2022, https://cmsimpact.org/program/documentary-representation/

21. Caty Borum, Paula Weissman, and David Conrad-Pérez, "The Lens Reflected: What Stories and Storytellers Get the Greenlight in Documentary's Streaming Age?," Center for Media & Social Impact, American University School of Communication, Washington, DC, 2022, https://cmsimpact.org/program/documentary-representation/

22. Sahar Driver and Sonya Childress, "The Evolution of Impact: The Future of Social Change and Nonfiction Storytelling," *Filmmaker Magazine*, August 23, 2022, https://filmmakermagazine.com/116071-the-evolution-of-documentary-impact/.

23. Sahar Driver and Sonya Childress, "The Evolution of Impact: The Future of Social Change and Nonfiction Storytelling," *Filmmaker Magazine*, August 23, 2022, https://filmmakermagazine.com/116071-the-evolution-of-documentary-impact/.

24. Sahar Driver and Sonya Childress, "The Evolution of Impact: The Future of Social Change and Nonfiction Storytelling," *Filmmaker Magazine*, August 23, 2022, https://filmmakermagazine.com/116071-the-evolution-of-documentary-impact/.

25. Sahar Driver and Sonya Childress, "The Evolution of Impact: The Future of Social Change and Nonfiction Storytelling," *Filmmaker Magazine*, August 23, 2022, https://filmmakermagazine.com/116071-the-evolution-of-documentary-impact/.

26. More information about *In My Blood It Runs*, and the team behind it, can be found at: https://inmyblooditruns.com/impact/

27. Shared by film team, email communication, February 14, 2024.

28. Rachel Naŋinaaq Edwardson, interview with author, June 8, 2022.

29. Rachel Naŋinaaq Edwardson, interview with author, June 8, 2022.

30. Alex Kelly, interview with author, June 8, 2022.

31. Rachel Naŋinaaq Edwardson, interview with author, December 21, 2022.

32. Rachel Naŋinaaq Edwardson, interview with author, December 21, 2022.

33. Maya Newell, interview with author, December 21, 2022.

34. Rachel Naŋinaaq Edwardson, interview with author, December 21, 2022.

35. Anya Rous, interview with author, May 26, 2022.

36. Anya Rous, interview with author, May 26, 2022.

37. Anya Rous, interview with author, May 26, 2022.

38. Anya Rous, interview with author, May 26, 2022.

39. Anya Rous, interview with author, May 26, 2022.

40. Rosemarie Lerner, interview with author, May 16, 2022.

NOTES 231

41. Rosemarie Lerner, interview with author, May 16, 2022.
42. Rosemarie Lerner, interview with author, May 16, 2022.
43. Rosemarie Lerner, interview with author, May 16, 2022.
44. Rosemarie Lerner, interview with author, May 16, 2022.
45. Rosemarie Lerner, interview with author, May 16, 2022.
46. Rosemarie Lerner, interview with author, May 16, 2022.

Chapter 8

1. Beadie Finzi, in-person interview with author, November 30, 2023.
2. Beadie Finzi, in-person interview with author, November 30, 2023.
3. C. Borum Chattoo, P. Aufderheide, K. Merrill, and M. Oyebolu, "Diversity on U.S. Public and Commercial TV, in Authorial and Executive-Produced Social-Issue Documentaries," *Journal of Broadcasting & Electronic Media* 62, no. 3 (2018): 495–513, https://doi.org/10.1080/08838 151.2018.1451865.
4. Beadie Finzi, in-person interview with author, November 30, 2023.
5. Louis Menand, "The Rise and Fall of Neoliberalism," July 17, 2023, https://www.newyorker.com/magazine/2023/07/24/the-rise-and-fall-of-neoliberalism.
6. Robert Kuttner, *Can Democracy Survive Global Capitalism?* First edition (New York: W. W. Norton & Company, 2018).
7. Victor Pickard, *Democracy Without Journalism? Confronting the Misinformation Society* (New York, New York: Oxford University Press, 2020), 174.
8. Shoshana Zuboff, *The Age of Surveillance Capitalism* (New York, NY: PublicAffairs, 2019).
9. Yanis Varoufakis, *Technofeudalism: What Killed Capitalism* (Brooklyn, NY: Melville Publishing, 2024).
10. Caty Borum, David Conrad-Pérez, and Bryan Bello, "Creative Independent Investigative Documentary Storytellers in the Streaming Age: Toward a Community of Practice Framework," *Journalism Practice* 18, no. 7 (2022). https://doi.org/10.1080/17512786.2022.2126993.
11. Beadie Finzi, in-person interview with author, November 30, 2023.
12. Alex Pritz, interview with author, June 13, 2023.
13. Nanfu Wang, Zoom interview with author, June 12, 2023.
14. CMSI, "Making Social Change with Documentaries: What Works, Why and How? And She Could Be Next Case Study," Center for Media & Social Impact, August 2023.
15. Chloe Genga, Zoom interview with author, December 22, 2023.
16. Wilfred Okiche, "Kenya's Docubox Builds a Thriving Doc Community in East Africa," *Documentary*, September 20, 2022, https://www.documentary.org/feature/kenyas-docubox-builds-thriving-doc-community-east-africa.
17. Lauren Wissot, "'I Believe That Stories Need to Try to Communicate Beyond Their Intended Audiences': Sam Soko on His Sundance Doc *Softie*," *Filmmaker Magazine*, January 29, 2020, https://filmmakermagazine.com/108979-i-believe-that-stories-need-to-try-to-communicate-beyond-their-intended-audiences-sam-soko-on-his-sundance-doc-softie/.
18. Wilfred Okiche, "Kenya's Docubox Builds a Thriving Doc Community in East Africa," *Documentary*, September 20, 2022, https://www.documentary.org/feature/kenyas-docubox-builds-thriving-doc-community-east-africa.
19. Judy Kibinge, email communication with author, June 28, 2024.
20. Kristin Feeley and Shira Rockowitz, "Announcing the Recipients of the 2024 Sundance Institute | Amazon MGM Studios Producers Awards," Sundance Film Festival, January 21, 2024, https://festival.sundance.org/blogs/announcing-the-recipients-of-the-2024-sundance-institute-amazon-mgm-studios-producers-awards/.
21. Wilfred Okiche, "Kenya's Docubox Builds a Thriving Doc Community in East Africa," *Documentary*, September 20, 2022, https://www.documentary.org/feature/kenyas-docubox-builds-thriving-doc-community-east-africa.
22. Wilfred Okiche, "Kenya's Docubox Builds a Thriving Doc Community in East Africa," *Documentary*, September 20, 2022, https://www.documentary.org/feature/kenyas-docubox-builds-thriving-doc-community-east-africa.

232 NOTES

23. Wilfred Okiche, "Kenya's Docubox Builds a Thriving Doc Community in East Africa," *Documentary*, September 20, 2022, https://www.documentary.org/feature/kenyas-docubox-builds-thriving-doc-community-east-africa.

24. Tom White, "Documentary's Role in Reclaiming Sub-Saharan History and Culture," *Documentary*. October 3, 2020, https://www.documentary.org/blog/documentarys-role-reclaiming-sub-saharan-history-and-culture.

25. Wilfred Okiche, "Kenya's Docubox Builds a Thriving Doc Community in East Africa," *Documentary*, September 20, 2022, https://www.documentary.org/feature/kenyas-docubox-builds-thriving-doc-community-east-africa.

26. Neo-Griot, "Interview: Judy Kibinge," Kalamu ya Salaam's information blog, September 20, 2014, https://kalamu.com/neogriot/2014/09/20/interview-judy-kibinge/#:~:text=of=%20each%20character.-,"I%20don%27t%20like%20stories%20that%20don%27t%20mean,was%20dealing%20with%20real%20issues.

27. Chloe Genga, Zoom interview with author, December 22, 2023.

28. Abigail Arunga, "Sam Soko on 'Free Money' and Finding Intrigue in the Complexities of Real Life," Sinema Focus, October 11, 2023, https://www.sinemafocus.com/sam-soko-on-free-money-and-finding-intrigue-in-the-complexities-of-real-life/.

29. Caty Borum Chattoo, *Story Movements: How Documentaries Empower People and Inspire Social Change* (New York, NY: Oxford University Press, 2020), 197–199.

30. Alex Pritz, Zoom interview with author, June 13, 2023.

31. Sushmit Ghosh and Rintu Thomas, Zoom interview with author, July 18, 2023.

32. Robert Bahar, Zoom interview with author, September 29, 2023.

33. Emily Roseman, interview with author, May 15, 2023.

34. MacArthur Foundation, "Press Forward Will Award More Than $500 Million to Revitalize Local News," September 7, 2023, https://www.macfound.org/press/press-releases/press-forward-will-award-more-than-500-million-to-revitalize-local-news.

35. Nishant Lalwani, interview with author, May 18, 2023.

36. Caty Borum, David Conrad-Pérez, and Bryan Bello, "Creative Independent Investigative Documentary Storytellers in the Streaming Age: Toward a Community of Practice Framework," *Journalism Practice* 18, no. 7 (2022): 1867–1885, https://doi.org/10.1080/17512786.2022.2126993.

37. Anthony Kaufman, "Let's Make a Deal—Or Not: More than 80% of Docs Don't Sell at Top-Tier U.S. Film Festivals," Distribution Advocates, January 19, 2023, https://distributionadvocates.substack.com/p/lets-make-a-dealor-not.

38. Anthony Kaufman, "Let's Make a Deal—Or Not: More than 80% of Docs Don't Sell at Top-Tier U.S. Film Festivals," Distribution Advocates, January 19, 2023, https://distributionadvocates.substack.com/p/lets-make-a-dealor-not.

39. Caty Borum Chattoo, *Story Movements: How Documentaries Empower People and Inspire Social Change* (New York, NY: Oxford University Press, 2020), 13–15.

40. Julia Bacha, interview with author, September 29, 2023.

41. Brandon Kramer, interview with author, December 19, 2023.

42. Beadie Finzi, in-person interview with author, November 30, 2023.

43. Caty Borum, Paula Weissman, and David Conrad-Pérez, "The Lens Reflected: What Stories and Storytellers Get the Greenlight in Documentary's Streaming Age?," Center for Media & Social Impact, American University School of Communication, Washington, DC, 2022, https://cmsimpact.org/program/documentary-representation/

44. Caty Borum Chattoo, *Story Movements: How Documentaries Empower People and Inspire Social Change* (New York, NY: Oxford University Press, 2020), 110–113.

45. Julia Bacha, interview with author, September 29, 2023.

46. Center for Media & Social Impact, *Negotiating Social Impact Rights in Documentary Film: A Best Practices Guide*, Center for Media & Social Impact, American University School of Communication, 2023.

47. Nanfu Wang, Zoom interview with author, June 12, 2023.

48. Danielle Turkov Wilson, Zoom interview with author, July 26, 2023.

49. Peter Noorlander, Zoom interview with author, May 23, 2023.

50. Beadie Finzi, in-person interview With author, November 30, 2023.

51. See Victor Pickard, *Democracy Without Journalism? Confronting the Misinformation Society* (New York, New York: Oxford University Press, 2020), 164–176.

52. Beadie Finzi, in-person interview with author, November 30, 2023.

Index

For the benefit of digital users, indexed terms that span two pages (e.g., 52–53) may, on occasion, appear on only one of those pages.

Figures are indicated by an italic *f* following the page number.

Aam Admi Party (AAP), 1
ABC, 30–31
About to Die (Zelizer), 53–54
Abrams, Stacey, 33, 34, 149–50
absolute power, 28
Academy Awards, 42, 56, 69, 87, 142–43
activism, 6, 25, 50–51, 134, 139–40
  centering solutions, 145–48
  centering stories of, 142–45
  citizen engagement and, 33
  climate, 148
  colonial roots of, 141
  digital, 15
  ethos, 11–12
  human rights, 12, 111–20
  "impact producer" and, 13–14
  learning and, 21–22
  LGBTQ+ community, 116–18, 154
  power and, 21–22, 142
  power of, 32
  social justice and, 60, 140–41
  stereotypes and, 145–48
  undercover reporting and, 111–20
The Act of Killing (documentary), 109–10
A-Doc. *See* Asian American Documentary Network
advocacy, 142–43
AFAC. *See* Arab Fund for Arts and Culture
Afghanistan, 75–76, 121, 123
AFLAMUNA, 16
AFP. *See* Agence France-Presse
African Union Summit, 123
Agence France-Presse (AFP), 132–33
AI. *See* artificial intelligence
Akeyulerre Healing Centre, 168
All In (documentary), 30–35, 34*f*, 46
#AllInForVoting, 34*f*, 34
Álvarez Junco, José, 37

Always in Season (documentary), 25–26, 156–59, 196
Amazon, 6–7, 19, 20–21, 34
Amazon Prime, 32, 88–89, 100
Amazon rainforest, 124, 125, 142–43
Ambulante, 16
American Civil Liberties Union, 96–97
American Conservative Union, 99
American Factory (documentary), 19
Americans for Prosperity, 96–97
Amnesty International, 25, 84–85, 111–12
Ancine, 144
And She Could Be Next (documentary), 25, 149–52, 153
"anti-documentary" perspective, 141
Arab Fund for Arts and Culture (AFAC), 16
Arab Spring, 12
Arizona State University, 99
Arrernte, 165, 168
artificial intelligence (AI), 81
  fake photos and videos, 71–72
  generative, 184
Asian American Documentary Network (A-Doc), 161
Associated Press, 68–69
Attica (documentary), 159–60
audience
  active role of, 9–10
  human rights figures, movements, and organizations with, 120–23
Aufderheide, Patricia, 7–8, 23–24
Australia, 14, 16, 25–26, 78, 154, 165, 168
authoritarianism, 15, 46, 71–72, 104–5, 131
  conditions for, 29–30
  contemporary, 27–28
  creeping tactics of, 47
  Franco and, 36

234 INDEX

authoritarianism (*cont.*)
  freedom of expression and free press with,
    17–18, 73
  free media and, 30
  Nanfu Wang films and, 103–4
  political trends toward, 82–83
  populism and, 29
  rise in, 6
  semiauthoritarianism, 17–18, 82–83
  The Silence of Others and, 44–46
  stealth, 27–28
Autlook Filmsales, 57–58
autocracy, 28
autocratic governments, 17–18

Bacha, Julia, 46–47, 198, 200
Bahar, Robert, 38, 41, 43–45, 194
Bahrain, 154
Balladares, Tata, 132–33, 135f, 135f
Ballour, Amani, 48, 49–50, 56, 59–60
BBC, 68–69, 86–87, 120
BBC News Russia, 118–19
Berlin Film Festival (2018), 41
Bertha Foundation, 138
Bharatiya Janata Party (BJP), 1, 84–85
Big Tech, 184
BIPOC communities, 161, 163, 177
BJP. *See* Bharatiya Janata Party
Black Birth (documentary), 163
Black Panther Party, 159–60
"Bloody Sunday," 30–31
Bolsonaro, Jair, 17–18, 124, 144, 145, 186
Born Perfect Campaign, 172–73
Borum Chattoo, Caty, 8–9, 23–24
Boycott (documentary), 46–47
Branovytska, Nina, 69–70
Brazil, 16, 25, 29–30, 123–26, 133, 142–43, 145,
    181, 186
Brennan Center for Justice, 31, 32
BRITDoc. *See* Doc Society
Brown Girls Doc Mafia, 161
Bruzzi, Stella, 61–62

Cambodia, 133
capitalism, global, 28
Carey, James, 128–29, 134
Carnegie Endowment for International Peace,
    81
Carracedo, Almudena, 38, 41, 43–45
casteism, 83
The Cave (documentary), 24, 48, 49–51, 58, 59,
    60, 194
CBFC. *See* Central Board of Film Certification

censorship, 2–3, 75–76, 90, 91, 203
  of *An Insignificant Man*, 5
  self-censorship, 81
Center for Media & Social Impact, 22–23
Central Board of Film Certification (CBFC),
    1–2
Chacón, Dulce, 35–36, 38
challenges, for documentary storytellers, 17–22
change
  global, 28
  social, 8, 16, 50–51, 60
Change the Name (documentary), 163
Channan, Michael, 7, 23–24
Chechnya, 111–20
chemical weapons, 49, 194
Chicago Media Project, 33–34
Chicken & Egg Accelerator Lab, 161
Chicken & Egg Pictures, 87–88
Children's Ground, 168
Childress, Sonya, 163–64
Chile, 14
China, 25, 80, 102–11, 131, 154
China Undercover (documentary), 46–47
Chouliaraki, Lilie, 109, 110
Cinema Novo movement, 124
citizen engagement, 33
civic motivation, 8–9
civil rights, 31
civil rights movement, 160
civil society, 6, 11, 25
civil wars
  Rwandan, 54
  Spanish, 35–36, 39
climate activism, 148
climate change, 124–25, 132–33, 136–38,
    146, 147
climate justice, 124, 126, 139, 148
Climate Reality Project, 136–38
CNN, 6–7, 20, 73
CNN Films, 20–21
coalition building, 98
Cold War, 27
collective action, 205
collective memory, 46
Colombia, 133
colonialism, 140–41
Color Congress, 163–64
Columbia Journalism Review, 78
"Common Man's Party." *See* Aam Admi Party
community collaboration, 166–67
community empowerment, 169
community healing, 25–26
El Confidencial (news outlet), 43–44

INDEX   235

conflict, witnessing stories of, 52–53
Constitution, US, 76–77
contemporary authoritarianism, 27–28
conversion therapy, LGBTQ+, 170–73, 175
Corporation for Public Broadcasting, 161–62
corrective histories, 159–65
Cortés, Lisa, 32, 33, 35, 47
Council of Europe, 59–60
counternarratives, transmitting, 11
Court, Maria Ignacia, 176
COVID-19 pandemic, 19–20, 88, 103–4, 193–94
Crack (documentary), 162
Crimea, 70
crimes against humanity, 74
criminal justice reform, 92–95, 98
Crip Camp (documentary), 19
Cultura (news outlet), 43–44
cultural memory, 52–53
Curi, Juliana, 124, 125, 126

Dalit community, 83–84
Dartmouth College, 116–18
Decentralized Independent Story and Cultural Organizers (DISCO), 185–86, 199, 203
deforestation, 144–45
Delikado (documentary), 25, 134–42, 135f, 135f, 137f, 137f, 153, 195–96, 201–2
democracy, 17–18, 27, 30, 43, 46
    liberal, 29–30
    media freedom and, 77–78
    multiracial, 35
    voting rights and, 32
Democracy Index report, 5
Democracy Report (2023), 27
Democratic Republic of Congo, 66
Denmark, 49
Department of Justice, US, 31, 161
Desktop Entertainment, 100
Devaney, Jess, 171
Devi, Kavita, 84
Devi, Meera, 87f
Diaz, Ramona S., 75
digital activism, 15
digital media, 81
digital surveillance tools, 81
digital technology, 12
disagreement, 95–96
DISCO. *See* Decentralized Independent Story and Cultural Organizers
disinformation, 81
Disney+, 49, 88–89

The Dissent and Endangered (documentary), 75–76
distribution, 7, 21, 101, 128–29, 131, 197–201
    dual distribution model, 90, 200
    for Netflix, 82–83
    for *One Child Nation*, 130
    in Philippines, 138–39
    royalty, 167–68
    seeking, 115
    for *Writing with Fire*, 88
Divine Nine, 161–62
Docedge Kolkata Asian Forum for Documentary, 16, 87
Doc Sao Paolo, 16
Doc Society, 14, 87–88, 90, 115–16, 125–26, 138, 144, 181, 185–86
    "documentary community" meetings of, 13–14
    Good Pitch program, 13, 41
    Safe and Secure resource guide, 204
DocuBox, 16, 189–91
Documentary Filmmakers With Disabilities (FWD-DOC), 16
Documentary Film Program (Sundance Institute), 15–16
Documentary Power Research Institute, 22–23
Documentary Story Lab, 181
Dream.org, 92
dual distribution model, 90, 200
Duterte, Rodrigo, 74, 132–33, 138–39
"duty of care," 138–39

The Economist (newspaper), 5
The Edge of Democracy (documentary), 46–47
editorial independence, 8–9, 193–95, 198
Egypt, 27
Egyptian Revolution of 2011, 19
8Above, 96
empowerment
    community, 169
    voter, 33, 34
Encarnancion, Omar, 37–38
Engage Media, 16
entertainment media, 22–23
entertainment value, 8–9
"Erased Heritage," 190–91
Estonia, 181
ethics, commitment to, 8–9
Etilaat Roz (documentary), 75–76
European Union, 136–38
Exodus International, 170–71

Facebook, 74

236 INDEX

FACT. *See* Film Certification Appellate Tribunal
Faulkner, William, 32
Fayyad, Feras, 48, 49–51
FCRA. *See* Foreign Contribution Regulation Act
feudalism, 184
The Fight (documentary), 46–47
Film & Campaign, 16
Film Certification Appellate Tribunal (FACT), 2–3
Filmmaker Magazine, 163–64
financial insecurity, 203–4
financial resources, 201–5
Finzi, Beadie, 181, 182, 183, 184, 185–86, 204
Firelight Media, 160–61
First Amendment, 76–77
First Nations, 165, 168–69, 170
The First Step (documentary), 24–25, 91–101, 93*f*, 93*f*, 198, 200–1
First Step Act, 92, 97, 99
Fondation AlterCine, 87–88
forced sterilization, 176–79
Ford Foundation, 15–16
Foreign Contribution Regulation Act (FCRA), 80
"forgetting," 37–38
For Sama (documentary), 24, 56–58
Fotogramas, 42
Foundation for the Study of Democracy, 49–50
France, 14, 41, 46–47, 49, 75–76
France, David, 112, 113–15, 118, 128
Franco Bahamonde, Francisco, 36–38
Franklin, Maxyne, 181
Freedom House, 17–18, 27, 78
Freedom in the World Report, 17–18, 27, 78, 81
freedom of expression, 24–25, 27, 73–76, 183
  authoritarianism and, 17–18, 73
  under duress, 76–101
  Writing with Fire and, 83–91
Freedom Riders (documentary), 159–60
Freedom Summer (documentary), 159–60
Free Money (documentary), 192
free press, 17–18, 30, 52, 76, 183
free speech, 17–18, 74
F@ck This Job (documentary), 186–87
Fuller, Robert L., 158
funding, 21, 50–51, 115, 130, 138, 147–48
  experimental models of, 187–88
  global models for, 101
  for independent media, 79
  as media repression tool, 80
  nonprofit, 67
  for *Writing with Fire*, 87–88
FWD-DOC. *See* Documentary Filmmakers With Disabilities

Fyre Fest (documentary series), 19–20

Galante, Jose Maria "Chato," 40*f*
Game Changer (documentary), 163
Garzon, Baltazar, 38
Gautem, Devi Dayal, 84
generative AI, 184
Gessen, Masha, 112, 195–96
Getting Real conferences (IDA), 14
Ghosh, Sushmit, 85, 86, 87*f*, 87–88, 90, 194
GIPA. *See* Global Impact Producers Assembly
GiveDirectly, 188–89
GLAAD, 171
global capitalism, 28
global change, 28
global documentary community, 13
Global Impact Producers Assembly (GIPA), 14, 185–86
global networks, 185–93
Global Witness, 136–38
Good Pitch India, 87, 90
Good Pitch program, 13, 41
Gorokhovskaia, Yana, 78, 79–81, 101
Goya Awards, 45
Grant, Oscar, III, 158
grassroots engagement, 123
grassroots networks, 15
grassroots organizing strategies, 12
Great Britain, 29–30
Grigoriev, Maxim, 49–50
Guetschow, Lindsay, 33–34, 120–21, 122
Guggenheim, Davis, 22–23
Gulley, Titi, 158

Haiyan, Ye, 103–4
Hale County This Morning (documentary), 163
hate crimes, 114
HBO, 19, 21, 115, 118–19
He Named Me Malala (documentary), 25, 120–23
Hinduism, 83
homosexuality, 153, 154. *See also* LGBTQ+ community
Hong Kong, 130–31, 132
Hooligan Sparrow (documentary), 25, 103–4, 106–7, 186–87
Hoop Dreams (film), 94–95
A House Made of Splinters (documentary), 69
How Democracies Die (Levitsky and Ziblatt), 47
How to Lose a Country (Temelkuran), 29–30, 47
Hulu, 6–7, 19, 49
Human Flow (documentary), 130–31
human rights, 7, 10, 24, 38, 74, 102–11, 120–23
  abuses, 105
  activism, 12, 111–20

INDEX 237

campaigns, 16
films under threat, 128–31
Universal Declaration of Human Rights, 76–77
violations of, 25, 39, 54–55, 81, 103, 107, 111–20
Human Rights Commission, 136–38
Human Rights Watch, 68–69, 74, 120
The Hungarian Playbook (documentary), 46–47
Hungary, 27, 29–30, 181
Hungary: Viktor Orban's Illiberal Democracy (documentary), 46–47

I Am Not Your Negro (documentary), 163
I Am Samuel (documentary), 25, 153–54, 190
ICC. *See* International Criminal Court
ICTY. *See* International Criminal Tribunal for the former Yugoslavia
IDA. *See* International Documentary Association
idealism, 3–5
identity, 63–65
IDFA. *See* International Documentary Festival Amsterdam
IDFA Bertha Fund, 87–88
I Did Not Want to Make a War Film (documentary), 68–69
IFPIM. *See* International Fund for Public Interest Media
"impact producers," 13–14
incarceration, mass, 92, 96–97, 98
independent documentary storytelling, 181–85
distribution and, 197–201
editorial independence and, 193–95
essential infrastructure for, 201–5
global and regional networks and, 185–93
journalism synergies, 195–97
independent media, 79
India, 1–2, 16, 24–25, 83–91, 121, 123, 154, 181
Indian Constitution (1950), 83
Indian Supreme Court, 2–3
India: The Modi Question (documentary), 130–31
Indigenous people, 83, 124, 132, 136, 142–43, 165, 168–69, 170
In-Docs, 16
Indonesia, 14, 16
Industrial Revolution, 6–7
informed consent, 178
In My Blood It Runs (documentary), 25–26, 165–70, 167f
INN. *See* Institute for Nonprofit News
The Innocence Files (film), 94–95

An Insignificant Man (documentary), 1–6, 2f, 2f, 3f, 4f
Institute for Nonprofit News (INN), 196–97
"Intermediary Guidelines and Digital Media Ethics Code Rules 2021," 88–89
International Criminal Court (ICC), 75
International Criminal Tribunal for the former Yugoslavia (ICTY), 54–55
International Documentary Association (IDA), 2–3, 14, 75, 86–87
International Documentary Festival Amsterdam (IDFA), 13–14, 16, 87–88, 185–86
International Fund for Public Interest Media (IFPIM), 11, 27, 79–80, 196–97, 199–200, 203–4
International Press Institute (IPI), 90
International Rescue Committee, 54
International Resource for Impact and Storytelling (IRIS), 12
internet-based organizing tools, 13
The Interrupters (film), 94–95
In the Same Breath (documentary), 103–4
investigative journalism, 61–62, 73
investigative nonfiction, 10
IPI. *See* International Press Institute
Iran, 48, 154
Iraq, 130–31
Ireland, 75–76
IRIS. *See* International Resource for Impact and Storytelling
Iron Butterflies (documentary), 68–69
isolated communities, 176–79
Israel, 14
ITVS, 138

Japan, 14
Jatav, Meera, 84
Al Jazeera, 86–87
Je Suis Charlie (documentary), 75–76
Johnson, Lyndon, 31
Jones, Danye, 158
Jones, Van, 92, 93f, 94–95, 98–99
Jordan, 154
Joshua (documentary), 130–31
journalism, 10, 17–18, 52, 54–55, 70–71, 78. *See also* media freedom
investigative, 61–62, 73
scholarship, 22–23
synergies, 195–97
traditional, 52–53, 55, 70, 124, 143, 152–53
undercover, 61, 111–20
wire, 133
Judgment at Nuremberg (ABC broadcast), 30–31

238 INDEX

JustFilmsBUILD Network, 15–16
JustFilms program (Ford Foundation), 15–16
justice
climate, 124, 126, 139, 148
criminal, reform, 92–95, 98
restorative, 43
Just Mercy (film), 94–95

Kadyrov, Ramzan, 112, 113, 114
Kamau, Toni, 189, 190
Kartemquin Films, 94–95
al-Kateab, Waad, 56–58
Kaufman, Anthony, 198
Kazin, Michael, 29
Kejriwal, Arvind, 1–2, 2*f*, 3*f*
Kemp, Brian, 33
Kenya, 25, 121, 123, 153–55, 181, 187–89, 192
Kenya Film and Classification Board (KFCB), 154
Kesavan, Mukul, 84–85
KFCB. *See* Kenya Film and Classification Board
Khabar Lahariya, 84–85, 86, 90, 91
Kibinge, Judy, 189–91
The Killing of a Journalist (documentary), 75–76
Kingdom of Silence (documentary), 46–47
Kramer, Brandon, 94–95, 96, 198
Kramer, Lance, 91–92, 94–95, 96–97, 99, 100
Krichevskaya, Vera, 186–87
Krishnan, Murali, 84
Kuttner, Robert, 27, 28
Kuwait, 154

Lacy, Lennon, 156
Lalwani, Nishant, 27, 79, 80, 82–83, 196–97, 203–4
land defenders, 132–36, 195–96
Laney, Ryan, 116–18
Lapunov, Maxim, 119
The Last Men in Aleppo (documentary), 46–47, 48
Law of Historical Memory, 37–38
The League, 149–50
Lebanon, 16, 181
legal threats, 203
LGBTQ+ community, 112, 113–15, 116–18, 119–20, 154
LGBTQ+ conversion therapy, 170–73, 175
liberal democracies, 29–30
LightBox Africa, 67, 188–89, 191
long-term movement building, 151–52
Los Angeles Times (newspaper), 86–87
Lula da Silva (president), 145

Luminate, 144
Lumumba, Patrice, 66
lynching, 156–57, 158–59
Lyra (documentary), 75–76

de Mabior, Akuol, 62–68, 65*f*, 188–89
de Mabior, John Garang, 62–63
de Mabior, Rebecca Nyandeng, 63, 64*f*, 65*f*
Making a Murderer (documentary series), 19–20
Maksymenko-Dovhych, Zhanna, 70
Malakunas, Karl, 132–33, 134–39, 201–2
Malala Fund, 120–21, 122
Malaysia, 154
Marie Claire (magazine), 86–87
mass incarceration, 92, 96–97, 98
McKinnies, Melissa, 158
media. *See also* social media
digital, 81
entertainment, 22–23
public, 103–4, 161–62, 199–200
public interest, 10, 11
streaming, 15, 19, 20, 88–89
systems, 6
media freedom, 84–85, 86, 101
democracy and, 77–78
under duress, 76–101
megacorporations, 82–83
memory
collective, 46
cultural, 52–53
Law of Historical Memory, 37–38
Mertes, Cara, 12, 14, 15–16, 19–20, 21
The Messy Truth (series), 94–95
Mexico, 16, 75–76, 133, 181
Ministry of Information & Broadcasting (India), 88–89
misinformation, 81
"modes," of nonfiction storytelling, 7–8
Modi, Narendra, 1–2, 84–85
Le Monde (news outlet), 41
Moscow Community Center, 119
MSNBC, 6–7
MTV Entertainment Studios, 20
multipart documentary series, 19–20
multiracial democracy, 35
Multitude Films, 171
Muratov, Dmitry Andreyevich, 73
The Murder of Emmett Till (documentary), 25–26, 159–60
Musya, Kisilu, 146–48
Mwangi, Boniface "Softie," 188–89
Myakotin, Igor, 114

INDEX 239

Namour, Salim, 49
Nash, Kate, 23–24, 108–10
Nasrin (documentary), 130–31
National Center for Lesbian Rights, 171
National Geographic, 49, 58–59, 145
Nazi Germany, 30–31, 73
NDTV. *See* New Delhi Television
Nelson, Stanley, 159–60, 161–62
Netflix, 6–7, 18–21, 42, 82–83, 88–89, 162, 175
Netflix Africa, 192
the Netherlands, 16
neutrality, 52–53
New Delhi Television (NDTV), 84–85
Newell, Maya, 165, 170
New Sudan, 63
The New Yorker (magazine), 41, 68–69, 105, 106–7, 112
The New York Times (newspaper), 41, 86–87, 95–96
New Zealand, 16, 154
Nigeria, 121, 123
Nobel Peace Prize, 73
nonfiction storytelling, 9–10, 30
    investigative, 10
    "modes" of, 7–8
nonprofit funding, 67
Noorlander, Peter, 202
No Simple Way Home (documentary), 24, 62–67, 64f, 64f, 65f, 65f, 188–89, 196
Nowhere to Hide (documentary), 130–31
NPR, 84–85

Obama, Barack, 92
objectivity, 52–53, 71
Occupied (documentary), 68–69
#OccupyWallStreet, 12
O'Keefe, Ben, 33–34
Olive, Jacqueline, 158–59
Oman, 154
One Child Nation (documentary), 25, 102, 103–4, 106–7, 130, 186–87
one-child policy, 102, 103–4
Opango, Pauline, 66
OPCW. *See* Organisation for the Prohibition of Chemical Weapons
Oppenheimer, Josh, 22–23
opportunities, for documentary storytellers, 17–22
oral learning, 147–48
Organisation for the Prohibition of Chemical Weapons (OPCW), 49–50
Orozco, Natalia, 62
Osman, Wazhmah, 109

von Ossietzky, Carl, 73

"Pact of Forgetting," 37–38
El Pais (news outlet), 41
Pakistan, 120, 121, 123, 154
Palawan, the Philippines, 132–33, 134–36
participant wellness models, 170–76
PBS, 6–7, 91, 161–62
PBS Frontline, 57–58, 68–69, 75
Peace for Nina (documentary), 24, 69–70
Peacock, 20–21
Peck, Raoul, 140–41
Perspective Fund, 33–34
Peru, 25–26, 176–79
Pew Research Center, 95–96
PFLAG, 171
the Philippines, 24–25, 27–74, 132–36, 138–39, 195–96
Pickard, Victor, 10, 184
A Place of Our Own (documentary), 159–60
Plan C (documentary), 130–31
Pop Culture Collective, 149–50
populism, 17, 24, 30
    authoritarianism and, 29
    right-wing, 29
    in US, 29–30
Portugal, 36
power, 13, 79–80, 205. *See also* empowerment
    absolute, 28
    of activism, 32
    activism and, 21–22, 142
    challenging of, 6
    institutions of, 17–18
    networked tiers of, 184
    social critique of, 197–98
Pray Away (documentary), 25–26, 170–76, 172f, 173f
Press Forward, 196–97
Press Law (1938), 37
Pritz, Alex, 142–44, 145, 186, 194
propaganda, 13, 49–50, 71–72
proximity, 52–60, 61–70
Public Culture (journal), 108–9
public dissent, 1
public good, 10
public interest media, 10, 11
public media, 103–4, 161–62, 199–200
Putin, Vladimir, 112, 113, 114, 119–20

Qatar, 154
Queendom (documentary), 130–31
queer people, 124–25, 154. *See also* LGBTQ+ community

240 INDEX

The Quipu Project (documentary), 25–26, 176–79, 196, 200–1

Raben Group, 33–34
racial violence, 156, 157, 158
racism, 140–41
Radio Silence (documentary), 75–76
Rafiki (documentary), 153
Rally the Vote bus tour, 35
Ranka, Khushboo, 1–3
Raoul Wallenberg Prize, 59–60
Rappler, 73, 74, 75, 79
La Razon (news outlet), 43–44
Regarding the Pain of Others (Sontag), 113
regional networks, 185–93
Renov, Michael, 7–8, 23–24
Reporters Without Borders, 78, 84–85
resistance, witnessing stories of, 52–53
Ressa, Maria, 27, 73–74, 75, 79, 81
restorative justice, 43
Rial, Martha, 54
Al Rifaiy, Rania, 49–50
"right to rights," 106–7
right-wing populism, 29
risk-averse decision-making, 21
Romania, 154
Rous, Anya, 171, 172, 174
The Routledge Companion to Media and Human Rights, 107–8
royalty distribution, 167–68
RTVE (public broadcasting network), 42, 43
Russia, 25, 58–59, 112–13, 118–19, 130–31, 154, 181, 195–96
 OPCW and, 49–50
 propaganda and, 80
 Ukraine and, 68–70
 US and, 48
Russian LGBT Network, 119
Rwanda, 54

Safe and Secure resource guide (Doc Society), 204
Sarda, Jyoti, 149–50, 152
Saudi Arabia, 46–47, 48, 154
Scheduled Castes, 83
Schomburg Center for Research in Black Culture, 160
Scotland, 16
Scott, William, 23–24
Search, Jess, 15–16, 181
second Industrial Revolution, 6–7
security resources, 201–5
self-censorship, 81
Selma, Alabama, 30–31

semiauthoritarianism, 17–18, 82–83
Serbia, 14
Servini, María, 39
SFFILM Documentary Film Fund, 87–88
Sheffield Meet Market, 87–88
Shelby v. Holder, 31–32
Showtime, 20
Shukla, Vinay, 1–5
Shulgin, Alexander, 49–50
The Silence of Others (documentary), 35–47, 39f, 40f, 40f, 42f, 194, 195–96
Singapore, 154
The Sleeping Voice (*La Voz Dormida*) (Chacón), 35–36
Slovakia, 75–76
Smith, Marcia, 160, 161–62
social change, 8, 16, 50–51, 60
social control, 75
social impact engagement, 200–1
social-issue documentary storytelling, 11
social media, 41, 74
 campaigns, 2–3
 early days of, 12
social reform, 7
Softie (documentary), 67, 188–89
Soko, Sam, 67, 188–89
solidarity, acts of, 110
A Song of Grace (documentary), 163
Sonita (documentary), 109–10
Sontag, Susan, 113
Sotoudeh, Nasrin, 130–31
Southern Poverty Law Center, 32
South Sudan, 24, 52–53, 62–67
Spanish Civil War, 35–36, 39
Spanish National Court, 38
SPLM/SPLA. *See* Sudan People's Liberation Movement/Army
The Square (documentary), 19
#StandwithMalala, 122
status quo, 8–9
stealth authoritarianism, 27–28
Story Movements (Borum Chattoo), 8–9, 23–24
Story Syndicate, 33–34
streaming media, 15, 19, 20, 88–89. *See also specific platforms*
Strong Island (documentary), 62
subscription video on demand (SVOD), 19
Sudan People's Liberation Movement/Army (SPLM/SPLA), 62–63
Sundance Film Festival, 19, 75, 86–88
Sundance Institute, 15–16, 138
Supreme Court
 Indian, 2–3
 Shelby v. Holder, 31–32

INDEX 241

SVOD. *See* subscription video on demand
Syria, 24, 46–47, 48, 49, 52–53, 56, 57–58, 59, 194
Syrian American Medical Society, 60

Tahrir Square, 19
Taiwan, 181
Tandav (series), 88–89
Tell Them We Are Rising (documentary), 161–62
El Tema (documentary), 186–87
Temelkuran, Ece, 29–30, 47
The Territory (documentary), 25, 142–43, 144–45, 153, 186, 194
Thailand, 136–38
Thank You for the Rain (documentary), 25, 146–48, 148f, 149f, 153
Think Film, 59–60
Think-Film Impact Production, 202
13th (film), 94–95
This Evening (documentary), 163
Thomas, Rintu, 85, 86–88, 89, 90, 194
A Thousand Cuts (documentary), 24–25, 75–76
Thunberg, Greta, 111
Thurgood Marshall Fund, 161–62
Tiger King (documentary series), 19–20
Till, Emmett, 160–61
Time Magazine, 86–87
Times of India, 83
Tlaib, Rashida, 149–50
Together Films, 16
Toronto International Film Festival, 1
Townsend, Kate, 18–20, 21
traditional journalism, 52–53, 55, 70, 124, 143, 152–53
transgender people, 124–25. *See also* LGBTQ+ community
trauma, 63–65
Trevor Project, 171, 172–73
The Trials of Muhammad Ali (film), 94–95
Tribeca Film Festival, 87–88
Trump, Donald, 17–18, 94–95
TTT (news outlet), 41
Tulsa Burning (documentary), 159–60
The Tunnel (propaganda video), 49–50, 72
Tupi Kagwahiva (language), 144–45
turf wars, 184
Turkey, 14, 27, 29–30, 47
20 Days in Mariupol (documentary), 68–69
Twitter (X), 88–89
"two-tiered system," for documentary makers, 21

Ukraine, 24, 52–53, 68–70, 130–31

undercover journalism, 61, 111–20
underrepresented communities, 123–26
UNGA, 123
United Arab Emirates, 154
United Kingdom, 16, 29, 41, 181, 187, 202
United Nations, 42, 54–55, 60
United Negro College Fund, 161–62
United States (US), 5, 14, 16, 24–26, 41, 154
    Constitution, 76–77
    Department of Justice, 31, 161
    mass incarceration in, 92, 96–97
    populism in, 29–30
    racism and colonialism in, 140–41
    Russia and, 48
Universal Declaration of Human Rights, 76–77
universal rights, 106–7
Unquiet Collective, 16
"untouchables," 83
Uru-eu-wau-wau people, 142–43, 144–45
US. *See* United States
Uttar Pradesh, India, 83–91
Uýra, The Rising Forest (documentary), 25, 123–26, 125f, 126f, 127f, 200–1

vérité movement, 6–7
Violence (journal), 43–44
voter empowerment, 33, 34
Voting Rights Act (1965), 31
La Voz Dormida (*The Sleeping Voice*) (Chacón), 35–36

Walt Disney Company, 49, 58–59, 145
Wang, Nanfu, 102–6, 107, 111, 130, 131, 186–87, 201–2
Wanja, Emily, 146, 148, 189
war crimes, 54–55
wars
    civil, 35–36, 39, 54
    Cold War, 27
    turf, 184
    Yugoslav, 54–55
Washington Post, 86–87
We Are Not The Machine, 190, 191
Welcome to Chechnya (documentary), 25, 111–20, 116f, 117f, 128–29, 195–96
We Will Not Fade Away (documentary), 68–69
WhatsApp, 43–44
Wheatley, Thalia, 116–18
When Spring Came to Bucha (documentary), 68–69
When the Guns Go Silent (documentary), 62
While We Watched (documentary), 75–76
white supremacy, 158–59
Winter on Fire (documentary), 19

wire journalism, 133
"witness," 70–71
women and girls, Dalit, 84–85
Working Films, 161
World Press Freedom Index (2023), 52, 71–72, 78, 84–85

Writing with Fire (documentary), 24–25, 83–91, 87f, 194

X. *See* Twitter

Yousafzai, Malala, 120

About the Authors

Caty Borum is Executive Director of the Center for Media & Social Impact and Provost Associate Professor at the American University School of Communication. She is an award-winning documentary producer, book author, engaged scholar, professor, and strategist working at the intersection of social change communication, documentary, and entertainment storytelling. She is the author of *Story Movements: How Documentaries Empower People and Inspire Social Change* and *The Revolution Will Be Hilarious: Comedy for Social Change and Civic Power*, and coauthor, with Lauren Feldman, of *A Comedian and an Activist Walk into a Bar: The Serious Role of Comedy in Social Justice*.

David Conrad-Pérez is a journalist, media historian, and Research Director of the Center for Media & Social Impact at American University, working at the intersection of journalism studies, journalism history, and social justice. He has worked as a producer for WNYC's *On the Media* and PRI's *The World*, and he has reported stories for news outlets that include the *Los Angeles Times, New York Times, Reuters, and the San Francisco Chronicle.*